SPORT AND TRAVEL IN INDIA AND CENTRAL AMERICA

SPORT AND TRAVEL IN INDIA AND CENTRAL AMERICA

A. G. BAGOT

GYAN

Published by

Gyan Publishing House
5, Ansari Road
Daryaganj, New Delhi-110002
Phone: 011-47034999, 9811692060
E-mail: books@gyanbooks.com

Distribution Network
gyanbooks.com
India, USA, Canada, UK, Australia

ISBN: 978-93-6780-061-4 (PB)

First Published, 1897

2nd Impression 2024

Printed at: Gyan Press, Delhi.

SPORT AND TRAVEL IN INDIA AND CENTRAL AMERICA
Author: A. G. BAGOT

SPORT AND TRAVEL

IN

INDIA AND CENTRAL AMERICA.

"MY BULLET CAUGHT HIM IN THE CENTRE OF THE FOREHEAD."

Page 342.

SPORT AND TRAVEL IN INDIA AND CENTRAL AMERICA.

BY

A. G. BAGOT,

LATE 60TH RIFLES ("BAGATELLE"),

AUTHOR OF "SPORTING SKETCHES," "MEN WE MEET IN THE FIELD," "SHOOTING AND YACHTING IN THE MEDITERRANEAN," ETC.

LONDON: CHAPMAN & HALL, LD.

1897.

PREFACE.

THESE reminiscences of sport and travel, which I now for the first time publish in book form, have for the most part appeared in the columns of the *Asian*—the *Field* of India. And to the courtesy of the genial editor and proprietor of that journal, I am indebted for leave to reprint them. It may be argued that they deal with the "long ago," and that everything has changed now for the better, or worse. On that point I must leave others to judge. I have only done my best to describe, so far as my memory serves me, the scenes of sport in the past, in the hope that they may be found of some slight interest.

THE AUTHOR.

CONTENTS.

PART I.

INDIA.

PART II.

CENTRAL AMERICA.

PART I.

INDIA.

SPORT AND TRAVEL IN INDIA AND CENTRAL AMERICA.

CHAPTER I.

THE P. V. H.

Tempora mutantur, et nos mutamur in illis is no doubt as true in the present day as it was when the sentence was first penned. Indeed, if anything, it becomes more applicable every year. For, as the days go on, we seem to live more rapidly, and changes consequently increase in proportion. In sport this is certainly the case. The rapid transition from the old flint lock to, first, the percussion cap, then the breech-loader with a pin-fire cartridge, from thence to central fire hammerless guns, and, as if that did not give sufficient powers of slaughter, lastly, magazine guns, which will fire five shots without taking the weapon from the shoulder—all show that shooting is a very different thing in 1897 to what it was five-and-twenty or thirty years ago. So in hunting. The pace is hotter, and the fields larger. Two and three horses out a day is nothing out of the common. No hacking your animal slowly to cover and riding home perhaps twenty miles after a hard day. No! that is far too slow for the present generation. Horses are sent on, you gallop all the way to the meet, or drive well wrapped up, *bien entendu* in a brougham, which probably waits somewhere within a reasonable distance to take you back. Or, the universal train becomes the cover hack, and you dash down from London by an express for a *gallop.* (I will not call it hunting) with the stag hounds, and are back in town by four o'clock. And so on through every class of sport, from pitch and toss to battle and murder. One and all are changing day by day as we ourselves are also altering our habits to suit. This being the case, a few reminiscences of sport in India, as it was some twenty odd years ago, may not be out of place, and I will begin with a memorable run with the P. V. H., which, as all in India know, stands for "Peshawar Vale Hounds."

Those who have been to Peshawar will not want a description of the country. To those who have not, I can only say that at first sight it is about as rum a country to get over as any I have ever been in. There are methods of irrigation (or were) which in their way are a triumph, so far as being snares to the unwary. They consist (perhaps, after all, I had better put things in the past, as everything may be different now), and so I will say they consisted of three deep narrow ditches, V-shaped and close together, too big to fly, and unless you had a clever nag, scarcely room between each ditch for him to drop his hind legs on to, and so take in two. Sometimes there was a wall of mud in front, or rather, on one side, and sometimes they were open, and you came upon them before you knew what was before you: and, if you did not come down, it was the horse's fault and not yours, for until one became accustomed to them it was next door to impossible to avoid catching one's animal by the head with, in nine cases out of ten, the inevitable result. Part of the country, however, was really good, and was looked on as the Leicestershire portion; and, consequently, when the meet was advertised at Shubkudder, there was sure to be a big field. It was from this place that the run I am about to describe took place, and as on that—to me—memorable occasion I happened to be officiating as second whip, I have a claim to know a little about it.

At the time I am speaking of the master was a well-known sportsman, who we will call Ben Richards. I dare say not a few will recognize under that name who it was that swayed the destinies of the pack. However, of one thing I am certain, that all agreed a better sportsman or more popular master could not have been found. With a very keen eye, and a thorough knowledge of what hounds were doing, he was always there at the moment he was wanted. Nothing stopped him when hounds were running, and the way they flew to his horn or holloa showed they were fond of him, and proud to work under such a kind master. I think, so far as I remember, he was the first huntsman I ever heard whistle to his hounds when drawing, though I have since come across two others who did the same; but I can remember, as well as if it was yesterday, the first time I saw him mounted on his favourite old chestnut, with the hounds in cover, and heard him as he rode through alternately cheering them and whistling. I thought it a novel idea. But "forard on."

It was a bright cold morning in February when I turned out to ride on to Shubkudder with the hounds. It was fifteen miles from the station, and necessitated an early start, as the fixture was 10 a.m. and hounds do not travel to cover sixty miles an hour. As I rode up to Richards' bungalow to breakfast, there was ice on the roads and a sprinkling of snow above the Kyber Pass, and it looked all over like a good hunting day. Breakfast did not take long, and by 7 a.m. Richards, Walters (first whip), and myself (second whip, officiating) were on the way. We had sent the syces on overnight with the horses, and rode our hacks out—a circumstance which nearly caused trouble, for about halfway out a jackal jumped up right in front of the pack, and before we could turn them they were off in full cry. Happily he was a ringing village brute, and turned short back, so we managed to stop them, not, however, before I had got mixed up with my "tat" in a ditch, and precious nearly broken my leg. Nothing further occurred *en route*, and by the time the field arrived, I had managed a "wash and brush up," not to mention a cup of hot coffee.

Ten fifteen punctually (Richards would never give more than a quarter of an hour's law), we threw off, and the first two covers being blank, allowed most of the late contingent to come up. As we were trotting on to our third draw, a thorn cover by the side of a stream, Richards' quick eye caught sight of a dark object stealing about two fields off under a wall. Turning to Walters, he said, "Gallop on to that knoll and try and view him away over the river," and then with a nod to me to put them to him, and a chink of the horn, he lifted the pack almost on to the back of a stout hill jackal, who we knew would run as straight as an English fox.

"Tally ho, gone away!" from Walters, and we were on the line in a crack with a breast high scent: the first obstacle being a small river pretty nearly bank full and as cold as—well it could give an iced peg two stone—I can feel it now—the sensation, as we all, that is, Richards, Walters, and self, plunged in with the pack. Some of the field thought they would go round to a ford that some one knew or pretended he knew of; others thought they would await further developments, while the remainder hardened their hearts and took the plunge. It was a steepish bank on the other side, which bothered us a bit, and by the time we got out, the hounds were racing away a quarter of a mile in front, and we had to gallop hard to get up to them, which, however, was by no means a bad thing after such a cold lead off. For another mile we flew as straight as a die over a delightful bit of grass country, intersected with small brooks and a wall or two, with now and again a sort of hedge of thorn, till we came to our first check in a bed of rushes. Here a slight diversion was caused by the arrival of an Irish medico, whose horse, having got the upper hand of him, charged straight into the centre of the pack, and stopping dead short, deposited his rider over his head into the rushes, where, the ground being boggy, he stuck fast, whooping and holloaing like a maniac. "For Heaven's sake, stop that row!" shouted Richards. "Hold hard, sir," yelled Walters. "Ware hounds," quoth I. "Is it shtop? Is it hould hard now that you'd be asking me? To the divil wid your hounds," was all the reply we received, and eventually Walters and I had to dismount, and, laughing fit to kill ourselves, managed to pull him out of the bog, with the loss of his hat and one boot. Meanwhile Richards had made a long swinging cast forward, and, hitting off the line to the left of the reeds, it was forard away again. Over a wall with a ditch to and from, followed by a deep drop into a lane, we went; and then, turning sharp to the right, we set our heads straight for the hills, distant about seven miles.

Twenty minutes without a check thinned the field considerably, and there was more than one sportsman running after his horse, while scarce a coat but what showed signs of having made acquaintance with mother earth. I confess it was a welcome moment to me when I saw the hounds suddenly throw up, for my nag was cutting things uncommonly fine at every fence, and showed pretty evidently that the pace was beginning to tell. However, the breathing-space was not long, as old Reveller (one of the Grafton lot) hit off the scent down the middle of the lane we had crossed some time before, which, like all country roads, had taken a long sweep only to return to its original intention or destination, and we were at it hammer and tongs again.

At this spot, trying to turn some young hounds, I got a rattling fall jumping out of the road, and Walters, who essayed the same performance about thirty yards further on, met with the same fate, unfortunately laming his horse so badly that he could not go on; consequently Richards and I were left alone. Luckily there was little to do but to ride, for the scent was burning, and the hounds simply revelled in it, running almost mute. As we neared the hills, the country got more cramped, and it was a case of jumping every minute. Moreover, we were considerably bothered with some irrigation works of the nature of those I have already described. Both Richards and myself came down in the same ditch, where we were promptly joined by four others, and it took us nearly five minutes to get out, during which time the hounds had run clean away, giving us a rare job to get up to them.

It was a treat to see the field, for, with the exception of some four or five who were well up, the rest were miles behind, and our line was clearly marked by loose horses and galloping forms. On we went, however, every fresh hundred yards being productive of more grief, and every instant our horses showing more signs of distress, till at last Richards, viewing our quarry stealing along half a mile ahead, made a last despairing attempt to lift the pack on to his back. He was about fifty yards in front of me, and

I was doing my little best to bring up the stragglers, when suddenly I saw him disappear, and, before I knew what had happened, I felt my nag pull himself together, and with a tremendous effort he landed me safe on the other side of a deep nullah full of mud and slush, at the bottom of which I saw Richards and his gallant old chestnut rolling about. As might be expected of him, the first thought in Richards' mind was sport, for in answer to my inquiry if he was hurt, he shouted, "Here, get along, and take the horn; kill if you can. I'm all right: I'll follow as soon as I can get out of this hole." And he threw up the horn, which I caught, not that it was much use, for it was choke-full of mud, and somewhat bent in the fall. Besides, there was not any time to clear it out, for the pack, having caught sight of the jackal, were racing in view. One more wall, and then victory, thought I, as I charged it. I got over myself on my head, but my nag succumbed with a sob on the far side, and picking up the pieces I started to finish the run on foot. A hundred yards further it was over, and the pack ran into their quarry at the foot of the hills. I had just wind enough left to sing his requiem, and blow as much of the mud out of the horn as I could, when I was joined by another figure, covered from head to foot with mud, also on foot, with no cap, and one spur gone, and then Richards' voice (for it was him) rang out clear as a bell. "Who-whoop, whoo-who-o-op," and the great run was over. One hour and thirty-five minutes; distance about thirteen miles.

The field came dropping in by twos and threes in various stages of *deshabille* and discomfort, and in some cases I doubt if our own fathers would have recognized us. To give every man his due, I must say that the Irish medico turned up among the first, having ridden the whole run since his catastrophe, without either his hat or boot; a pretty figure he presented, too, with a red silk handkerchief tied round his head, and a face of much the same hue as his improvised head-gear. "By the Lord Harry!" he shouted as he came up. "It bates county Meath entoirly, and if I could foind mi bhoot and get a dhrop of the crayter, I'd be the phroudest lad out of Oireland this day!"

Having gone back to look after my steed, I was lucky enough to find him, together with the old chestnut, and as they both had recovered their wind, neither were the worse for the bucketing. By this time it was getting on for half-past three, and twenty-four miles home to the kennels, while a count showed two couple absent without leave. A nice prospect for the second whip, said I to myself, as I made ready to start off in quest of the truants. As luck would have it, however, a couple and a half turned up, and a late arrival brought word from Walters that he had taken back one of the youngsters with him.

So ended one of the best days' sport I ever remember, either in India or in the Old Country, and those who were out that day (perhaps some are still drawing the nimble rupee) will, I am sure, fully endorse my sentiments. I know both Richards and myself were pretty well tired, not to say cold, by the time we got back and had seen the hounds cared for; and I am afraid we both went fast asleep after dinner and a bottle of "the boy" (though in those days champagne had not acquired that name); and as I got up to say good night—for I was dining, or rather supping, with him—I remember I was so stiff I could hardly get back to my quarters. Still, as I tumbled into bed, I congratulated myself on having been one of those who had taken part in the run; and now, as I write, I should be very glad to brave all the stiffness possible—ay, even coupled with a touch of rheumatism—if I could only be certain of such a grand day's sport as we had in those old days with the P. V. H. and their excellent master.

CHAPTER II.

"A BOBBERY PACK."

In the last chapter I endeavoured to give an account of a memorable run with the Peshawar Vale hounds, and in so doing was dealing with the genuine article, where everything was orthodox and carried out to the letter of hunting law. But as it is not, or was not, in everybody's power to be within hail of that sporting pack, and some sort of hunting having been from time immemorial necessary for human nature, other methods of pursuing the wily jackal and obtaining a gallop had to be devised. The solution of the problem was found in the establishment of what was known as a "bobbery pack," and as the transition from the sublime to the ridiculous is comparatively easy, I make it the subject of this sketch.

At the time of which I am writing, "bobbery packs" were pretty plentiful in India, and most up-country stations had them more or less. Where I happened to be, we had one in the major degree, and it fell to my lot, in connection with Howard of the Hussars, to organize and hunt the same. I remember we had souls far above the system of "Trencher feeding," which, as every one knows, means each member of the hunt keeping one or two dogs and bringing them to the meet. No; we considered it quite beneath our notice; so, as mud was cheap, and labour plentiful, we built kennels for the comfort and housing of the pack, and kept a regular staff of attendant "mehters" to wait on them.

I cannot, with any degree of truth, say that our pack was a particularly level lot, or, indeed, handsome, but it was generally admitted that, "though rum 'uns to look at, they were beggars to go," and, considering the amount of trouble we took over them, it would have been hard lines if they did not do something to earn their soup. We had two couple of old hounds, which Howard had picked up in Calcutta, the sole survivors of a draft, all of the others having succumbed to the trials of the Red Sea. Then there were a couple of half-bred pariahs, containing a dash of foxhound, a dash of greyhound, three parts of pariah, and the rest what you like. Then some pariahs, pure and unadulterated, four or five smart fox-terriers, a bull pup, a couple of greyhounds from the North, a spaniel or two, and lastly a good honest old English retriever, who constituted himself a sort of honorary member. He belonged to me, and used merely to join in when he thought there was any fun going on. It will be seen from the composition of our pack that we could not rely much on their powers of picking out a cold scent, though in cases of difficulty we certainly had the foxhound element to fall back on, and two of the terriers had wonderful noses; still I am fain to confess a good deal of the hunting was guess-work, and, when not running in view, riding to holloas.

All through the hot weather we were hard at work trying to get our unruly subjects in order, and at 4 a.m. either Howard or myself, with the native whip in attendance, might have been seen daily exercising the pack in couples. And what a time it took them to learn the proper use of those said couples! or to recognize, if their onward career was suddenly checked by a post which they had tried to pass on opposite sides at the same time regardless of the chains between them, that it was not the fault of their neighbour, and was not, therefore, a good and sufficient cause for action! The amount of whipcord expended in the first month was something prodigious, and I began to despair of ever teaching them the difference between their proper quarry and the native pig, for directly one of the village "soors" crossed the path, away would go the whole pack in full cry, upsetting women, children, and chatties, till they got so mixed up with their couples that they could go no further, and were brought up all standing. On one occasion both Howard and myself were out riding slowly through the cantonments with the pack, when they took it into their heads to be off after a pariah, and being open ground, with the exception of overturning the native whip, did little damage at first. But they so frightened the "pi" that he bolted through an open door in the married quarters, followed by the whole lot, and then the row began. First a terrible smash of broken crockery, followed by appalling screams; then more smash as of furniture overturned, more screams mingled with barking and howls from the pariah; and on our coming up and rushing into the room, we found a veritable chaos. The table was overturned with all the breakfast-things smashed on the floor. A large filter in the corner was endways, having imprisoned one couple in its fall. Chairs were all over the place, and the pariah half murdered under the bed; while on the top of the latter piece of furniture lay a sergeant's wife in a dead faint; the worst of it all being that she was shortly "expecting," and the scene that had just been enacted precipitated events and necessitated the prompt attendance of the doctor. Of course we had to pay the damage, which was by no means a small item, and the sergeant was not best pleased when he came back to his quarters and saw the ruin that had taken place. Luckily, however, there were no complications so far as the lady was concerned, otherwise the consequences might have been more serious for us, and whatever else might have happened it would certainly have put a summary end to the "bobbery pack."

Towards the commencement of the cold weather we had got things into fair working order, and there was a marked improvement in the deportment of our charges. They had learnt to abjure the attractions of pork, and also to come to the horn. Moreover, we were able to dispense with the use of the couples, and in a few preliminary scurries with bagged jackals they evinced a positive taste for the article, and were blooded in most orthodox manner. This was very satisfactory for us, as we were for some time rather hopeless, and inclined to grudge the payment of the weekly "bunniah's" bill. One animal we were forced to draft out of the pack, namely, the bull-dog. We could do absolutely nothing with him, for his whole soul was wrapped up in fighting, and no sooner were the pack laid on than he immediately had his teeth into whatever dog happened to be nearest at the time. One day it was a hound, the next one of the half-bred pariahs, or a greyhound, and sooner than not have a go at something he would fly at the native whip or a horse's heels. The latter, however, he was not quite so keen about, as on one occasion he got lifted about fifteen yards by a judicious and well-directed kick. Run he would not, but followed some half a mile in rear of the chase at his own pace till they came to a check, when another impromptu mill was the order of the day. We had named him Tomboy, and never was I so glad of anything as the day when Howard agreed to strike his name off the books and allow me to make him a present to the Quartermaster-Sergeant.

A month later and we advertised our first regular meet, "7.30 a.m., the cemetery"—being a fine cheery place to commence with, but pretty certain for a find, though to make quite sure of the fact we had put two native "shikaries" in different sugar khates with each a basket containing the necessary animal—to wit a bagman. Having settled the matter by, not the hazard of a die, but spinning the all-powerful rupee, it devolved on me to carry the horn on our opening day, Howard officiating as first whip. The native whip, arrayed in a new pink, was mounted on a "tat," and precious uncomfortable he seemed; but sustained by pride, and swelling with importance and the desire to show off among his fellows, he tried his best to look as if he liked it, and manfully rated the hounds on every possible and impossible occasion. "Git away, Travellah, ware, oss," he had learnt by heart, but it was generally followed by a few choice epithets in the vernacular, and a wild endeavour to crack his whip—a proceeding infinitely more dangerous to those unfortunates who happened to be within reach, than to any individual animal of the pack. In one of these flourishes he managed to fetch his steed a sounding smack across the head, and the next moment it was a case of "*profundit humi.*" However, he picked himself up, and having dusted his coat and questioned the paternity and maternity of the unfortunate "tat," besides addressing a few cutting remarks to "Travellah," he remounted, but took good care to keep his whip quiet, while he made up for it by a more liberal use of that unruly member called the tongue.

We had a tremendous field (for an up-country station), and no less than seven ladies graced the proceedings, the whole garrison turning out *en masse*, both mounted and dismounted. There was the Commissioner and his daughter, the Cantonment Magistrate and his belongings, besides various other civil servants, including the Postmaster, an exceedingly fat baboo, who ran the native whip to a head for bad riding and—tell it not in Gath—bad language. Some had come out to scoff, more especially those who had lately joined from England, and in consequence were inclined to make disparaging remarks and to compare our turn-out with the Quorn or some other crack pack. But we paid little heed to them, being far more taken up with the all-important questions as to whether we should find, and, if so, how our heterogeneous assortment of animals would acquit themselves. The first draw was some high flag rush grass, lying just outside the Cemetery, where we had had "Khuber" of more than one jackal, and with a chink of the horn off we trotted in grand style. I took care to impress on the field the necessity of keeping well back and leaving the lower side open, while I took the pack to the far end and got them (or as many of them as I could) into cover as quick as possible. A whimper, gradually swelling into a chorus, from the hounds soon showed that the grass was tenanted, and then the sharp shrill yapping of the terriers joined in the anthem as a sort of treble motive, while the half-bred pariahs occasionally treated us to an alto. One jackal broke away back, closely followed by the couple of greyhounds and the honorary member (the retriever), but the rest of the pack stuck to their first love like angels. So, sending the native whip off to try and stop the honorary member and his friends, I went on with the main body, who were evidently making it pretty warm for their quarry. A couple of turns up and down, and then "gone away" from Howard, who had stationed himself at the bottom left-hand corner, proved that they had forced him away. Galloping down as hard as I could, I blew the hounds out of cover, and had the satisfaction of seeing the Calcutta draft lay down to their work as well as if they were in the shires, and, what is more, as if their example had brought out the whole of the foxhound strain in them, the half-bred pariahs did likewise, and with heads well down ran the line as if they had been used to it all their lives. Then followed the terriers, the rear being brought up by the tag-rag and bob-tail, such as spaniels, pariahs, etc., who I am fain to confess did nothing more than follow their leaders. However, that they followed at all was something, and I felt quite proud as we sailed away over the open towards one of the large sugar khates where we had planted a "shikarie."

"I hope to goodness that idiot won't loose a bagman when he hears us coming," said Howard to me as we galloped along. "I think I'll get on and see; besides, I may be able to view our brute over the other side of the khate." And with that he turned his horse over a mud wall and made a short cut for the khate. As good luck would have it, our jackal made a considerable detour, and having to cross some rising ground I caught a glimpse of him as he topped the summit before making his point. I dared not lift the pack, for they were running very well, and I argued if I once got their heads up that they might never get them down again. My fleeting vision of master jack, however, was of great service, for they threw up at the foot of the rising ground, and consequently without making a cast I was able to put them on to the line again in a jiffey.

When we arrived at the top of the small hill I saw, to my intense amusement, Howard riding after a native who was legging it like a maniac, losing portions of his very scanty attire as he ran. It was of course the "shikarie," who, like the ass he was, had slipped his bagman and was now flying for bare life from avenging justice. Happily Howard had spotted the hunted jackal, and was able to tell me exactly where he had gone into the khate, which was some little help, though when I saw how thick it was I never imagined we should get the brute out of it. The pack did not fancy it at all, and would not face it for some time, save and excepting always, as they say in legal documents, the terriers, who were now of great use, for being small they were able to get through the bottom, and actually forced the jackal out, and ran him in view for a hundred yards or so to a small river. Here I got "Travellah" & Co. to work, and the honorary member with the two greyhounds having rejoined, the whole pack were at it and took up the running along the side of the bank. The stream itself was not broad, but both banks were very steep, and if one did happen to make a mess of it in jumping, it would be a case of ropes etc., to get one's horse out.

I had just said to Howard that I hoped the jackal would not make across the stream when we had an optical proof of the dangers of a false step, for the Postmaster, who had not long turned up, having funked the mud walls, and consequently having been thrown out, incautiously ventured too near the edge, and the bank giving way both horse and rider disappeared beneath the anything but limpid water. When he emerged he was indeed a woe-begone spectacle; and the language he used was something quite beyond description. Some of the field good-naturedly fished him out, but he had to send for aid from the nearest village to extricate his steed. Luckily, as we went on, the stream narrowed, and the banks became less steep, so that it was no longer a formidable obstacle, and at the very nick of time Howard caught sight of our friend stealing away on the opposite side. I say the nick of time, for the "small dog" portion of our pack were beginning to give up the game, and for the last five minutes I had been keeping them going by an occasional bit of music. To holloa them over the stream was the work of a moment, and galloping with the pack at my heels across a dry paddy field, over a wall and a nullah, the latter of which brought me to grief, they viewed their jackal, and, led by the honorary member, were away full cry before half the field were over the stream. As soon as I had picked myself up and collected the various articles I had dropped about, I remounted, and made the best of my way after them; but Howard, who had seen my catastrophe, was already with the pack, and cheering them on, he clapped them right on to master jack's back, and before I could come up it was "who whoop." So much for run No. 1, which was eminently satisfactory to us, and was even admitted by the scoffers to have been "a first-rate burst for the sort of thing, don't you know." It had lasted about thirty-five minutes, and though by no means straight, there had been plenty of jumping, and the pace at times very fair, while the pack had surprised us all by the way they stuck to the line.

By this time the sun was getting hot, and if there was to be any more hunting that day we had to set about it at once, so, after a hurried consultation with Howard, we agreed to trot off to "khate" No. 2, where we had our second reserve bagman. Of course we did not want the field to find out our little game, so as we rode along we told the native whip to get into the cover and give the "shikarie" the office directly we got up. These instructions he carried out to the letter, and the "shikarie," being possessed of more than the usual quantum of brains, turned out the jackal close to the edge of the cover with his head to an open plain some three miles across, and only here and there a wall or nullah, and then only near the end. There was no cover whatever to be seen, and it was, moreover, in a direct line for home. Almost as soon as I had thrown the hounds in it was a case of "forard away," and there we were, all galloping and shouting like a pack of emancipated schoolboys across the maidan. No mishap at the first fence with the exception of the native whip, and he did not count. The second, a deep nullah, was also negotiated in safety, but the third emptied more than one saddle; and two of the ladies came to grief, but luckily no bones broken. Everybody seemed highly pleased, so I thought the fun might as well be kept up, and as by this time neither myself nor the pack had the remotest idea of the line, or the jackal's whereabouts, I simply galloped ahead, choosing the most direct route for home, and with Howard driving the pack along, we made a regular steeplechase of it till we came close to the cantonment, where we pretended to lose the jackal in a thick cactus hedge, and after pottering about for the look of the thing, we gravely asserted that the sun was so hot that the hounds could not own the scent, and gave the order for home. This was a signal for a general stampede to the various messes for pegs wherewith to cool the parched throats, and at the same time to drink success to the chase; and one and all said they had had some real good sport, declaring the pack to be first-rate, and the institution thereof a great success. We had many a good scramble after that, during the cold weather, but somehow we never had so good a day as the opening one; and even Tomboy, the bull-dog, looked ashamed of himself as we passed him and his new master on the way to the kennels, and seemed as if he deplored the fact that he was not considered worthy of being a member of our bobbery pack.

CHAPTER III.

A SKY MEETING.

I DOUBT if there is any other country in the world where sport flourishes to the extent that it does in India. Whether it be hunting, shooting, racing, cricket, or whatever else may occur to the mind, one has only to arrive in what is known as the "Gorgeous East" at the proper season, to find each and every one in full operation. Certainly, so far as racing is concerned, India is a veritable nursery garden. Every station has its meeting at some time or other during the year, and those who were never known to back a horse in England will be found buying their fancy at the lottery, and even donning the silk as full-fledged jockeys. Besides the regular meetings, there are institutions known as "sky meetings," sort of impromptu scratch affairs, which, though they do not bring out any crack performers in the way of horses, are great fun, and consequently very popular. They used to be got up in the station itself, while a few men from neighbouring places would send a horse or so, and a native gentleman's purse, subscribed for by the leading natives about, was generally a feature. The term "sky races," as applied to these meetings, I fancy, must have originated in "scurry races;" but of this I am not sure, nor is it a matter of vital importance.

In common with other stations, the one at which I

found myself in 186— naturally had its sky meeting, and from the amount of galloping done early in the morning, and the racy conversations that filled the air, one would have thought that one of the classic races at least was about to be decided. In those days I was not overburdened with the "too, too solid flesh," so was in request for training purposes. Three and four horses a morning, and as many more in the afternoon, I had to put through the mill; while the respective owners (those who did not ride, I mean) would, stop-watch in hand, criticize the performances of their nags. Very knowing, too, they tried to appear, and some of them would go any lengths to time an adversary's animal, if they thought by so doing they could gauge his form. Personally, I never had any great faith in the stop-watch, though I confess there is more chance for it in India than at home; but to suppose that by timing a horse galloping by himself over any named distance could give any sort of line to his powers when running in company, struck me as absurd, and I have seen no cause to alter my opinion since. However, it pleased the various owners, and did no harm to any one else, besides encouraging the trade of the chronometer maker, so let it pass.

Now, in my bungalow, where three of us used to "chum," we had two or three smartish nags—one, a country-bred, which owned me for a master, and was about as good a beast across a country as it has ever been my good fortune to turn my leg over; another, an Arab galloway belonging to Tilson, which could make most of them gallop; while a third, the property of our Assistant-Surgeon, though not anything particular to look at, we had privately tried to be a flyer at a mile. There was also one other, a "waler," which I had not long bought, but of him more anon. With this galaxy of talent, we looked upon three races as already won. The steeple-chase we proposed for my country-bred, the galloway race for Tilson, and the hack race we allotted to the Dr. McSweeney by name. Of course we had to be careful in our training, for it would not do to show the trumps we held to the world, and thereby increase the prices we should have to give at the lottery. So, having found an excellent bit of turf in a secluded spot some three miles away from the station and racecourse, one of us would go off very early and get our gallops over before the other sporting owners had shown a leg. Now and then, just for the look of the thing, we would give our nags a spin (half-speed) on the recognized training ground; but the real preparations went on unobserved and on the quiet. It was no doubt hard work, and both Tilson and myself were training as fine as a hair; but, as we anticipated a grand *coup* by our stratagem, we did not mind a bit of extra trouble.

As the time fixed for the races drew near, everybody got more and more knowing, and, better still, as every owner of a steed imagined his own crock a certainty, he did not mind putting his hand in his pocket for a handsome subscription, looking on it merely as so much money lent for a short time. "Bound to get it back over the hurdle race, or the this, the that, or the other event," they argued; consequently, the added money, as well as the entries, made quite a respectable show. Indeed, the stewards found themselves in such funds that they added another item to the card, viz. "a hurdle race, two miles, over eight flights of hurdles, for horses the *bonâ fide* property of officers belonging to the garrison; catch weights, owners up." Directly McSweeny heard of this, he came bucketing over to me and said, "Look here, my boy, you must enter the waler for this at once." "But," I objected, "Mitchell of the Artillery has one that can beat me in a canter." "Never mind, you enter your nag; I'll see to the rest," replied McSweeny, and accordingly entered he was, so that we had pretty well the whole stud engaged, though how McSweeney was going to ensure a win for me I did not quite see, unless he meant exercising his surgical skill on either Mitchell or his horse.

By this time the racing mania had communicated itself to the "syces," who were, if possible, warmer partisans than their respective masters, and on more than one occasion the argument became so heated that words were found ineffectual, and recourse was had to blows, when the dusky attendants endeavoured to do battle for their charges, by hitting, scratching, pulling, kicking, and wrestling with a rival, yelling the while as if pandemonium was let loose. Unfortunately, they were wont to select our "compound" as the native Tattersalls, and the row was often so great that one of us had to rush out and quell the disturbance with a dose of "lakri," or hunting-crops. However, it had the advantage of making the syces as keen as mustard, and woe betide the unfortunate grass-cutter who neglected to do anything that might conduce to the welfare of the stud to which they were attached. Prompt vengeance, swift and unfailing, was their reward, and meted out with unsparing hand.

The day before that fixed for the races we all assembled in the evening at the Recreation Rooms to draw the lotteries, and very plentiful was the chaff as the various animals were put up for auction and bought generally by their owners. I remember, by the way, there was a little unpleasantness over the lottery on the pony race, as a certain owner who had two entered bought his second best for a song, leaving the other, which was a real good thing, to run loose, and a rumour (afterwards confirmed, I am sorry to say) went round that he had arranged matters with his jockeys to win with No. 2—as clear a case of roping as could well be imagined. Our bungalow were particularly fortunate, for in the steeplechase I drew my own horse, the country-bred, named "The Prophet" by McSweeny's express desire, for he said that a prophet generally went before, and therefore the name was a good augury, though to my mind a somewhat hazy definition. As he was not much fancied, I managed to secure him for a small sum. McSweeny's animal, being quite unknown, also went for next to nothing, and the Bard, as he called him, was knocked down to the doctor. For Tilson's galloway we had to pay a stiffish price, as he had a reputation, but as two others in the same race were almost equally fancied, it did not so much signify, as it made the lottery well worth winning, and we were quite certain that the Pippin, as Tilson's nag was called, held everything else quite safe. For the hurdle race (extra), McSweeny, against my advice, bought my waler, The Buck, though "Mitchell's" animal was a red-hot favourite. On my remonstrating with the worthy medico, he only replied with a knowing wink: "I tell you I know something; you leave me alone. If you chaps don't like it, I'll have it all on my own account" (you see, we had formed a sort of little company, and all bets and stakes went to the firm). So confident was he of success, and as the amount involved was very little, we agreed that it should go into the pot, and after a peg or two we retired, well satisfied with the prospect of our investments. Tilson and self proceeded to turn in at once, as we both had a hard day before us, but McSweeny rode off to the Artillery lines, where he had a mysterious appointment, about which he was as silent as the tomb. Evidently it amused him, though, for he kept chuckling to himself like an asthmatic hen, till his syce brought his "tattoo" up, and he disappeared round the corner of the bungalow, returning in about an hour, and, much to our disgust, waking us both out of our first sleep.

The morning of the races was, as it generally is at that season, as fine as could be wished; not too hot, and not too much sun, and everybody was astir betimes. The course itself presented quite a gay appearance, with the natives in their best-coloured raiments, and a choice assortment of buggies, dog-carts, ekkas, and bullock hackerys were drawn up alongside the rails. Moreover, a troupe of niggers, recruited from the regiments, enlivened the proceedings with the latest comic songs, while the band of the European regiment was located in the paddock to play between the various events that figured on the card. The first of these was the big event, the steeplechase, and a field of ten faced the starter. We all got off well together, and came down to the first fence, a stiff hurdle, in a bunch. Here we lost four of the competitors, two coming down at the fence, one refusing, and one getting over himself but leaving his steed on the wrong side. For half the distance there was not much to choose between any of us. All the horses were jumping like angels, and I confess I did not feel quite so comfortable about winning as I had done the previous evening. However, the next quarter of a mile made a vast difference; the pace began to tell its tale, and, with the exception of the Prophet and a great raking chestnut belonging to the vet. of the hussar regiment, the rest were gradually tailing off. Neck and neck the vet. and I rode till we turned down to the water jump, which had been made a real good bath for any one who got in, not the ordinary—

> "Shallow dug pan with a hurdle to screen it,
> That cocktail imposture the steeplechase brook."

but a right-down honest piece of water between six and seven feet deep, and quite as broad as one wanted. Coming down the hill I let the Prophet have his head, and side by side we raced at the obstacle; both in the air together, and then a mighty splash—a volume of water glancing in the sun, for all the world like that caused by the explosion of a submarine mine, then one horse alone appeared in the straight—and that one being the Prophet. I cantered in an easy winner. McSweeny, radiant and beaming, rushed out to escort me into the paddock, accompanied by Ram Bux, my syce, who from the satisfaction lurking in his eyes and the corners of his mouth, had evidently gone a "raker" on his "gee," thereby spoiling the Egyptians in the shape of his brother syces, Just as I had weighed and "all right" was pronounced. the dripping vet. came in, only having managed to secure the third place, and, whether by design or accident, oddly enough, as he appeared amid shouts of laughter, the band struck up the well-known tune of "Wrap me up in my tarpaulin jacket," which so disgusted him that he rode straight home, and did not turn up again till the races were nearly over.

The next was an ekka race, to be driven by natives, half a mile, and the casualties were something surprising. Never before or since have I heard such a shindy as the natives kicked up. Both the drivers and their partisans running alongside yelled and screamed at the very top of their voices, while from time to time wheels would get locked, and then over would go the ekkas, and plaudits gave place to vituperation. It was eventually won by a boy of about nine, who was driving an extraordinary coloured steed belonging to one of the resident Baboos, the said steed rejoicing in a milk-white body, with pink eyes and nose, the mane and tail having been dyed a bright scarlet. As the winner received quite an ovation, I suppose the win was a popular one, and I noticed the youthful jockey regaling himself to his heart's content with a choice assortment of that peculiar class of sweet-meat so dear to the native soul, all of which was being poured upon him by enthusiastic admirers as a tribute to his skill.

Following this came the galloway race, which brought out a field of seven, among them the redoubtable Pippin, who looked fit to run for a man's life, and being beautifully ridden by Tilson, won the race for us by about two lengths.

The pony race, which, as I have already said, was the subject of some unpleasantness, resulted in the engineer being hoist with his own petard, for the jockeys, who the owner thought he had satisfactorily squared, refused to be parties to the transaction, and both his ponies were ridden out to win; the better of the two (which he had not bought himself) eventually coming in an easy winner. Of course, the owner could say nothing, as, if he opened his mouth, he would only have proclaimed his roguery; but his face showed that he did not like it. Moreover, as the jockeys were not so reticent, the whole matter came out, and the stewards taking the matter up, his racing career, for a time at all events, came to an abrupt termination.

So far our stable had done well, and now the third event in which we were engaged was at hand, for the saddling bell, or rather, the bugle which acted as such, rang out for the hack race. We had had a tremendous argument with McSweeny, trying to induce him not to ride the Bard himself; but he was obdurate, and declared no one knew the horse as well as he did, and ride he would. Accordingly we had to give in, and the doctor made his first appearance in silk. I forget how many went to the post, but it was a large field, and, being an open race, there were all sorts, shapes, and sizes, among them being a half-caste sportsman who fancied himself no end. After no less than three false starts they got off, the half-caste nobleman poaching two lengths. The Bard lay second, and we could see McSweeny riding all he knew. Close home he caught his adversary, when, to our amazement, we saw the half-caste suddenly rise in his stirrups and administer a sounding back-handed cut across the Bard's face, and then jamming both spurs home, shot right across him and landed his horse first by a neck. McSweeny's face was a picture! He was very much out of breath and crimson with rage as he came into the paddock, vowing vengeance.

"I'll have his blood, the hound! How dare he?" he shouted; and then launched a few choice epithets into space.

"All right, old man; keep your hair on!" said Tilson. "Just get your objection ready; it will be settled in a moment; every one saw it."

But so irate was the doctor, that it was all we could do to make him behave like a rational being, and to prevent him administering a sound thrashing to the offender on the spot. Of course the half-caste, much to his disgust, was disqualified for foul riding, and the race awarded to McSweeny, thus giving the firm the three races we had made up our minds to have.

Before the extra race the interval was filled up by a "tattoo" race, and a race where every man rode his adversary's tat, that is to say, he held the reins of his own animal, but was mounted on that of some other competitor, the inevitable consequence being that as the animals edged away from each other the luckless riders got spills.

After these were over, I proceeded to get ready for the last item on the card, and just as I was about to mount the Buck, McSweeny appeared, and said he wanted a word with me. Having assured himself that no one could hear him, he commenced: "Look here, you must ride this race, as I tell you, you will just wait on Mitchell till you get into the bottom, and then come away best pace and win. Mitchell's horse is the only one I am afraid of, so all you have to do is to keep your eyes on him."

"But," said I, "suppose I can't come away from him; what then? He has got the legs of me; I know, so I don't see how your little plan is going to work."

"Bosh!" replied the medico; "Mitchell's horse is a charger, and going through the school always makes them slow. You do as I tell you, and it is a certainty."

I could not for the life of me see the force of his argument, but promised, so far as I was able, to carry out his instructions; and up I got. The waler was not in the best of tempers, and having been kept some time standing about, resented it by commencing a series of uncompromising bucks, the third of which landed me well over his head almost at McSweeny's feet.

"By Jove! that's not part of the programme," said that worthy, as soon as he had ascertained that there was no damage done. "If you are going to fall off like that, we have not a ghost of a chance."

"Fall off, be hanged!" I retorted; "who the deuce is going to stick on a buck jumper in a seven-pound saddle? I should like to see you try."

Not a whit abashed, he remarked that if he had not something else to do he would; and, as it was time for me to go to the post, I remounted and rode off, feeling rather sore and somewhat indignant withal.

Only four went to the post as it was considered a moral for Mitchell, and from the supercilious way he eyed my mount I could see that he was himself of the same opinion. Another exhibition of temper on the part of my beautiful Australian delayed us for some time, but at last a start was effected, and we were off. It was no more use my trying to wait on Mitchell than fly, for directly the flag fell the Buck took the bit between his teeth, and with a mad plunge that precious nearly deposited me a second time he dashed to the front, and was over the first hurdle some five lengths in advance of anything. The more I pulled the more determined he seemed to be, and the pace accordingly was a cracker. About half the distance, however, I managed to sober the gentleman down a bit; and Mitchell, who had been forced to ride his horse out, gradually drew up, the other two being quite outpaced. As we descended the hill to the bottom indicated by McSweeny we were neck and neck, Mitchell if anything being a shade in advance, and as we neared the hurdles he let his horse go, evidently meaning to come away and win as he liked. It had just flashed through my mind as to what on earth McSweeny meant by telling me to make the running from here, when I saw his well-known form standing by the hurdle, and cheering me on, while from out of a clump of trees that lay on the right of the course, rang out sharp and clear, a trumpet call—"The halt!" No sooner did

Mitchell's horse hear it than, planting both his forelegs in front of him, he stopped as if he had been shot, right under the hurdle, over which his rider described a beautiful parabola known as a "voluntary." A wild unearthly yell from McSweeny of "Gang awa, gang awa-a-a, mon" (he was wont to relapse into broad Scotch when excited) gave me the office, and over I went, racing up the hill as if the devil himself was behind me. On getting into the straight I looked round, and saw that Mitchell had again remounted and was doing his best to make up for lost time. But it was too late, as I had got a good quarter of a mile start, and jumped in an easy winner. In fact, it was the Buck first, the rest nowhere. Perhaps there was not a shine when Mitchell arrived! I have seldom seen a man so wild, and being unable to do anything only made him worse. He could not lodge an objection, because under no rules of racing had he any grounds for so doing, and though he talked very big about what he was going to do, and about the d—d robbery, etc., etc., it came to nothing, more especially as I told him I was as innocent of the transaction as a babe unborn. Oddly enough, Mitchell had not noticed McSweeny at the hurdle, and when the doctor turned up in the middle of the rumpus and asked what it was all about, he gave him, in all good faith, a history of the "infernal trumpet," as he called it, with a few adjectives added—not of the politest. "Dear, dear, what a pity; and you were winning too!" said the unabashed medico. "I'll tell you what it is, Mitchell, it only shows what a mistake it is to teach a dumb animal music! Now I once had a dog——" What further disclosures McSweeny would have made concerning his dog will never be known, for amid shouts of laughter from every one who was near, Mitchell, highly incensed, stalked off, muttering anathemas against horses, trumpets, and dogs in general.

That evening, when Tilson and myself tackled McSweeny in the privacy of our bungalow, he confessed that he had suddenly remembered that Mitchell's horse was famed for knowing every call and acting thereon at once, so, by bribing a trumpeter to sound the halt at that particular moment, he had carried out his little plot And when we remonstrated with him on the iniquity of the transaction, he only said: "I have owed that fellow one for ages; he has got a thundering sight too much cheek. I fancy now, though, it will take him some time before he forgets this little game. My word, but he was savage!" And then he went into such fits of laughter at the thought of his own villainy that he nearly choked, and it took both our united efforts to bring him to his sober senses, which we did by pounding his back as hard as we could. Needless to say, Mitchell did all he knew to find out who the guilty musician was who caused his defeat; but he never did, and, after a time, he came to see the ludicrous side of the matter, and used to tell the story against himself as a joke. And so ended the sky meeting which, taking it all round, was a great success—at least, our stable thought so, for we had carried off four events, and won quite a nice little sum of money between us. Though I am bound to confess that, although I was in no way an accessory before the fact, I felt certain qualms of conscience in taking a share of the bets and stakes appertaining to the extra race, which I had won solely and entirely by what, to give it a *quasi*-alliterative title, I may call McSweeny's stratagem.

CHAPTER IV.

A DAY'S PIGSTICKING.

THE first time that I made acquaintance with that most exciting of all Indian sport, yclept pigsticking, I confess I was somewhat sceptical on the subject. I had not long arrived from the "old country," and the glorious memories of a quick forty minutes with a straight-going fox were thick upon me. I did not believe for a moment that anything could compare with the helter-skelter rush for a place when the welcome "Gone away!" had sounded from the bottom of the gorse; or that the satisfaction of finding one's self sailing away in the van with a breast high scent and an eager pack could be equalled. Of course I had heard (who has not?) of the excitement of a race for the first spear, and the well-known song, of "The Boar, the Boar, the Mighty Boar," was not new to me. Still, for all that, I was not a true believer, and when after much preliminary discussion the Pigsticking Club was formed, I enrolled myself as a member, more out of curiosity than anything else.

It was at my first up-country station in the North-Western Provinces that I made my *début*, and, as it happened, formed one of a small company to inaugurate the sport of that locality. Certainly, in former days, there had been pigsticking there, but at the time I am alluding to no such thing had been seen or heard of for some years, and it was only the proverbial oldest inhabitant who remembered anything about either the ground or the sport.

We were fortunate in having in the station two old hands and enthusiastic sportsmen as leaders of the movement, in the shape of the Commissioner Sahib named Field, and the Magistrate, who answered to the name of Quick. The former was well known as one of the best spears in Bengal, while the latter, though not so renowned, followed close in his footsteps, and what he lacked in experience he made up for in extra keenness. Besides, Quick had a happy knack of instilling the native mind with a great respect for both himself and the majesty of the law. The Rajas and coolies alike considered him a great man, and as the management of affairs, especially the "honks," devolved on his shoulders, it was just as well that this should be so. The rest of us, with the exception of the officers of the hussar regiment quartered there, and who had been some time in India, were for the most part novices, made up of Civil Engineers, Indigo planters, Civil Service, and the remaining officers of the garrison. At the first meeting it was carried that every member should pay an entrance of twenty rupees, and as many as went out to the meet were bound to contribute to the expenses of the day besides, in equal shares. Other rules were made, which I scarcely remember now, beyond that for riding a sow there was a fine of, I think, ten rupees, and for slaughtering a squeaker double that amount, and some other penalty to boot.

Everybody, directly matters were settled, commenced to lay in a stock of spears and other paraphernalia, and my bungalow presented quite the appearance of either an armoury or an ironmonger's shop. There was plenty to do before the opening day, for it became necessary to increase the stud, and a good pigsticker was not to be picked up every day. Personally I was most fortunate, for some three weeks before the subject had been mooted, I had bought an animal from an officer of the hussars who was going home on leave, which said animal had the reputation of being, besides the finest fencer, one of the best pigstickers in the North-Western Provinces; and a second horse which I purchased out of a batch of artillery casters turned out nearly as good. There are some horses who are natural pigstickers, and seem to delight in it, and who, besides showing no fear, manage by intuition to take care of themselves and avoid being ripped, while others, no matter what their breeding or class may be, never acquire the art, and invariably get into trouble and badly cut every time they are taken out. Luckily my caster came under the former denomination, so that I had two horses requiring no training, and consequently had only to learn the tricks of the trade myself.

The programme for the opening day was to camp out the night before close to the ground, which was situated some six miles from the cantonments, so that we could make an early start of it the following morning. We ourselves proposed to ride or drive out to camp in the cool of the evening after dinner, while the horses would go on ahead with the tents and camp equipage. Of course, when the day arrived, there was the usual difficulty with the coolies and bullock hackeries; and though Quick had put the train under the charge of the jemadar of police and his myrmidons, the whole *posse* halted some little way out and engaged in either a political or social discussion, which, had not Quick himself suddenly appeared in their midst like the spirit of wrath, would doubtless have been continued *ad infinitum*. However, his arrival was the signal for a general stampede, and so scathing were his remarks, and such dire vengeance did he promise, that they never halted again till they reached the tope of mango trees which had been selected for our camp. The Commissioner and Quick wisely declined to join us younger spirits at dinner; but having made an early repast cantered out to the camp as soon as the sun was low. I say "wisely," because the dinner was not the best preparation for the sport to come. The "Simkin" circulated freely (in some instances rather too freely), and when at last we did make a move it was at a much later hour than that originally intended.

There was a great assembly in the mess compound of "tats," with their attendant syces, buggies, dog-carts, and "ticka gharries," and there was no little confusion as to which was what and whose was whose. At last affairs righted themselves, and amid a series of "view holloas," and other discordant noises, we started, a joyous cavalcade, led by two ticka gharries full inside and out and tooled respectively by young Gordon of the hussars, the last joined cornet (they were cornets in those days), and Percy of the artillery. I am sorry to say that both these young gentlemen were among the instances in which the Giesler had circulated too freely, and how they steered out of the compound gate is to this day a mystery to me. No sooner, however, were they well clear and in the road, than occurred the inevitable challenge to race, and away they went yawing about all over the place, and leaving behind them bits of harness, or rather, pieces of rope that acted as such, every ten yards. I was driving in a buggy just behind with Colville, an Indigo planter, and directly his horse saw the gharries start he took it into his head that he must do likewise, and though we both "tailed on" to the reins, nothing would stop him, and there we were bounding along first on one wheel and then on another, till at last we ran into the hindermost "ticka" which had collapsed from the sheer expenditure of harness—there being nothing left for the unfortunate tats to pull with. Luckily, though we both shot out and the buggy turned over, there was no damage done, and having righted the ship and assisted in the operation of refitting and re-rigging the broken-down craft that had caused our mishap, we proceeded on our journey to catch up the remainder of the company who had passed us. We had not very far to go, for about a quarter of a mile further on we found them all assembled round a large tank, endeavouring to rescue the ponies and extricate the other gharrie therefrom. Young Gordon, it appeared, was so elated at the collapse of his rival that he never thought of looking where he was going, and, coming upon the tank suddenly, round a turn in the road, he had driven the whole bag of tricks full gallop into the middle of it, much to the discomfort of the insides, and to the eminent peril of the tats, who, hampered by the harness, were gradually being drowned by the water-logged *and fast-sinking* trap. However, with the aid of some ropes, partly from the other trap and partly heel ropes, we managed to make a fairly substantial cable, which two of the dripping gentlemen who had, thanks to Gordon, taken an involuntary bath, swam off with, and affixed to the gharrie. Then, with a "long pull, a strong pull, and a pull altogether," we got it close to the side, and finally up the bank on to *terra firma*, ponies and all. The damage to the harness was soon repaired with ropes, string, and pieces of strap, and, with the exception of having lost a door, a lamp, a cushion or two, and being soaking wet, the gharrie was not much the worse, and the crew having once more got aboard, off they started again; this time under the guidance of the native Jehu, who evidently looked on Gordon as a direct descendant of Shaitan.

No further mishap having occurred, we were soon at the camp, where we found Field and Quick awaiting us, and quite prepared to give us a lecture on our being so much behind time. But the history of our adventures, and the appearance of the shipwrecked crew, did for them entirely, and the lecture was forgotten in shouts of laughter, in which every one joined so heartily that it necessitated the opening of sundry "pegs," after which we turned in, and silence reigned throughout the camp.

Five a.m. the following morning we were aroused, and coffee, etc., was under way in the mess tent, where we all assembled in due course. We mustered eighteen or twenty spears, and were consequently divided into two divisions, the one being under the command of the Commissioner Sahib, and the other in charge of Quick. Both commanders further sub-divided their troops into bodies of three, who were bound to stick to each other throughout the day, and then came the ceremony of drawing lots to determine which party should have the first run, the lot falling to the commissioner's army corps, which numbered amongst its ranks my humble person. This being over, and chota hazzi finished, the signal to mount was given, and we filed off in two columns, followed by our respective syces. There was a certain amount of awkwardness shown by a great many of us I am afraid, in the handling of our spears; at least, so far as I am concerned personally I am sure of it, for I well remember now what an encumbrance I found it in the management of my too eager mount, but happily no accident occurred, and we reached the margin of the jungle in safety and full of expectation.

Here we took up our positions right and left, and Quick went forward to where we could see the red turban of the jemadar of police conspicuous among the army of beaters, in order to give his final instruction about the "honk." As soon as he had finished his confabulation with the jemadar, the signal was given, and the beat commenced. Pandemonium let loose would be a joke to the row! Tom-tom-wallahs drumming, men shouting, guns firing, dogs barking, horses plunging, all combined to assist in one grand chorus quite worthy of Wägner at his best.

Presently we heard the welcome sound of "Soor, Soor," and a little later a sounder broke away, led by a fine old tusker, after whom, at a given signal, my party started. Now, as the said party consisted of Field the commissioner, one of the hussars, also an old hand at the game, and myself the novice, it stood to reason that my chance of obtaining a spear was a very small one; but away I went, best pace, determined to do or die. From the nature of the ground I thought it would result probably in the latter, but there was not much time for reflection, because the pace a pig can go when fairly on the job is surprising, as is the awful ground in which a good pigsticker will travel in perfect safety—ground which to look at in cold blood would make—

> "Each particular hair to stand an end,
> Like quills upon the fretful porcupine,"

as the bard has it.

We were all then pretty well matched, as far as pace went, so were making a neck-and-neck race of it, and I had just begun to think that after all there might be a chance for the novice, when the boar suddenly "jinked" right under my horse—a proceeding which took me completely by surprise, and as nearly as possible unshipped me altogether. I was riding the animal with a reputation, and directly he saw piggy's manœuvre, he jumped clean over him as high as if he was clearing a big post and rails, and thereby avoided being ripped, but so unexpected was the sudden bound into vacancy, that it was all I could do to keep my seat, and when at last I recovered myself I had the satisfaction of seeing my competitors with a long lead, and recognized that I was out of it altogether that time. However, I made the best of a bad job, and followed in their wake, arriving just in time to see Field obtain the first spear, the hussar having come a cropper at a nullah some fifty yards back. "Look out for the charge!" shouted Field as I passed him, thirsting to flesh my maiden spear, and almost before the words were out of his mouth the boar was round and charging slap at me. Again my stud showed his wisdom and saved his bacon, enabling me at the same time to deliver a well-timed, though somewhat fluky, thrust. "Good," said Field, who was watching the *denouement*, and I was as proud of that monosyllable as if I had received the thanks of the commander-in-chief at the head of the army. Our enemy, the boar, then got his back up against a small tree, and evidently intended to make a fight of it and to die game—an intention he carried out to the bitter end, for our party having been augumented by a further detachment, who had accounted for their quarry, we all took it in turns to ride at him—a proceeding which resulted in two horses being badly ripped and having to be taken away. Eventually, however, he succumbed to the inevitable, and the fighting old boar breathed his last, with his face to the foe, like the valiant old soldier that he was.

Meanwhile Quick's party had not been idle, and bacon being plentiful, they had had on their side some excellent sport, and three boars had bitten the dust. Gordon, who by the way belonged to our lot, had wounded a sow, and accordingly came in for a deal of chaff, besides having to fork out the fine. It was no use his protesting his innocence. There were too many witnesses against him, most of them I noticed being those who had suffered from his "Jehuship" the previous evening. So he had to pay up and look pleasant.

After a short interval for rest, we moved on to the next beat, for which, being in more open ground, we were able to utilize a couple of elephants which Quick had brought out, and which were found very useful adjuncts for directing the operations. Unfortunately, in this "honk," we had a native badly ripped by a pig that broke back through the line, and if our doctor had not been on the spot and taken prompt measures, using a couple of turbans as bandages, I believe the man would have bled to death. As soon as he had been attended to and sent back to camp, we proceeded, and, forming a line, went steadily across the open. We had only gone about half a mile, when on the left flank, occupied by Quick and his army, there broke away a huge sounder among them, being four or five boars which, having been separated from the rest, gave the whole of his party employment. Shortly after our lot were equally busy, and to my great delight, as well as surprise, more by good luck than good management, I managed to obtain the spear from the Commissioner Sahib, and there and then became a convert and embraced the worship of the "Soor." Field, though I could see he did not quite like being beaten by a novice, was very generous about it, and congratulated me heartily on my success, and as we dismounted and turned our horses' heads towards the wind after the fray, I felt myself quite a hero.

The wind-up of our day's sport was a general race towards the camp by the whole hunt after a solitary boar, over some of the worst ground in the district, and many were the falls, and plentiful the anathemas, though luckily no one was really hurt. The honours were equally divided between our two commanders, who both got home simultaneously, at least so close together that no one could say which was entitled to the first spear, and then we cantered off to the camp, and to a welcome tub, fully prepared, after a change, to do ample justice to the breakfast which had been prepared during our absence. And such a breakfast (or rather I should say a tiffiin) as it was! Some of the ladies had come out from the station and graced the table with their presence, so a merrier party could not well be imagined. The commissioner made an excellent speech, as also did Quick. And Gordon, who had to return thanks for the ladies, was very happy in his remarks when he apologized for his want of chivalry in wounding one of their sex. The champagne cup was iced to perfection, and when it came to cigars and coffee, every one acknowledged that they had had a most charming day, and our Pigsticking Club was voted a great success. Indeed, though I subsequently saw a good deal of the sport, carried out probably in a more othodox manner, I don't think I ever enjoyed it better than on the occasion of my first experience, when I went prepared to ban and remained, like a better man, to bless.

CHAPTER V.

A TRIP TO THE HILLS.

For some months before we made a start for three months' shooting in the hills, our plans and arrangements had been the subject of long and anxious consideration; over and over again our route had been changed and a new one devised, only to return again to our original intentions. Tents and shouldarees had been ordered and counter-ordered, till at last for very shame we were obliged to buy one that was entirely useless, and had we set out with the amount of stores that we had put down on paper as requisite, we should have required the greater portion of our Indian army to carry them. Eventually, however, we actually did come to a definite conclusion, and one fine day found Newcombe, Fairleigh, and myself preparing to follow our goods and chattels, which we had already sent on to Naini Tal. Newcombe was an old shikarie, though he had never been in the Himalayas before, but Fairleigh and myself were by no means such mighty hunters, our experience being at that time limited, so far as big game was concerned, to the slaughter of the graceful black buck and an occasional blue cow or nilgai. Consequently we were obliged to agree to everything that Newcombe suggested, and he did not forget to take advantage of our ignorance by making us do double the amount of work we ought to have done, while he entirely shirked any share of the labour that fell by rights on his shoulders. Of course, so far as expenses went, it was share and share alike, and the like proportion should, in all fairness, have been maintained in the work; but the old shikarie knew a trick worth two of that, and though profuse with his orders and advice, he took exceeding good care that whatever trouble it caused us, nothing should interfere with his *otium cum dignitate.* Doubtless, however, had the positions been reversed and the experience laid on our side, we should have done exactly the same, so it cannot be said that he was much to blame.

But to continue. Part of our way we had to go by dâk. It was my first introduction to that method of travel, and I cannot say I fully appreciated its beauties. Either our gharries were more than usually defective in the arrangements of their springs, or our "rezais" were not sufficiently thick to save us from "the thousand natural shocks that flesh is heir to" when once under way, for at the end of the journey we were all bruised black and blue, and so stiff and sore that we could hardly move. Could a cricket ball feel, I can quite understand its sensations on being hit to leg for four, for on that occasion in the dâk, metaphorically speaking, I was hit to leg every five minutes, and hit very hard too. The first stage, being along a decent road, was not so bad, but when it came to lighting straw under the bellies of the ponies to get them to start over a track rather more "nubbley" than the streets of a Mexican town, Oh, Lord! However, it certainly gave plenty of employment to the mind, for besides the uncertainty of the harness holding out, or the wheels keeping on, it was always a matter for conjecture which part of the vehicle, back or front, roof or sides, would be visited by your unfortunate person at the next bound or jolt. How the driver managed to stick on I never quite fathomed, for it must have been worse than riding on the limbers of a gun at full gallop across country. Stick on, though, he did, and, unlike myself, at the end of the journey seemed little, if any, the worse for it; and while I could scarcely crawl he was, what the Americans would call, "waltzing around" quite happy, on the look-out for the sahib's bucksheesh.

Very glad indeed was I when the torture came to a termination, and from their faces I could see that my companions in misfortune shared my joy. We had a pleasant ride up the hill, and finally installed ourselves at the Lake Hotel, where we found our advance guard had arrived about four days previously. Naini Tal in those days was a very different place, I fancy, to what it is now. It was before the terrible accident and landslip, and it was then by no means so much frequented or so fashionable a resort as it afterwards became. However, the hotel was particularly comfortable, and the rest and cool air very refreshing, so for two or three days we thoroughly enjoyed ourselves, and abandoned everything to the pleasures of *dolce far niente.* Every morning we had a swim in the cold water of the lake, which gave us an appetite for breakfast of a hundred horse power, and that meal being over, we smoked and idled the time away according to our several lights. Newcombe was the first to awake to the fact that the lotus-eating existence we were leading was not conducive either to travel or sport, and so once more we set to work arranging, collecting, buying, and packing. Newcombe would fain have played his old game, and merely directed the operations, pipe in mouth, from the depths of a comfortable armchair; but, luckily, by this time we had gained some experience, and, much to his disgust, we refused to do more than our proper share, so he was forced to buckle-to with the rest of us.

It took us three hard days' work to get everything ready, and there was some little difficulty about procuring the necessary number of coolies to carry our goods. But "it is a long lane that has no turning," and at 8 a.m. on the fourth day things were all ship-shape, and the coolies loaded and despatched under the command of Newcombe's Madrassee boy, John by name. Two hours after they had gone, we ourselves prepared to follow, and having given our rifles to our two shikaries, we shouldered our guns and set out to march our first stage of ten miles. We had wisely determined to make short marches at first, till we got into condition, when our daily journey was increased to fifteen, and in some instances twenty miles. When we arrived at our camp the first day out, which we did about three in the afternoon, we found John had already pitched our tents, and was busily engaged plucking a fowl for our dinner. We had one fair-sized but light shouldaree tent for ourselves, and a smaller one, which was given over to John as his kitchen, pantry, and sleeping-place, three small camp beds with waterproof sheeting, and the ever-useful rezais being the only furniture carried; but although we were travelling in light marching order, our coolies presented a formidable cavalcade, and we soon saw that when we got beyond Almorah we should have to reduce our baggage considerably, or, notwithstanding any amount of perwanhas and other official documents, we should be left stranded for want of sufficient transport.

I am sorry to say that our first night's sleep was by no means so peaceful as it might have been, for John took the opportunity of misbehaving himself to the extent of getting hilariously drunk. John, I may state, prided himself on being a Christian, an excellent thing to be, no doubt, but as the form of his religion occasionally showed itself through the medium of the bottle, one sometimes could not help wishing that he had been a follower of the Prophet or a worshipper at the shrine of Vishnu. Anyhow, on the night in question, he had evidently poured out libations to the success of our trip far too frequently, and the consequence was that no sooner were we all comfortably in bed, than he burst into song. "What the devil's that?" asked Fairleigh. "Jackals," I replied, half asleep; but on a louder and still more discordant note being sounded, Newcombe fathomed the mystery by exclaiming, "It's that brute, John; he is tight, and trying to sing. I'll give him something to sing for, d—n him," and then he got out of his bed, grumbling all the time, and, having found a bamboo cane, went out into the night in the direction of our Christian friend's sleeping-place; and presently we heard sounds issuing therefrom that told us plainly John was being subjected to some forcible remonstrances, emphasized by a bamboo accompaniment. Unfortunately the cure only lasted a short time, for Newcombe had scarcely turned round once in his couch when the noise began again. And it was not until past three o'clock in the morning, notwithstanding our united endeavours, that the singer ceased from troubling, and the weary were at rest.

Of course John next morning was very penitent, and so profuse in his promises that such a thing should not occur again (which promises, I am glad to say, he kept with only one falling away), besides suffering so evidently from hot coppers and headache, that we forgave him with a solemn warning, and started him off with the camp directly we had finished chota hazri, meaning to get to our next camping-ground in time for tiffin, which of course we did not do, and, consequently, were pretty nigh famished before we could get anything to eat. Newcombe was furious, and laid all the blame at our door. "This comes of going out on a shooting expedition with a couple of green hands; I thought I was a fool when I started," he growled. But Fairleigh cut him short by saying, "I don't know what you thought when you started, but I can tell you what I think, and that is that you are an infernal fool now to talk such rot;" and as I backed him up, we were two to one, and the old shikarie had to cave in.

We stayed two or three days in Almorah, where we were delayed getting a perwanhah and rupees, both of which articles were essential to our well-being, but the time passed pleasantly enough, for the officers of the Goorkas who were there treated us most hospitably, and undertook to look after everything we left behind. It was no easy matter to select what we should discard, for we were bound to take a fair amount of stores with us, as Almorah was the last place at which we could expect to obtain anything like tinned soups or articles of that description, and we were sorely puzzled. John's tent was the first to go, much to his disgust; as for the future he would have to make a lodging for himself out of boughs, or sleep under the fly of our shouldaree, where, Fairleigh said, "he would be near at hand, and within easy reach if he ventured to turn on the minstrel tap again."

Then we dispensed with two cases of brandy, some tins of flour, and a quantity of spare ammunition, all of which we argued we could send back for if we found we required them. Even then we had more to carry than we knew what to do with; but by surreptitiously increasing the individual load of each coolie, and distributing odds and ends judiciously among them, we managed to get along, though at first it was a tight fit. For the first four or five marches we had little or no sport, beyond an occasional shot at black partridge and a snap shot at some gooral, one of which we wounded but failed to bag—somewhat of a disappointment, as fresh venison would have been a treat of no mean order. At last, however, we arrived at Kilgoong. I think the name of the place was Kilgoong, but am not certain, and writing from memory, with no data to refer to, I may be mistaken. Anyhow, it was close under the snow hills, and we reached it after a heavy day's walking, just as the sun was setting. Never shall I forget the beauty of the scene as we suddenly came over the crest of a small hill and saw the whole of the snowy range laid out before us like a map—the high peaks towering into the sky, majestic, silent, and grand beyond expression, while the setting sun turned the whole into one lovely pink hue, the colour of the most delicate blush rose. All around us were scattered quantities of small ripe Alpine strawberries, which I, who had been suffering from a touch of fever, ate with avidity, and a little lower down the opposite slope we could see numerous bushes of yellow raspberries on the banks of a mountain stream, close to which, on a small level plateau, John had pitched our camp. "By Jove, how beautiful!" I exclaimed. "It is like Paradise; I vote we stop here for a bit."

"So do I; it's like a dream," said Fairleigh; and then we turned to Newcombe for an expression of his opinion, but were rather surprised to find him intently surveying through his glasses some bushes about two hundred yards down the hill to our right. Presently he beckoned to one of the shikaries, and directed his attention to the same spot, and the pair of them stood looking for a few moments without speaking. At last Newcombe shut his glasses with a snap and said, "I thought so; it's a bear." And the shikarie corroborating his opinion, we were all of us immediately on the *qui vive*, and the beauty of the scenery was at once forgotten in the excitement of the chase.

Our plans were soon formed. Fairleigh was to make a detour to the right with the second shikarie, I was to move a short way down the hill to our left, while Newcombe and the other shikarie delivered a direct attack. As we cautiously approached the bushes, we saw to our great delight not one but two bears, male and female, both of whom, quite unsuspicious of evil, were making their evening meal of fruit and berries. As soon as I arrived at the spot where I had been told to wait, I sat down, and, keeping my eye on the bushes, watched the development of the centre and right flank attack. From my position I could see Fairleigh in the distance, but from the nature of the ground, Newcombe was invisible. Presently, however, I heard the "crack, crack," of his rifle, and the largest of the bears suddenly sprang up in the air, and then stumbled off to the right, evidently hard hit, while the other, after a moment's hesitation, came best pace towards where I was seated. I confess I was tremendously excited, and my hand trembled so that I could scarcely hold my rifle. However, I pulled myself together, and as Mrs. Bhaloo emerged from a clump of thick bushes, I took a steady aim at the white spot and pulled. The smoke hung so that for a moment I did not know whether I had missed or no, but as it cleared away I had the satisfaction of seeing a dark mass lying on the ground, and from the shouts of the men who were left on the summit of the hill, I knew that I had killed my first bear.

Before I could load again I heard Fairleigh's rifle ring out, both barrels, and then a single shot from Newcombe, followed by a shout of "Look out on the left!" Jamming two cartridges into my rifle, I ran a little way down the hill to get a better view, when I came suddenly face to face with the second bear, badly wounded. Directly he saw me, however, he turned short back, and made upwards as fast as he could. I dared not fire, for I did not know where either of the other guns might have got to by this time, so contented myself with shouting, and then laid myself flat down behind a big stone to avoid any stray bullets that I expected would soon be flying about. After a few moments' silence, crack went Newcombe's rifle again, and his loud "who-whoop" told me that all was over, and that by the greatest piece of luck in the world we had bagged two bears in less than half an hour. Oddly enough, neither Newcombe nor Fairleigh, when we rejoined each other, knew that I had killed my animal. They had heard me fire, but being unable to see, and only hearing a single shot, they thought that I had missed, and that the bear had got off scot free. When I told them, therefore, that I had scored, I came in for much congratulation, and Newcombe insisted on blooding me, for luck, as he put it. Anyhow, we had a great night in camp, and having deprived the bears of their jackets, securing at the same time some tit bits, we had an extra tot of grog round, and having gladdened John's heart with a stiff "nor-wester," we turned in and slept the sleep of the just.

The next day, acting on the advice of our head shikarie, we arranged to make an expedition into a neighbouring valley to try a drive for deer; so, leaving our camp standing, and taking with us only our bedding and waterproof sheets, we started to descend some fifteen hundred or two thousand feet, and arrived at our destination about five o'clock in the evening. Under the direction of the redoubtable John, a very comfortable bower was erected of bamboo, which, with a thick carpet of leaves and grass, looked most inviting. But the heat was tremendous, for we were surrounded on all sides by hills which entirely excluded every breath of air. It was as if we were at the bottom of a well, and we felt it the more from having suddenly come down from an altitude of over ten thousand feet. Sleep was almost out of the question, and when at an early hour the following morning the head of the village or district came with a noble army of beaters to place us in position before he went off with his men to drive the hills round, I fancy we one and all wished him at the devil. The result of the drive was not a success, for although the men said they had started no end of deer, not a sign of anything came near us, and we were forced to chronicle a blank day, at the same time registering a vow that we would try no more of these sudden descents into the awful heat of the valleys.

It was a very different matter going up to our camp again, for the two nights had so taken it out of us that we could scarcely get up the hill, and in places where the ascent was steeper than ordinary we were obliged to sit down and gasp. When at last the white side of our shouldaree hove in sight we could have shouted for joy, and it did not take us long after we arrived before all three were revelling in a bath in the mountain stream. That and a cool peg put us in better spirits, and we soon forgot the troubles we had endured in the valley, though it was some days before we recovered our strength entirely, and, what is more, the whole party who went down suffered more or less from a slight attack of fever.

Two days later we pushed on towards the snows, and some pretty rough ground we had to pass over, sometimes having to swing round an awkward corner by holding on to a bush with a sheer drop of some thousand feet into the khud below if by chance we let go or the bush came out by the roots. On these occasions John's face was a picture—a picture of despair—and he had to summon up all his Christian fortitude, which was not much, before he could make the attempt. He would generally bid us all farewell as he grasped the branches over his head, preparatory to swinging himself across, saying, "Good-bye, sahibs, good-bye; me Christian man, sahib, but me be killed, and what my wife say?" and then when he found himself safe on the other side he would draw a deep breath of satisfaction and exclaim, "Ah me, all right this time; but next time me die!" When we reached about twelve thousand feet by the barometer we found a convenient spot for our camp, and decided to stay three or four days there in order to try for some burrhel or mountain sheep. Very hard work it was too, for these animals are exceedingly wary, and require very careful stalking. The first morning I went out with our head shikarie by myself, Newcombe and Fairleigh being lazy, and our second shikarie being laid up *pro tem.* with a bad foot, for the cure of which, like all natives, he had bound up his head. It was always a mystery to me when I was in India what first put it into the native mind that an injury in any part of the body was only to be cured by binding up the head. But so it was; no matter what the malady might be—fever, dysentery, a broken leg, or a sprained ankle—it was always the same. The patient's head was at once enveloped in bandages, and I never was able to convince them that it could not possibly have any good result. After we had gone about two miles the shikarie suddenly pulled me down, and pointing eagerly to a cluster of rugged-looking rocks about three hundred yards off, whispered in my ear, "Burrhel, sahib, burrhel." For some time I gazed intently at the place, and for the life of me could see nothing, but as he was so confident, I put myself under his guidance, and we commenced a long and difficult stalk in order to get down wind of our quarry; eventually he led me within a hundred yards of them, behind a projecting ledge, and on looking over the edge I saw two fine beasts facing me, evidently suspecting something, but not quite sure from what quarter the danger was to be apprehended. Carefully pushing my rifle in front of me I took a steady aim, when "click" my right-hand barrel missed fire, and the two burrhel simultaneously gave a bound in the air and vanished over the side of the rock. Cursing my luck, I dashed forward and managed to get a snap shot with my second barrel at the hindermost, just as he was disappearing. By the greatest fluke in the world the bullet took effect, and down the khud rolled the burrhel stone dead. It was hopeless to try and get down to him then, so, having marked the spot, we returned to camp and got some men and ropes, with which, after a two hours' job, we succeeded in getting the head and skin. We had to lower two men down the precipice by ropes to where the animal had stuck in a cleft of the rock, and they had to skin him as best they could and cut off his head, bringing the trophies with them when they were drawn up again. The following day we all three went out after gooral, and succeeded in bagging two, Newcombe and Fairleigh getting one apiece, while I distinguished myself by missing one of the easiest shots imaginable. On our way home a serraow deer jumped up in front of us, and though we all fired a volley at him and brought him down on to his head, he eventually escaped after giving us a good two hours' job following up his tracks, which were very plain from the blood he left on the long grass. We spent three more days in our camp, during which time I got one more burrhel, as also did Newcombe, and Fairleigh bagged a bear, which was quite an unexpected event, as we had not seen any signs of the animal about, and there was not much in the way of food for them where we were. We then packed up our traps and pushed forward for the pass, supposed to be between thirteen and fourteen thousand feet altitude, though I think that is over the mark. However, when we arrived we found the pass still blocked, and after a council of war decided to return by a different route and shoot our way back to Almorah. I don't think any one was sorry, for it was bitterly cold in the snows, and the atmosphere was so rarefied that we found great difficulty sometimes in breathing, besides which our men showed signs of knocking up, and John, who was getting more miserable and shrivelled up daily, and declared every hour would be his last, pointed out that our stores were giving out—"no flour, no soup, no brandy sharab soon, what we do? We die. I die any way, but if no food sahibs die; what then?" he said, and so the order to retreat was given.

We travelled over the same ground again as far as Kilgoong, or Gilgoong, and then struck off to the left, taking a track at a somewhat lower altitude. The second night after we left Kilgoong we had a rare scare. Our camp had been pitched on the side of a hill overhung by some trees, and about three in the morning we were woke up by the most infernal shindy. Everybody was holloaing and shouting at the same time, while in the midst of it all John dashed into our tents, yelling like a maniac, and catching his foot in a box which was doing duty for a table, he landed on to the top of Fairleigh's bed, which immediately collapsed under the double weight.

"Get out, you drunken beast," roared Fairleigh, as soon as he had extricated himself from the *débris*. "Get out, or I will flay you alive." (Of course we thought John had been at the bottle again.) But John remained where he was, howling with fear and pain, for he had barked his shin against the box, and the row outside still going on we could not for the life of us make out what had happened. At last Newcombe, by the application of his slippers in default of a better article, managed to bring his retainer to his senses, and in reply to his query as to what all the row was about, John stammered out, "Bhag come, tiger come, eat me, very bad, master." "Tiger be hanged!" I said, getting up. "Yes, sahib, big tiger. I Christian man, I speak true; he come just now, eat me bad," persisted John; and so we all groped for our rifles and ran outside. When we at last obtained a hearing, we found that it was as John had said, only substituting leopard or panther for tiger. It appears that John had built himself a snug little bower of branches, under which he had curled himself up in his blanket fast asleep, when he was suddenly woke up by the collapse of his house about his ears, and a heavy body falling on the top of him, which he saw to be, in the dim morning light, what he called a tiger. The yell that he gave woke the whole camp, and the shikaries saw the brute bound off, and then all the men began to shout to help him on his journey. One of the branches had scratched John's arm, and in his terror he thought he had been seized by the tiger, *hinc illæ lacrymæ.* Whether the brute had bounded off a bank or tree, and so dropped by accident on to the roof of John's shanty, or whether, attracted by some fowls which we had there, it had endeavoured to seize them and so caused the collapse, we never could make out. Certain it was, however, that the animal had been there and had managed to frighten the Christian man well-nigh into a gibbering idiot, besides depriving us of all chance of further sleep, for the occurrence was too much of an event not to be thoroughly debated in general council by all our men, and of course the house must needs assemble to be addressed by the hero of the disaster, just in rear of our shouldaree.

The next day, notwithstanding our broken night, we had a long march of twenty odd miles, and we had tiffin halfway and then shot up to camp. I had only taken my smoothbore, and though I had taken the precaution to put a few cartridges loaded with bullets in my pocket, I did not intend to do more than pick up, if possible, a partridge or so for dinner. I was very fortunate, for I managed to bag two brace of black partridges and a jungle cock, and when I rejoined the others I found that Newcombe had shot a little kakar, or barking deer, so that our larder was well stocked. It was just as well that it was so, for that night it came on to rain, and for the next two days it poured in torrents. To improve matters, John managed to smash three out of our four remaining bottles of brandy, and when he came to inform us of the accident, bringing with him the broken bottles, it was very evident that he had been screwing his courage up to sticking point by the help of the "heel taps" that remained. It was no good, however, crying over spilt milk or spilt brandy, and the only thing to be done was to despatch a messenger by a short cut to Almorah to meet us with another case, which we immediately did, and then put ourselves on short allowance till his arrival.

Our route the next day lay through a forest of pine, the scent from which in the sun was quite overpowering. We had halted for our midday meal on the banks of a small stream, and having bathed were just preparing to make a move, when suddenly there appeared on the opposite side a fine sambur with a magnificent head. Of course our rifles and guns were well out of reach, and after looking at us disdainfully for a few seconds he trotted off and was seen no more. It was very provoking, as it was the only one we saw the whole time we were out; but it could not be helped, for no one ever expected his visit, more especially as we were at the time laughing and talking and making more noise than usual. That evening, after sundown, Newcombe had a shot at a skulking hyæna, but missed, and I shot my first and last monkey. I wanted a skin, and seeing a fine old gentleman within range I fired and brought him down. Unfortunately, however, I had not quite killed him, and his behaviour was so piteous and so human that I felt as if I had committed murder, and vowed I would never be guilty of such a crime again.

We bagged one more bear and some barking deer before we got to Almorah, and then, after a three days' rest, started off direct to Naini Tal, where we arrived one evening at six o'clock, all of us, as well as men could be, having thoroughly enjoyed our trip. The Christian man John was immensely pleased to get back to the hotel, where he was, from having been to the snows, quite a hero, and he celebrated his return in his usual manner. I am sorry to say, however, that on this occasion we were unable to reprimand him, for his masters were not free from drink themselves, having one and all of us passed the line of demarcation which separates sobriety from intoxication. It was hardly our fault, though, and happened thus. When we sat down to dinner we thought we should like some beer, which we had not tasted for so long, and accordingly ordered a bottle apiece. Whether it was from being in a room after so long a sojourn in the open air, or for what other reason I cannot say, but very soon after finishing his bottle Newcombe had to be assisted to bed. The next to follow in like case was Fairleigh, and the last of all to claim the kind offices of the hotel servants and the faithful Christian John was—though he blushes to own it—the writer.

CHAPTER VI.

AMONG THE SNIPE.

NOWHERE else is such sport to be obtained amongst the *tenuirostres* as in India. Whether it is the climate or the succulent paddy fields that attract them I am unable to say, but certain it is that, like the Irishman's trout, "they simply swarm," and wherever you go, no matter what the district, you are pretty certain of making a good bag, provided always that you can hold decently straight. The one great feature in this class of sport which recommends itself strongly to the mind of a junior officer who is not too much overburdened, as a rule, with the riches of this world, is its inexpensiveness. Unlike tiger-shooting or pigsticking, there are no costly accessories. A couple of natives to carry your cartridges and lunch and to bring back your game, and an occasional *douceur* to a boatman who may have to ferry you across some jheel, are all the "extras" required beyond your gun and cartridges; and, as the same complement will suffice for two or even three, the expenses when divided come to little or nothing.

The only difficulty that we—by we I mean myself and brother subs—experienced on landing in India was the finding out of the best spots for shooting. The residents and old hands were very chary of taking out a youngster with them, for fear that he might form too intimate an acquaintance with the locality, and utilize his knowledge, by taking the cream off their preserves on the days when they were unable themselves to go out.

To obtain information from the native shikaries was next door to impossible, they having been one and all heavily bribed to hold their tongues; and to ask the ordinary villager anything about a snipe was worse than useless, as not one in a thousand ever knew what the creature was, and were wont to call a paddy bird, a heron, and a snipe by the same name.

This being so, Crawley and self determined to set our wits to work and prospect for ourselves, and for a fortnight or three weeks we scoured the country on our tattoos in every direction, hoping to alight on some hitherto unknown preserves. At first we met with but little success, for, although we came upon some very likely-looking ground, there were certainly not a sufficient number of snipe to be seen to account for the large bags that our civilian acquaintances were wont to bring home, much to our envy and disgust.

"I tell you what it is, old man," said Crawley to me one day after an unsuccessful ride, "the only way we shall ever find out anything is to get in with some of the old stagers and get them to show us the ground."

"That won't wash," I replied. "I tried it on with Jones, the magistrate, and he dried up at once."

For some little time Crawley remained silent and buried in thought, and then, suddenly jumping up, exclaimed: "I have it; I know he and McPherson, the doctor, are going out to-morrow. I'm blessed if I don't play detective and follow them."

It was no use my objecting that they would be certain to see him, and sooner than let him into the secret would forego their day's shooting. Crawley was determined, and went off at once to make his preparations. Now it so happened that Crawley, besides being a very good actor, was also an accomplished linguist, that is to say, that languages came to him without any trouble, and partly from studying Hindustani on the voyage out, and partly from his natural gift, he had already passed the lower standard and could chatter like a native.

Accordingly, the following morning, having hired an ekkah in the bazaar, and having made himself up as a high-caste native, he slipped out of our bungalow unperceived and started off past the doctor's house as if he was going to the town. When he got to the corner from whence he could command a view of the station, he pulled up under a tope of mangoe trees and waited till he saw the two sportsmen set out on their ponies, accompanied by their retainers with their guns. Letting them pass, he followed slowly in their tracks for about four miles on the main road, when they turned off sharp to the right through the jungle for another two or three miles down a path which led them to the borders of a large lake or jheel. On arriving there he found the two ponies picketed, with the syces enjoying the ever-present "hubble-bubble," and by a few careful inquiries in the vernacular managed to elicit the fact that the "sahib logue" had crossed in a boat to the other side, and that the ponies were to meet them at the far end of the jheel, some three miles further on.

Leaving the syces to the enjoyment of their fragrant (?) weed, he then drove on to the end indicated, and had the satisfaction of seeing a beautiful stretch of snipe ground, with paddy fields as far as the eye could reach, and evidently swarming with birds. A village close by gave him the name of the locality, and also the information that the jheel extended about the same distance in the opposite direction; and then he returned to the station without being discovered, and, after a deal of greasing and hard scrubbing, reappeared in his original character of the British subaltern, well pleased with the success of his undertaking.

"We will give the ground two days' rest," he said, "and then we'll just go and have a try what *we* can do; and, by Jove! won't Jones and McPherson be mad?"

That evening the two sportsmen returned with a bigger bag than usual, some thirty-two couple, giving themselves great airs in consequence, while we were chuckling all the time to ourselves and longing for the next two days to go by. I was for not waiting, and wanted to start out the very next day; but Crawley was inexorable, and, as I could do nothing without him to show me the ground, I had to give in, and exercise that most difficult of virtues called patience. Never did the time pass so slowly; but there is much truth in the French saying that everything comes to those who know how to wait, and, accordingly, on the third day, very early in the morning, everything was ready for a start. I had taken my bheestee, who was a very keen shikarie, and we had one other local man to help to carry the game, besides Crawley's chokra, who was in charge of the lunch. These and our two syces completed our army, and we set out full of spirits, and that article which we are told on good authority springs eternal in the human breast, viz. hope.

We had not gone very far before a slight *contretemps* occurred, in the shape of Crawley getting kicked over his pony's head, gun and all. The little brute suddenly took to kicking and plunging like a mad thing, and Crawley, being considerably hampered by his weapon, besides being taken quite unawares, described a beautiful parabolic curve into the road, which, luckily for him, was some six or eight inches deep in dust. As soon as he had picked himself up and made sure that his gun had received no damage, he remounted, and with a few gentle reminders soon convinced the erring tattoo of his iniquity; and then we proceeded on our route, arriving at the edge of the jheel without further mishap.

Unfortunately, however, we could find no boat to ferry us over (we found out afterwards that it was necessary to order one to be in waiting), so we had to ride down to the end and commence shooting back. This delayed us a little, and gave our syces a long tramp; but, as we had started early, and we had the whole day before us, we did not so much mind. Having taken a pull at some cold tea just dashed with whisky, we sent off our crocks, and, forming a line, prepared for action. The boy with the lunch we sent on to a village we saw in the distance, as near as we could judge, about halfway between us and the far end of the preserve.

The first blood fell to Crawley, who bagged a right and left in fine style. Then up got a whisp of seventeen or eighteen right in front of me, and I am fain to confess that the temptation was too strong, for I pulled into the brown of them, with the result that there were six down to the first barrel, and I nailed one more with my second. "Wholesale and retail" Crawley called the two shots, and chaffed me considerably, but I reminded him that the bigger the bag that we brought back with us the more irate and jealous Jones and McPherson would be; and as we had already got four and a half couple in four shots, if we went on like that there was every prospect of their having jaundice. Things went on swimmingly for the next half-hour; there were plenty of birds, and we were both holding straight, and, consequently, were in high feather, with a gradually swelling bag, when suddenly I felt the ground disappear from under my feet, and souse I went into a hole some eight feet deep. I scrambled out again in a second, and luckily had the presence of mind to keep my gun above water; but I was more like a drowned rat than anything else myself, and was forced to get a fresh supply of cartridges from my bheestee.

"*Facilis decensus*, eh, old man?" said Crawley, as soon as he stopped laughing. "Yes," I replied, "but it was softer falling than the road," which rather shut him up, and then we started again.

My next victim was a large water snake, which nearly frightened me out of my life, as I stood on it, and of course thought it must be a cobra of the worst kind. Crawley followed by contributing a large paddy bird to the bag, which he said he wanted to stuff and send home, but the bheestee did not see it in the same light, and being possessed of a mind capable of discriminating between a hawk and a handsaw, let it drop, quite by accident (?) on the way. With varying luck we at last arrived at the village, and, coming out of the water, we found a decent bit of grass on the windward side where we determined to lunch. By this time the sun was well up and pretty hot, so, taking my coat and flannel shirt off and wringing them out, I hung them up to dry, much to the edification of the village damsels, who watched the operation from afar off. I then proceeded to count up our bag, and found it consisted of twenty-three and a half couple of snipe, one snake, and a paddy bird (the two latter missing). Not a bad morning's work for two beginners, we thought, and the best of the ground before us.

We were far too enthusiastic to waste much time over our lunch, and as soon as we had finished our pipes we made a fresh start, accompanied this time by a large contingent of young men and boys from the village, who were a most infernal nuisance, and nearly got us into a bother which might have brought our day's sport to an abrupt termination. It happened thus: A single snipe got up rather wide on Crawley's right, and after a preliminary twist or two flew right back towards the village. Bang went Crawley's first barrel and down fell the snipe. I had just shouted "Good shot!" when there arose a most appalling and blood-curdling yell, and we saw a native dancing about as if the devil had kicked him, and screaming blue murder at the top of his voice. He was about eighty yards off, so it was certain he could not have been very badly hurt, though from his position he had been evidently directly in the line of fire; but, of course, we had to go back and inspect him, and the nearer we came the louder he groaned, till, as we got almost up to him, he fell down and made a pretence of yielding up the ghost.

In less time than it takes to write, we were surrounded by a host of villagers, all talking at once, and led by the head man. Where they all came from goodness only knows; but there they were, and amidst the general clamour and manifestations of sympathy for the sufferer, we managed to make out that a claim was put forward by the next-of-kin for a sum of two hundred rupees, as a sort of salve or compensation. After a quarter of an hour's bickering, and the application of a shooting-boot to the dead victim of the tyrannical sahib logue, which caused a sudden and satisfactory return to life on the said victim's part, the matter was finally settled at three rupees, one of which was confiscated by the head man, while the other two went to heal the supposed wound, if it could be found, which was extremely doubtful: and so the incident terminated, and we were allowed to continue our shooting amidst the benedictions of the populace, who now preferred to keep a respectable distance, and eventually disappeared in the same mysterious manner in which they suddenly turned up.

As soon as we had got clear of the crowd and their jabber, we set to work in real earnest, and for a couple of hours were firing away as fast as we could load. The snipe were in hundreds, and as the sun was hot they lay like stones, so by the time we had got within half a mile of our destination, viz. the far end of the jheel, we had only about a dozen cartridges left between us, while the bheestee and the other natives began to complain of the weight of the bag. When we counted out at the close of the day, we found that our total was fifty-one couple actually gathered, and I am sure that we failed to pick up quite ten couple more. Naturally we were in great spirits as we mounted our tats with the bags across our shoulders for our homeward journey, and *en route* we decided to ride up to the racquet court, where we were sure to find Jones and McPherson, before unloading our game at the bungalow. "My word! won't they be savage?" said Crawley, as we rode along. And he was right, for if ever "envy, hatred, and malice" were depicted on the human countenance, it was when the worthy magistrate and his colleague witnessed our arrival and heard the result of our day's shooting.

That night we were besieged with inquiries as to when, where, and how we had managed to find the ground, to all of which we turned a deaf ear, as we now considered ourselves quite on a par with the older residents, and, therefore, entitled to keep our knowledge to ourselves.

The great joke was that, after a good deal of beating about the bush, Jones offered to disclose his preserve if we would do the like with him, proposing at the same time an offensive and defensive treaty between us four against all comers. We tossed up who should speak first, and our side losing, Crawley began a detailed description of the ground. "But that is ours," said the annoyed Jones. "Yours be hanged!" replied Crawley. "How can it be yours? Isn't the country open to all of us? No, no; you tell us another pitch, or we will give ours away to all the other chaps." Jones was forced to comply with our demand, so that we got another preserve to shoot, besides the one that we, or rather Crawley, had found for ourselves. Many a good day we had afterwards; sometimes all four going out together, but we never beat our first bag; and, on the principle that "stolen kisses are the sweetest," I don't think we ever really enjoyed the shooting so much as on the occasion when we outwitted the old hands and covered ourselves with glory.

CHAPTER VII.

AN UP-COUNTRY CRICKET MATCH.

CRICKET is acknowledged to be the national game *par excellence* of Englishmen. Wherever they may be, north, south, east, or west, sooner or later, provided a sufficient number are gathered together, there is certain to be a cricket match; and climate has little or no effect on their ardour, for you will find them playing on the burning sand of the desert with as much zest as if it was the best possible pitch in the Old Country; and even an expedition to the North Pole is not considered complete without a consignment of bats, balls, and stumps. Nowhere, perhaps, does the game flourish with more vigour than in India, and already we in England have witnessed a team of native Parsees who have by no means disgraced themselves, even when pitted against very fair county elevens.

At the time of which I am writing, or rather about to write, the native mind had not grasped the delicacies and intricacies of "Yorkers," "long hops," and "half volleys," but were rather apt to look on a cricket match as a proof of the lunatic propensities of their masters the sahibs, and to wonder what possible enjoyment they could find in running about in the sun all the day after a leather ball. Certainly at Calcutta, where, by the way, there was, and I believe is still, the most beautiful cricket ground in the world, there used to be a "Fecknee waller," or thrower, who was by no means bad practice; very straight and very fast, of course with no break and little variations of either length or pace, but with six annas on the wicket, apt to be very deadly if you did not play with a straight bat. Many a rupee has he had out of me in the old days, and would doubtless do so again if he is still in the flesh; but, beyond that, and being a tolerable field on emergency, provided the ball did not hit his legs, he was useless. Batting with him was an unknown science, and one he did not care to learn. He threw and earned his "talub," picking up unconsidered trifles also in the way of tips, and there his cricket ended. His day's work over, I have no doubt over his hubble-bubble he was wont to dilate on the folly of the sahibs to an admiring circle of his fellow-countrymen. Still, cricket in those days was great fun, and a match looked forward to with great interest. I remember when going on tour up-country with the mofussil team, what sport we had living in tents, and being well (too well very often) cared for by our hosts. What nights we used to have in camp or at mess, and what practical jokes used to be played! One evening we put a young donkey into one of our team's bed, and he, returning to his tent in the early morn, perhaps with the slightest suspicion of unsteadiness in his gait, thought the devil had taken possession of his temporary domicile, and yelled and hallooed blue murder till everybody within a radius of two miles had been aroused and had sent to inquire what all the shindy was about. Another time, on a small branch line we had a special train, and passing some likely-looking snipe ground, we stopped the train and had an hour's shooting, continuing our journey at the end of the *battue*. Of course we arrived after dusk, when every one had given up expecting us. But our triumphal entry into cantonments on ponies in line at a hand gallop was nevertheless imposing, and would have been more so if some wretched wags, who had heard of our arrival from afar, had not stretched a rope across the road about two feet from the ground, and so caused the downfall of more than half our party. The following day, though, we had our revenge, for we kept them out in the field all the time, and put together over four hundred runs for the loss of six or seven wickets. On that tour I nearly got into serious trouble, for I was within an ace of slaughtering an unoffending baboo, whose curiosity got the better of his discretion. I was practising at a net, around which was gathered a select little crowd of native gentlemen, who, though warned more than once not to come too near, kept on gradually edging in and making their remarks: "Aree dheko, etc.," till at last I got a half-volley fair to square leg and landed the leader of the band plumb centre, which doubled him up into a ball and he was carried off in a moribund condition. Of course it was quite unpremeditated on my part, and a pure accident, but they were all very indignant, and vowed that they would have me in the lowest dungeon, and, if my friend had "handed in his checks," as our American cousins call it, I verily believe they would have had a real good try for it. Happily, however, after about an hour or so he came round, and matters began to assume a more roseate hue; but he did not come anywhere near the practice nets again, and I fancy the game of cricket fell considerably in his estimation. It was after this match, I think, that we were all nearly drowned, for, as far as my memory serves me, we had a somewhat cross-country journey to reach our next fixture, and our mode of progress comprised both train and dâk. For some reason or other we were delayed with the dâk, which had not been properly laid, and when we started it was getting dusk. About halfway we found we had to cross a river, and the gharries were taken bodily over on a frail raft constructed on the top of three boats lashed together, which somehow came adrift nearly in the middle of the river, and we slowly began to sink with all hands. It was only by bundling the natives and the ponies overboard that we managed to keep afloat at all, and by vigorous pulling, hauling, baling, and sculling that we got across just in time and fairly wet through, and then we had to wait for more than an hour, while the ponies, who had of course, with their natural "cussedness," landed on the other side, were fetched over and hitched on. It was a narrow squeak, but we all made light of it, and looked upon it as a gigantic joke, at least the "sahib logue" did, though I doubt if the retainers who had had to swim for it saw such a vast amount of fun in the adventure. This, however, has not much to do with the subject-matter which appears at the head of this chapter, namely, an up-country cricket match. So to business.

It was at the commencement of the cold weather that we had challenged the N.W.P. eleven, and when I say "we," I mean the station where I was quartered, and of which I formed a unit or atom. It was looked upon as pretty tall cheek on our part to endeavour to tackle an eleven picked from some ten or fifteen other stations, all of which were nearly double the size of our own; but we knew what the others did not, viz. that between the three regiments which formed our garrison and the battery of artillery we could pick out a team which would hold its own in most places. There were two "Varsity" eleven men, one of whom was a civilian, the other in the cavalry, and most of the rest of us had been in one or the other of the public school elevens, and, what is more to the purpose, had kept up our cricket after joining the army.

Our bowling was certainly above the average, and Q., the civilian, had only just come out from England, where he had been playing for his county all the summer, and where he had made an average of thirty-nine, and scored over a century twice. Our opponents numbered amongst them some very fair players, but they had the disadvantage of not having played together, whereas we were almost like a school, and two or three times a week managed to get up a game where the eleven played the next eighteen or something of that sort. So that we all knew each other's little ways, and all worked together like machinery. We had taken a great deal of trouble with the ground—watering, rolling, etc., and had got the pitch about as good as it could well be—our indefatigable secretary having looked after things as if he had solved the problem of "the whole duty of man."

On the morning of the match we deputed some of the non-players to meet our antagonists at the station about two miles off, and to bring them in gharries, which they accordingly did, and about eleven o'clock a.m. they turned up, and having been billeted amongst us, after a "peg" or so we all went off to the ground and proceeded to toss for the innings. They won the toss, and elected to go in, sending two steady bats to the wickets, who commenced by giving us a heap of trouble before we separated them. Not that they ran up many runs, but by a persistent system of blocking every ball, they made our bowlers so mad that they could not bowl a rap. At last one of the pair started to run, a short run, and the ball being beautifully fielded and returned, I had the bails off (I was keeping wicket) before the gentleman was home. The next comer was a swiper, who started to crack our somewhat demolished bowling all over the place, and very soon brought on a change. The second ball from our slow trundler the swiper tried to cut, and I, thinking he had touched it, yelled, "How's that?" To my astonishment, before the umpire could say a word, off he started to run, having mistaken my question for a call to go from his partner, and to make quite certain of things I had the presence of mind to whip off the bails, and appeal to the umpire at my end, who promptly gave him "out." He was in a tearing rage, and swore it was a swindle, sharp practice, and I don't know what else besides; but there was no help for him, he had to retire, and he eventually did it with a very bad grace, grumbling and swearing the whole way into the pavilion.

After him came the captain of the N.W.P., a fine bat, who, before we dismissed him, managed to put together sixty-eight runs, and the telegraph showed a hundred and four runs, three wickets, last man sixty-eight.

Following was the fat man of the side, and the wag of the party. He was a good bat, but an almighty thirsty customer, requiring refreshment after every other over. However, our astute captain saw what he had to deal with, and promptly put on our fast bowling. The first ball kicked, and caught our stout friend about the third button of his flannel shirt, knocking all the wind out of him completely. The second did likewise, and took him just above the kneecap, and the third bowled him neck and heels. He informed me, as he was leaving the wicket, that he never was so pleased at anything in his life as to hear the row in the "timber yard" behind him; for he felt certain another over from Douglas (our slinger) would have been fatal, and would have cost the insurance offices a mint of money.

We managed to get them all out by four for a total of two hundred and ten, and then sent in our representatives, the two first of whom did so well that we had one wicket down for ninety runs, and when stumps were drawn for the evening the score stood at one hundred and twenty for two wickets.

That night at mess was what might be called a heavy one, and the black pool in the billiard-room was anything but brilliant. We took good care of our guests, as may be supposed, and towards the small hours one or two of them were comfortably asleep with their heads resting on half-finished brandies and sodas.

The stout gentleman, who was so nearly demolished by our fast bowler, fell to my charge, and as he had "done himself" more than well, a pretty time of it I had getting him into my bungalow. We started all right, working what they would call in nautical language "short traverses," but about halfway across the compound he tripped over a stick and fell heavily. Whereupon he vowed he had been bitten by a snake, and commenced to weep bitterly, insisting on taking an affectionate farewell of myself every two seconds. No amount of persuasion on my part could get him on to his legs again. There he sat sobbing as if his heart would break, and begging me to be kind to his family after he had gone, and eventually I was forced to send for my bearer and the chowkedar and remove him *vi et armis* to his couch, where he very soon sank into a peaceful slumber. Next morning he remembered nothing about it, but admitted that he had a mouth like a lime-kiln and a head that felt as if it would burst. However, by 11.30, he was himself again, and all the rest being in like condition, we resumed our unfinished innings punctually to time. Certainly their bowling was not so straight as on the previous day, and had lost a considerable amount of "devil," the consequence being that before the last wicket fell our total amounted to two hundred and eighty-nine, or seventy-nine runs to the good.

After an interval of twenty minutes they went in for their second innings; and, although they led off badly, the first three wickets falling for thirty runs, before we had finished with them their total score was one hundred and seventy-two, leaving us ninety-three runs to get to win, and only an hour and a quarter to do it in, including waits. Our captain, like a sensible man, however, called us all together, and impressed on us the necessity of not wasting a second. "I would sooner lose the match a jolly sight than have it drawn," he said, "so let everybody be ready to go in at once directly a man is out." And, like obedient slaves that we were, we sat there watching the game, all fully attired in pads and gloves.

The first to go in were our champion hitters, and the way they swiped at everything and ran every possible and impossible run was a caution. As the time went on our adversaries took longer and longer between the overs, and it was patent that they were playing for the draw. But we were quite up to that, and all as keen as mustard, and as soon as a wicket fell, the next man took his place almost before the umpire could set up the stumps.

It wanted four minutes to time when I went in, the seventh wicket, and, as we still required four runs to win, the excitement was intense. The first ball was a trimmer, which I had to play forward and scored nothing for. The second the same. Two minutes now only were left, but the third ball happened to be my favourite—a half-volley to leg, and, putting my shoulders into it, I cracked it down to the boundary and won the match by four wickets for our side, almost on the stroke of time. How the soldiers did holloa—natives and all—though the latter, I am sure, did not know what it was all about. But we won the match, and after giving our guests a good "send-off" in the way of iced champagne cup, and three hearty cheers as they drove off to catch their train, we returned to the mess ourselves to drink our own healths and success to our cricket club.

I have played a good many matches since then, but I don't think I ever took part in a more exciting one, or felt prouder than when I got "well on" to that lucky half-volley which won the match and placed the necessary four runs to our side.

CHAPTER VIII.

OUR PIGEON CLUB.

It was just at the commencement of the cold weather, and those who had been fortunate enough to obtain leave had returned from the hills and rejoined their less-favoured comrades at an up-country station in Bengal. There was plenty to tell on both sides—of pleasant trips, good "shikar," and numerous flirtations on the one hand; and, on the other, tales of sickness, death, and intolerable heat. Some of our members, I am sorry to say, were absent for ever from their accustomed place at mess, and others had been invalided home. For those who had been obliged to stay in the plains it had proved a trying time, and the proverbial "oldest inhabitant" declared that there had not, in his experience, been such a terrible hot season known before. I am fain to admit that I have heard the same remark applied to the weather on more than one occasion—in fact, nearly every hot season is considered by those who have had to brave it, as worse than the previous ones, but in this instance there is no doubt that it had been exceptional. Personally, I am happy to say I had been on long leave and had escaped it, and felt all the better for having done so. Still, when I saw the somewhat dejected and washed-out appearances that my brothers-in-arms presented, I could not help feeling a twinge of conscience, and immediately decided that we must all pull together during the coming cold weather, and, to make up for lost time, organize all sorts of sports—good, bad, and indifferent. Certainly my comrades did not hesitate to make me work up arrears, for, I think, for the first month or so, I must have been a member of every court-martial, court of inquiry, or board that sat within a radius of train distance. However, after all, it was but fair, and none of us grumbled more than usual at the double labour imposed on us. Nevertheless I was not sorry when Tommy Atkins ceased from troubling and became a good boy, and the commissariat had exposed all their wares for inspection, giving us in consequence more time to devote to sport.

There had joined us from England about this time a senior lieutenant, who, after running through every known and unknown dodge to escape Indian service, had at last come to the end of his *repertoire*, and had been ruthlessly swooped on by the Horse Guards and promptly packed off. He happened to be a magnificent pigeon shot, and had made a clean sweep at Hurlingham and the Gun Club that summer, with much glory and profit to himself. Accordingly, almost the first question he asked on his arrival was, "Have you chaps got any pigeon-shooting here?" and on our confessing that we had not yet reached that acme of civilization, he undertook to organize a club at once. When I say he undertook to organize a club, I am perhaps a little premature in my statement, for the first attempt was a trial in my compound—a sort of scratch affair. We had sent out into the highways and byways for miles round in search of the necessary birds, and had been promised by a native shikari a consignment of veritable blue rocks from some adjacent temples, so we hoped that everything would go off swimmingly. Traps, of course, we had not, so we adopted the method of digging some holes and stowing a nigger in each with a string tied to his arm, giving him instructions to throw up the bird directly he felt his tether pulled.

After tiffin at mess, at which we had, of course, some champagne to inaugurate the affair, we adjourned to the compound, and a sweepstake of two gold mohurs each was soon made up. The ground was carefully marked out, and our crack shot, Percy by name, with a magnanimity worthy of a better cause, put himself at scratch. There were eight of us in the handicap, and it fell to my lot to lead off. Luckily for me, as it turned out, I was not up to the dodge of cutting the birds down a foot over the trap, and when the mystic word "pull" was given a white object appeared in the air for a second or so, and then commenced to flap slowly away. Of course I could hardly miss such a mark, and so scored No. 1 amid the laughter of the assembled crowd. The next bird was a duplicate of mine, only dark, and was easily grassed by the adjutant. Then came a real skimmer, which, going like greased lightning, got clear off, and left the gun staring blankly at the fast-vanishing speck and cursing his luck.

At last it came to Percy's turn to fire, and everybody held their breath, and with eager eyes watched carefully how to do it, determined to pick up a wrinkle if possible. Up came the champion to the mark, covered the traps (or rather, the place where the traps ought to be) carefully and scientifically. "Are you ready?" "Yes—pull." Bang! bang!—both barrels; and a *fac simile* of my bird to look at, unfurled itself and slowly flew a few yards, and then, as if in derision, turned head over heels; in fact, it was a tumbler. How we all did roar! And how savage Percy was! He d—d the shikarie, the birds, and everything within a hundred miles of him, winding up by asking indignantly, "What are all you fools laughing at?" Of course this only made us worse, and it was some time before we could go on; and when the performance was repeated, bar the tumbling, on the next occasion, I thought every one would have had a fit. Percy was trying, naturally, the orthodox method of firing over the trap, and the bird, being thrown straight up into the air in a ball, fairly bothered him, for he had fired both his barrels before ever the pigeon had started to fly. Eventually, by reason of a succession of easy birds falling to my lot, I managed to secure the sixteen gold mohurs, and thought myself rather a dog at the game. In fact, I was convinced that pigeon-shooting was going to pay my mess bills for the rest of my time in India, and consequently was as keen as mustard on the subject. When, however, we did get a few real blue pigeons from the temples, and not the bazaar brutes, I altered my opinion, and was not quite so certain of the pecuniary merits of the affair. But as I divided another sweepstake with Percy I did not do so badly for a commencement.

The next morning Percy was very mysterious, and shut himself into his bungalow, refusing to see any one. All we could get out of his bearer was that "the sahib was making something," and it was not till tiffin-time, when he emerged from his seclusion, that we discovered what he had been at. It appeared, then, that he had been all the forenoon manufacturing a pigeon-trap in wood, as a model for them to copy in tin in the bazaar. "No more of that infernal throwing the birds into the air for me," he said; "it ain't good enough. I am going to have proper traps made, and carry things out the right way;" and then he produced a circular he had drawn out to send round the station, soliciting subscriptions to form a gun club to shoot twice a week on the maidan, with tea and turn-out for the ladies, tents, etc., etc. Of course we all subscribed, and, being a new thing, it took directly, and every one became a member at once. I forget what the entrance-fee and subscription was, but nothing very ruinous, I think, the preliminary expenses of traps being the chief item. The tents we got for nothing, and easy-chairs were lent. Percy was president, and I was asked to be secretary, which meant doing all the work, and getting all the kicks, without receiving the more useful halfpence. However, after we had got the thing started, I argued there would be little enough to do, so I accepted, and to work we went. Never did I see such a mess as the native mind made of the traps. Generally they can copy anything that is given them, but in this case they seemed utterly at sea. Before we got anything that would act at all we had had five sets made, and I began to despair of ever getting what we wanted. I am not sure that a good deal of the bother was not caused on purpose, because it had been the "dustoor" to throw up birds by hand, and the good people did not see having any new-fangled arrangement.

Anybody who knows anything of India will recognize at once the terrible difficulty of inducing the natives to travel out of the beaten track. Whatever has been the "dustoor," or custom, good or bad, must be right, and must continue, without alteration or improvement, until the end of all things. I should say the two words which would be most likely to retard India (if it were allowed) in the march of civilization would be "dustoor" and "kismet." If a native has an accident with your property, or blows his leg off with your gun, it is never put down to his own carelessness; it is simply his fate ("kismet"), and if you point out to him the danger of carrying a bowl of powder for you to load your cartridges, with a naked light in close proximity thereto, should it be the "dustoor," or custom, in his family to do so, nothing on earth will induce him to desist therefrom; and it was just the same with the pigeon-traps.

At last, by dint of patience, accompanied by occasional threats and a certain amount of strong language, we obtained what we required, and for a week Percy was engaged in teaching a native to pull the strings. It was by no means an easy matter, for the astute nigger did not the least see why he should not pull them all at once, and make a "barra tamasha" of it right off, and he looked on one bird in the air at a time as clearly derogatory and quite a tame affair. Eventually, however, he was persuaded, and turned out quite a treasure.

Then came the choosing of the ground, the pitching of the tents, etc., and arranging about tea and music, also the keeping of the ground outside the boundary—a very necessary consideration if one did not want to bag three parts of the inhabitants of the bazaar, who we knew would crowd round to look on. Having settled all that, we got out the programme and fixed the opening day. Everything seemed to be going on as well as it possibly could, when late one evening, after mess, Percy came over to my bungalow where I had gone bound for bed, and, having dug me out, exclaimed—

"Look here, old chap, just come over and interview a shikarie for me. The beggar has come in with a long story about pigeons, but I can't understand a word of what he is saying, and my bearer is a bigger fool still."

Of course I put on my clothes and went over with him, where I found one of the men who had promised us to obtain pigeons in any quantity seated on his haunches pouring forth his grievances to Percy's bearer. I soon found out what was the matter—viz. that he had been unable to obtain more than three pigeons, and that there was no chance of his getting any more in time for our first day's shoot; at least, that was the brief summary of his tale, divested of the usual amount of excuses, lies, and persiflage.

"Here is a go," said I; "what are we to do?"

"Blessed if I know!" replied Percy, somewhat disheartened. "I never saw such a cursed country; one can't get anything. Ask that jabbering ape what he purposes"—pointing to the shikarie.

At first he had no idea, but if we gave him the order he would obtain anything, pigeons excepted, he said; and then he suddenly asked if any other birds would do, and suggested paroquets.

"By Jove! the very thing!" exclaimed Percy. "What fun! We'll cut their tails and they'll go like the wind, and how astonished everybody will be! Don't say a word about it; we will have a real lark," and there and then we gave orders to the much-relieved native sportsman for unlimited quantities of the little green birds, after which I again retired to my bungalow and bed.

Two days later saw the inauguration of our pigeon club, and early in the morning Percy was buzzing around like a blue-bottle. It so happened that I had shortly before this become the proud possessor of a horse and trap, which, so far as the latter article went, was by no means a bad turn-out; but about the horse, the least said the better. I had purchased, on a friend's recommendation, without ever seeing the animal, and therefore could not complain of my own judgment; but such a brute I never drove before. He had only one side to his mouth, not always that, and for shying would take a prize anywhere. Added to this he was a confirmed jibber, and if touched with the whip would kick for half an hour or so, bolting off in short rushes of about a hundred yards in the intervals. When Percy came and asked me to lend him my conveyance to go up to the ground, and to take his guns and ammunition up as well, I was somewhat loath to accede to his request; but as he persisted, and, notwithstanding my warnings, declared that he could drive any horse that ever was foaled, I at last gave in and allowed him to have his own way. To my surprise, at the start my beautiful steed behaved like an angel, and, having permitted them to load up the trap with all sorts of impedimenta, trotted off quite sedately, so much so, that Percy with an air of "I told you so," turned round and began to chaff me about my fears. At that moment the animal made a violent shy, and I saw Percy reach forward for the whip. I had just time to shout out "For Heaven's sake, don't hit him!" when the blow fell and the ball commenced. Kick! The brute kicked higher than I could have believed possible for any horse in the shafts to have done, and then with a rapid succession of violent plunges, which broke one trace, off he went up the road as hard as he could tear. To call for my tat and follow was the work of a minute, and the further I went the more plain was the trail. First of all, lying in the road, I came on a gun-case. Next a gun without a case, then a box of cartridges, a rug, and the scyce's turban. A little further on the scyce himself, sitting down rubbing his leg with a rueful countenance, and last of all the head and front of the offending, to wit, the animal down on his side, with the trap overturned, and Percy sitting on his head. Oddly enough, there was little or no damage done. So, having collected the pieces and righted the vehicle, we proceeded together to the ground without further mishap, and soon had matters in trim for the afternoon's sport.

At about half-past two people began to arrive, and the place looked quite gay. The first sweepstake was a big one, for nearly every member entered, and was prepared to do his best, or worst, as the case might be. The varied description of weapons would have somewhat astonished the men at the Gun Club in England, I fancy, for there were central-fire, pin-fire, muzzle-loaders, fired by both cap and tube, and an old converted flint-lock, which belonged to the Irish doctor, O'Brien—a real good weapon notwithstanding, being an old Joe Manton, or Egg, I forget which. Anyway he was as proud of it as possible, and was wont to hold long conversations with it before firing, such as "Arrah, mi darlint! you're not goin' to fail me;" "Sure ye could not do it, wid 'em all lookin' on, for the honour of the ould counthry." If he made a successful shot, he would hold the weapon high in the air with one hand and point to it with the other, exclaiming, "Look at the bheauty! sure it never can deceive me;" while, on the other hand, if he missed, he would look daggers at his piece, and say, "Bad luck to yer! where are your manners?" and retire amid the convulsive laughter of the bystanders. He was one of the best-hearted, most good-natured creatures imaginable, but excitable to a degree, and if roused was like the war-horse of old, "terrible in his mighty wrath," though I cannot go so far as to say that "the earth trembled as he walked." He had to fire the first shot in our opening match, and as he went up to the mark, confiding in his gun as usual, Percy and I could barely keep our countenances, for we knew what was coming. "Are you ready?" "Bedad I am that; pull, yer blackguard!" "Bang!"

as a small green paroquet, with no tail to speak of, shot off with a "chup, chup." "Murthur, what's that?" as "bang!" went the second barrel, and paroquet turned toes up. O'Brien's face was a perfect study as he stood there with his mouth wide open and his gun in the air. At last he spoke again, this time to the bird, "What is it yer are at all? Is it pigeons?" he said, and getting no reply, he added with a self-satisfied air, "Anyway Ould Ireland was too much for yer, yer thief, and it counts won (one);" and then he triumphantly returned to the tent, where he was received with such shouts of laughter that for a good ten minutes no one could go on.

Percy was much better at these birds than bazaar pigeons, and killed six running in grand style, only using his second barrel twice. I was soon hopelessly out of it, as were most of the others, and O'Brien, Percy, and one of the hussars—I forget his name—were the only three left with six birds each. O'Brien was the first to fail, for he missed with both barrels. Strange to say, it was infectious, for Percy followed suit, and it only needed a kill on the hussar's part to give him the stakes. He grassed his bird, but, unfortunately for him, it flew out of bounds, and so it was all "as you were" again. The wild yell of delight which O'Brien sent up when he saw the bird fall clear of the boundary was enough to deafen anybody, and the conversation he held with his trusty weapon was long and impressive. At last, however, he was ready, and with his second chance he dropped his bird just on the edge of bounds, where it lay fluttering. One second he looked at it, then put his gun down, saying, "Lie there till I tell yer," and started off in a series of bounds towards his victim, literally throwing himself full length on to the top of it from some distance off, and squashing it quite flat, at the same time knocking all the wind out of himself. When he had recovered sufficiently to walk, he came back, and, picking up his gun, without a word strode into the tent, never for a moment relinquishing the bird, which he laid carefully down, and then, with his eyes starting out of his head with excitement, he watched the next two shots. As it happened, they both missed, and O'Brien became the winner, which fairly sent him off his head, and he fell to kissing his gun like a lunatic. In a short time, however, he calmed down and asked for his bird. "What the plague do you want that thing for?" I asked, pointing to the flattened object. "Stuffing" (or, as he called it, "stoffin"), was his sole reply; and there and then he walked straight home to the cantonments to skin and "stoff" the little green paroquet which had proved so lucky to him.

After his departure we had three or four more matches, one of which I secured. I found with a little practice I soon got into the trick of it, but there was not so much fun without O'Brien's quaint remarks, and we shut up before it was dark, having had a very pleasant afternoon. During the cold weather, two or three times a week, we had our meetings, and always used paroquets, which were voted far better than pigeons. Whenever things flagged at all, O'Brien was always on the spot with a remark that made everybody scream, and no meeting was perfect without him. As a matter of fact, there were very few at which he did not turn up, for he found that his old gun grew in "manners," and seldom "failed or deceived" him, and that it was, in consequence, a very paying concern.

CHAPTER IX.

OUR FIRST POLO MATCH.

At the time about which I am writing polo had not arrived at such a pitch of perfection as it has in the present day. In fact it was, so far as English officers were concerned, almost in its infancy; and, although it had long been a popular game amongst the Mainpuri natives, it was only just commencing to spread down country. I am afraid if any of the teams who now face each other at Hurlingham and other clubs during the summer could have seen our somewhat crude efforts and limited ideas on the subject when we endeavoured to make a beginning, they would, judging from their present standard of excellence, have formed very poor ideas of our powers. Still, it is proverbial that Rome was not built in a day, and as everybody must walk before they run (though I admit that there are many who are inclined to reverse that order of procedure), I am not ashamed to chronicle the part I took in our opening match in India.

I forget who it was started the idea, but as far as my memory serves me the credit belongs to that corps who are entitled to use the motto "*Ubique*," viz. the Royal Artillery. Hall, who had seen the game played by the natives, came down to our station to join a battery there, and was never tired of dilating on the merits of the game (at least, I think he was the man). Somehow or another one evening at the racquet court or the bath, where he was holding forth as usual, it was suggested that we might possibly manage to get up some matches ourselves. No sooner said than done, and the motion before the house was carried *nem con.* A club was formed there and then, subscriptions invited, and Hall was asked to be secretary, and also to procure the requisite paraphernalia, which, after a little demur, he consented to do.

For a month everybody went mad on ponies, and the native bazaar, with that keen sense of turning an honest penny for which they are so justly celebrated, were quite equal to the occasion, and daily, strings of ponies, good, bad, and indifferent, of all shapes and sizes and of every imaginable breed, were to be seen going about the station to the various bungalows inhabited by the officers with a view of inducing "a deal." It must be remembered that "a deal" in India, no matter what the article may be, is a matter of time and importance, and perhaps a horse-dealing transaction takes more time than anything else. You will be expected not only to buy the animal but to listen to a speech or speeches of some length on his merits, the difficulty the vendor had in procuring him, how he knew that the sahib required it, and consequently had to bribe other dealers not to forestall him in the purchase thereof. And, after that is over, there will be an epilogue on the pedigree of the pony, going back into almost prehistoric times, for which, by the way, you will be asked to give an additional sum of money. Even supposing that the dealer accepts your offer of about one-fourth of the price asked, the matter is by no means concluded, for there will be a long haggle between him and your bearer and syce on the question of commission, which as likely as not will be referred to you, and if you tell the disputants to go to the devil, they will undoubtedly take you at your word, and, amid a volley of high words, disappear for three or four hours, during which period you are deprived of the services of your domestics, who will most likely reappear at the end of the time unfit for duty, dishevelled, and smelling strongly of "hubble-bubble," without which no bargain can possibly be completed.

Under these circumstances, of which I was aware, I determined not to make my purchases in the station, but went further afield, and was lucky enough to pick up two very good little animals for next to nothing, which, added to my Burmese tat already in the stable, fitted me out with a very fair stud. One of my new purchases, a bright chestnut, was a most wicked little beast, with an overpowering craving for pieces of his syce. It mattered not whether the piece came from a leg, an arm, or a thigh, so long as it was a piece of native flesh he was quite content and happy. He was all right when you were once mounted, but the difficulty was to accomplish that performance, for he would get up on his hind legs, and come at you open-mouthed, using his fore-legs all the time like a prize-fighter. I gave him the name of "The Putney Pet" from his fighting proclivities, and the way I mastered him was to square up to him and hit him on the nose with one from the shoulder as straight and hard as I could. This generally brought him to a horizontal position, and while he was shaking his head and wondering what had happened, I jumped on his back. At first, I own, I used frequently to bark my knuckles against his teeth, but after a little practice I became quite an adept, and managed to plant my blow on the nose, in nine cases out of ten, with telling effect.

Eventually every one had been accommodated with an animal of sorts, and the balls, made of solah or pith, as well as the polo sticks and clubs having arrived, we essayed to make a start. For the first few days we did nothing but practise both ourselves and our ponies in the art of striking the ball. Poor devils! They—the ponies—came off second best, for many a clout over the head and other parts of the body did they get in our wild endeavours to make a stroke. It was not an uncommon thing either to see a rider careering round in a circle sitting on his steed's neck, or else, when reaching out to strike, suddenly turn toes uppermost and disappear on the offside, where he would be left on the ground, a case of "*Profundit humi Bos.*" But no one was ever much the worse for their falls, and after a bit the ponies seemed to enjoy the sport quite as much as we did ourselves, and evidently came to look on the whacks they got as part and parcel of the game.

I remember on one occasion rather a ludicrous incident happening, which showed a certain colonel, who shall be nameless, that "off parade" Jack was as good as his master. The man in question was in command of a native infantry regiment, and as pompous and conceited an ass as it has ever been my lot to meet. He thought no one could do anything but himself, and applied that line of Shakespeare, *i.e.* "the divinity that doth so hedge a king," to himself, substituting the word colonel for king. Of course he must play polo, and when playing or attempting to play, equally of course, no one but himself was entitled to have any opinion. If you attempted to argue with him or put him right, he would look at you with a "do you know who I am?" air, and tell you he did not require your advice. Now it so happened that he was by no means a centaur, and when playing it was all he could do to stick on, much less hit the ball, consequently he was always in the way, and more often on the broad of his back, on the ground, than mounted. A few days before we commenced the first scratch game, there had joined his regiment a wing subaltern, who, besides being a good rider, had a very fair notion of playing polo. This somehow was gall and wormwood to the gallant colonel, and he signalled his junior out for attack by repeatedly shouting and holloaing at him. At last, in a run down, he came up full split on his off-side just as his sub was going to strike, and received the full force of the blow on the back of his neck. Of course it was an accident, but the colonel would not see it in that light, and completely lost his temper. "How dare you, sir, strike me?" he fumed. "I'll try you by court-martial, sir, for striking your superior officer. Consider yourself——" He would have said "under arrest," but at that moment one of our fellows, seeing what was going on, charged into the colonel at full gallop and sent him and his pony head over heels. This completed the gentleman's cup, and he promptly put both the officers under arrest, the result of which was that he got a good wigging from the officer commanding the station, and was immediately turned out of the club and not allowed to play again, and for years afterwards the story stuck to him, till I expect he wished himself at the bottom of the sea.

Well, after sundry pick-up games, we eventually considered ourselves competent to play a real *bonâ fide* match, and accordingly it was arranged that the cavalry should play the infantry. The horse artillery to rank as cavalry and the field batteries to throw in their lot with the infantry. We were pretty equally matched, and it was the subject of much betting before the event, as to which would win the day. The doctor, who had distinguished himself so greatly as a pigeon shot, was chosen as umpire for the infantry, and Burton of the hussars agreed to act for the cavalry, as it was deemed necessary to have two. I tried hard to induce the doctor to play himself, but unfortunately, two or three days before, I had offered to lend him the Putney Pet, and the offer was accepted. Of course when he came to mount, the little brute tried his usual pranks on, and the worthy medico, not knowing the dodge, kept dancing round him saying, "Arrah, be aisy, woh, woh, mi darlint. Bad cess to yer; wait till I'm on the top of ye, ye blackguard." At last he got tired of it, and boldly advancing tried to mount *nolens volens*. But the Pet knew a trick worth two of that, and, slipping under his guard, seized him by the shoulder, and though he did not manage to get a bit of flesh, took about five or six inches of coat and shirt off, and inflicted a bruise that lasted for weeks. After that the doctor said that no power on earth would induce him to go near the devil, and as he had only his own meek and quiet tat, he preferred not playing at all to risking his skin amid a lot of what he was pleased to term "screaming savages."

We had on our side a big heavy troop sergeant-major of artillery, who from his weight and quick eye was a host in himself; he was put as one of the backs, and, as long as he was riding a nag that he knew, was a tower of strength. We had at half-time got a goal apiece, and the game was as even as it could well be. Just as we had crossed over, one of our men, seeing the sergeant-major's pony was a bit pumped, offered to lend him one of his, adding, "If you can hold him," for the pony was a confirmed runaway.

"If I can hold him, sir!" replied the sergeant-major,

indignantly. "If I can hold him! I should like to see the horse I can't hold, much less a little bit of a tat."

"Very well, then," said the owner, "jump on;" and, calling to his syce, he handed over the animal to the non-commissioned officer's care. All went well for a space, as the ball was kept well up at the enemy's end, but at last there was a bit of a scrimmage rather near our goal, and the sergeant-major gave his steed the reins to see if he could make a diversion in our favour. A pretty diversion too he did manage to make! For directly the "tattoo" found his head loose, he was off like a rocket, and charging bang into the middle of the bully, scattered it like chaff before the wind.

Over went friends and foes indiscriminately, and nothing was to be seen for a moment or so but a confused mass of ponies' legs and men's arms waving about in the air. At last, from the centre, emerged the astonished and perspiring sergeant-major, with his pony's head well up in the air, sitting back sawing his mouth for dear life. One more unfortunate crossed his path, and paid the penalty for so doing by a summersault; and then away he went, swearing like the trooper he was.

Round and round the maidan he galloped, without seemingly slackening one iota, while we all stopped to see what the end of it would be. Presently he dropped his off-side rein and put all his strength into the near-side one, thereby pulling the tat's head quite round. Stop! Not a bit; it only diminished the size of the circle, and they both flew round and round just as fast, till it made one almost giddy to look on. At last, however, the end came, and, the girths snapping, the brave soldier deposited his thirteen stone on the grass, where he lay completely blown, the pony meanwhile galloping off perfectly happy to his own stable. All he said when we picked him up was, "Well, I'm d—d if that brute wouldn't pull a railway train!" and by this time his own animal having recovered his wind he remounted and prepared to continue the game, evidently feeling much safer on the back of the pony he knew, than careering round on the runaway like a lunatic teetotum. After a quarter of an hour's further play, a disputed point arose about a goal, whether it was or was not. It was against us, and Burton decided that it was one, but our worthy doctor swore it was not, and as neither side would give way, for the second time matters came to a standstill. (I mention this to show the primitiveness of our ideas.) What was to be done?

"Oh, play on," we said; "and let us settle it after." No; that would not do.

"Begad, we'll settle it before divil another sthroke is sthruck," insisted the medico, and after repeated arguments, all of no avail, he suggested that the two umpires should toss for it, or if he did not like that he would fight him for it. Eventually, seeing that there was no chance of any conclusion being arrived at between them, and the spectators becoming impatient, we took the law into our own hands, and driving the two disputants out of the way proceeded with the game without them. Luckily we shortly afterwards managed to obtain a decided and indisputable goal for the infantry, and the umpires, seeing this, agreed to allow the former one to the cavalry and call it quits—a somewhat lame but otherwise satisfactory method of getting over the difficulty.

Before time was called and the game was ended neither side obtained any further advantage, so that our first match ended in a tie, and neither side were able to crow over each other. How grateful was the iced peg, too, when all was over, and how stiff I was next morning, notwithstanding the fact that I was in pretty hard condition and training. The man who suffered most, however, was the unfortunate troop sergeant-major, for next day he could scarcely walk he was so stiff, while to bend his back caused him almost as much pain as he would have had to endure from a sharp attack of lumbago. Still, it was all great fun, and though, as I have already said, the play was somewhat crude and wanting in science, it was thoroughly enjoyed by every one, and we looked forward to the next match. I know that the doctor had a rough time of it that night after mess, when he announced his intention of retiring from the service and setting up in private practice—for he declared that if polo was going to become an institution, what with savage ponies and bad riding he would soon have so many patients on his hands that his fortune would be made. I don't exactly remember what penalty we inflicted on him beyond the fact that he had to stand drinks round, and to promise not to make rash statements in the future; but I do remember that it was late before we broke up, and that not a few of us showed a disposition to break into song on our way home to our respective bungalows.

CHAPTER X.

ON THE LINE OF MARCH.

It was not with the best grace in the world that we received the order to proceed by train and march route from the station where we were quartered, to Peshawar. For the news took us all quite unawares, just after we had settled ourselves comfortably and had arranged a full programme of sport for the coming cold weather. Some of us had recently purchased fresh steeds, with which we had fondly hoped to do great things in the pigsticking line, as well as securing an occasional race. Others had ordered from England new bats, guns, rackets, etc., which were supposed to be on their way out, and the unfortunate consignees knew very well that, should their goods fail to arrive before we started, they might look for them ultimately reaching them only in about six months' time.

The presidents and secretaries of the ice and gram clubs were also in dire distress, while the native apothecary, who had spent his all in setting up a sodawater-making machine, was understood to be seriously contemplating suicide. Indeed, I believe he would have committed the fatal deed if he could only have made up his mind in what manner he should make his exit —whether by some subtle poison extracted from the medical stores, the common or garden razor skilfully applied to the jugular, or a plunge into the dark waters of the nearest tank. The three alternatives, however, proved too great a conundrum to solve, and consequently he lived, and, for all I know, may by this time be a great man.

To me personally it was an intense bore, for our bobbery pack had to be broken up, and the "bunniah's" bills settled all in a hurry, to say nothing of the various other institutions of which I happened to be secretary, all of which had to be wound up or handed over. There being no appeal, and, like the laws of the Medes and Persians, the order to move being unalterable, the only thing to be done was to make the best of a bad job, and to put the best face on it that we could, and so for the next three weeks everybody was up to his neck in business. Of course the first thing that occupied our attention was the disposal of our respective bungalows, and *Lares et penates.* I am sure some of the descriptions that were forwarded to the incoming regiment of "desirable cottage residences, replete with every comfort, and beautifully embowered in the shade of stately spreading trees, with large and pleasant gardens surrounding the mansion," would have done credit to the most flowery advertisements of any West End house and estate agent. The four of us who inhabited, what I will call my bungalow, were in luck, for we got it off our hands at the first shot. I believe the name had something to do with it, for we called it "The Rectory," it being situated in close proximity to the church; and although we had on more than one occasion been ordered by the officer commanding the station to change the title, we steadily refused to do so; and it was snapped up by the colonel's mem sahib of the relieving corps, under the belief that at all events a house with that patronymic must be eminently respectable. The next thing to do was to send off our nags in advance, so as to meet us at the point where we detrained, no more than the authorized chargers being permitted to go with the regiment by rail. I managed to sneak one of mine in on the plea of being a musketry instructor, but no one else had a chance.

Never shall I forget the appearance our compounds presented as the day of departure drew near. Everybody was besieged by a perfect army of bunniahs, native bankers, and baboos of all descriptions, Jews, heretics, and Gentiles—some clamouring for the settlement of their little account, others endeavouring to purchase, for next to nothing, the various articles we had for sale, and all talking at the top of their voices. In every room you went into you were certain to find a greasy stranger who saluted you with an oily tongue at the commencement, and whose voice gradually acquired strength as he went on, *vires acquirit eundo*. You shouted for your bearer to turn him out, "Nickaldo gelde," and the worthy body servant opened the door to facilitate his departure. What was the result? Why, a long line of still more greasy gentlemen presented themselves to your view, all seated on their haunches in the verandah, and who, directly the door was opened, or the curtain raised as the case might be, considered it an invitation to them to enter, and commenced filing into your sanctum till distracted nature could bear it no longer, and you had to flee to the mess for safety.

However, everything must have an end, and by the time appointed we were all ready. Everything had been disposed of or given away, and most things settled, except perchance a few items between certain bearers and kitmagars and their creditors in the bazaar. The last stirrup cup had been quaffed, and there we were *en route* for the station, with the band of the new regiment playing us out. After the usual bother, which invariably accompanies the embarkation on a train, we at last settled down, and the signal was given for our departure. I had noticed when we got into the station that they had put the horse-boxes on in front of the train next to the engine, but although we remonstrated, the officials refused to alter it, as they declared it was perfectly safe.

Everything went well till about one o'clock in the morning, when we suddenly came to a stop at a small station, and were roused out by the cry of fire. Just as we had anticipated, the sparks from the engine had caught some straw or something in the front box, and there it was on the point of bursting into a blaze. To get the horses out was no easy matter, for, as every one knows, the smell of fire and smoke seems to almost paralyze them, and consequently, notwithstanding our united exertions, we could not make them budge an inch. To add to the difficulty, we could not get water, the station not being used to water at, except occasionally; the astute gentleman in charge had taken the key, and, like all natives, or the majority of them, directly there was an emergency where prompt action was needed, he lost his head. My bearer, Christian John (I had taken him over from his former master), of whom I have spoken before, certainly did his best, and, from the language he used when he found he could make nothing of the "muddle puddle porter," both in the vernacular and in the English tongue, I should say he must have piled up a heavy record against himself. Happily, the driver kept his wits about him, and shunting the burning box under the tank, with the aid of a crowbar he broke the chain, and two of the pioneers swamping up managed to get on the top, and a volume of water soon streamed on to the fire and put it out—not, however, before the unfortunate horses, or at least two of them, were badly burnt. We had a regular shindy when it was all over, for we promptly refused to continue the journey until a fresh horse-box was procured, and for some time they refused to send one down. In the end, though, we had our way, and, after a delay of some hours, we were off again, taking our damaged animals along with us. We had managed to get at the medical store-chest, and with the aid of our doctor I compounded a lotion of sugar of lead that gave them a certain amount of ease. One of the poor brutes was so bad that we had to almost pad his back with cotton wool on the top of flour and grease, and I never thought he would recover. I am glad to say, however, that they all got well in the end, and the railway company had to pay damages for their folly.

When we reached the first camp, where our tents were pitched ready for us, I was delighted to see my nags all safe and sound, and my head syce anxiously looking out for my arrival. He informed me that the whole party had been there three or four days, and that no casualty had happened, except the death on the road of the quartermaster's dog, which, as the animal was a vicious brute, who was for ever biting something or somebody, I don't suppose any one except his master regretted. Indeed, I fancy, if the truth was known, that the beast had been quietly put out of the way one night, though the syces attributed the demise to a snake bite.

I do not intend to describe the monotonous routine of a march so far as the military portion of it is concerned —the agonies of superintending broken-down bullock hackerys or wayward camels that insist on disposing of their loads every time they are put on, and make as much noise when expected to move as a whole army of pigs at slaughter-time.—No; let these unpleasant recollections be drowned in the remembrance of the matutinal coffee at the halfway house, or the cheery dinner at mess in the evening, to say nothing of the occasional day's sport picked up while on the road.

Of course a good many of us had got our guns with us somewhere handy, where they could be easily got at, and, as the regiment with the long train of baggage animals and carts toiled along the dusty road, we had to take it in turns to strike off to the right or left and endeavour to supply the mess with game of some sort from the neighbouring fields or *jheels.* The great field days for the sportsmen were those on which the distance to the next camp was short and the start early. At those times, as soon as the work was over and the men settled down, off they would go in parties in every direction, often not returning with their spoils until long after sundown. I remember at one camp we came to early in the day; we had "khubber" of some first-rate snipe-shooting to be had round the borders of a large tank some three miles off, and we were also told that the tank itself was as full of duck and all sorts of wild fowl as it could be. It being somewhat out of the beaten track, and not generally known, the place had seldom been shot over, so that there was every chance of a good day's sport. Now, as I happened to have my cart with me on the march, I immediately became a person of some importance, and I was much amused at the numerous innuendoes, accompanied by offers of refreshment, that were thrown out in order to induce me to give an invitation to make one of the drive out.

Johnson and McSweeny were eventually the two lucky ones selected, and, having obtained leave and got into our shooting kit, away we three went, with the syce and guide packed in somehow, in quest of the ground. For about a mile we returned over the road we had come that morning, and then we were directed to turn off to the left down a bye-lane, at least the guide called it a lane, but it was more like driving over the newly-dug foundations of a building than anything else, and precious glad I was when "the lane" came to an end, and we emerged into an open plain with only now and again a nullah to negotiate. In about an hour and a half, after one or two hair-breadth escapes, we arrived at the haven where we would be, and our eyes were gladdened by the sight of a first-rate bit of snipe-ground with the gleam of the water beyond shining through some high reeds. Having found a place under some trees to put up the cart, we disembarked, and immediately commenced operations. As we were walking up to the boggy ground, up got a covey of sandgrouse right in front of McSweeny, who being taken unawares, and not having seen any before, stood gaping at them open-mouthed. Bang, bang, bang—two barrels from Johnson and one long shot from myself, and three birds fell.

"Why the plague did not you fire, Mac; they were right in front of you?" I asked.

"Hoot, mon," he replied, "I just thought it was the divil. I was looking for wee bit snippets, and up gets monsters for a' the world like bubbly jocks."

Considering that a sandgrouse was not a particularly formidable article in size, McSweeny's astonishment must have played the deuce with his powers of vision I thought; and, having subjected him to a certain amount of chaff, we proceeded, and were soon hard at it among the "wee bit snippets."

The whole place was chokeful of snipe, and, what is

more, they were by no means wild, so it did not take very long for us to fill the bag pretty full. As we neared the tank we agreed to cease firing and go cautiously up for a chance at the duck, and after shifting our cartridges for some loaded with duck-shot we essayed a stalk, but we very soon found the water too deep for that game. Luckily our guide came to the rescue with a native owner of two dug-out canoes, into which we got and perched (I cannot call it seated) ourselves, while we were paddled gently to the rushes. As the boats entered them, up got a whole cloud of duck, and the result of our six barrels at close quarters was very satisfactory, eight coming down wallop. "Bhito, sahib, Bhito," whispered the guide as he shoved my boat into the thickest of the reeds, while the native owner did the same office for McSweeny and Johnson, and squat we did, for we could hear the wish, wish, wish of the returning duck as they circled back to where we hid. A minute or so of expectation, and then over our heads they came, four more losing the number of their mess. This made twelve ducks down in all, of which seven were dead and five cripples, the latter giving us a lot of trouble to retrieve. Eventually we picked up all but two, and then, as it was getting late, we rewarded our boatmen, and, having reached *terra firma,* made the best of our way back towards the trap.

Going back, Johnson shot a teal which fell into the middle of a small tank, and as none of the natives would go and fetch it, McSweeny offered to take his things off and swim out for the bird. Directly, however, the guide saw what he was about to do, he begged me to stop him, for he said no man could do it. The weeds were so bad that the moment you entered the water, after the first stroke or so, you would be dragged down and drowned.

And from what I heard subsequently I believe this would have been the case, though at the time I confess I was sceptical.

When we arrived at the trap, we counted the bag, which was somewhere about twenty-three couple of snipe, ten duck, and three sandgrouse—not so bad for an off chance. Before we reached the camp, I remember it was quite dark; and having missed our way twice and got turned over completely once, I thought we should never arrive at all. But on the principle of it being "a long lane that has no turning," we eventually got safe home, very tired and very hungry, but having thoroughly enjoyed our day's sport. I am glad to say that the proceeds thereof were duly appreciated by the mess, and the ducks were voted the fattest and best that had been eaten for some time.

The next excursion we made was somewhat of a different character, and did not redound so much to our credit as shikaries. We had camped somewhere below a range of small hills, in which tradition had it there were to be found both deer and hares, and now and again a panther; while in the jungle at the foot thereof, pig were supposed to "simply swarm." Of course this was too good an opportunity to be lost, so four of us went out—Johnson, Gordon, Tilson, and myself. McSweeny could not get away to his intense disgust, so was forced to remain in camp. I took Christian John with me to carry my rifle, and the other three also took out their attendant gun-bearers; so with a few natives of the district, and guides we made quite a formidable array. We commenced operations by beating the jungle for pig, and though a sounder was reported to have broken back, we never saw so much as a sign of pork. So we gave that up as a bad job. Certainly we bagged two or three hares, rather miserable specimens, and from what I had heard of their feeding propensities, I should not have cared to eat them. But they were better than nothing, and the men, who had no scruples on the subject, on our return to camp were very glad of the addition to their daily rations. Naturally we all devoutly hoped that we might come across the occasional panther, but although, under the direction of the native guide, we visited all the likely spots within hail, we had not the luck to come across the beast, and I am very doubtful if he ever existed at all, except in the mind of the imaginative native.

By the time we had finished our search after panthers, the day was far advanced, so we decided to strike over the hills and try for antelope, the universal name for all deer, female black buck included. We had toiled upwards for some little time, when on reaching a fairly extensive plateau our guide suddenly became greatly excited and pointed out a herd calmly feeding on the far side. This cheered our drooping spirits somewhat, and we immediately held a council of war as to the best method of stalking the animals. At last it was decided that Gordon and Tilson were to make a long detour to the left, and Johnson to go round by the right, while I was to make the best of my way across the plain on my stomach towards the herd. After giving the others sufficient time for their flank movement, for twenty minutes I waited patiently behind a rock, and then, considering that I had allowed ample time, I started on my journey. Pretty tired I was of crawling on my hands and knees before I had got halfway across. I dared not look up or stop, for fear of attracting the attention of the deer, and I was about played out, when a double shot in front told me that the game had commenced. On rising to a sitting position, I found everything had vanished like a beautiful dream, and presently I was joined by Tilson and Gordon, who informed me that they had both had a shot, and the former swore he had got home, but alas! the native guide pronounced against him and declared that they had both missed clean. It was getting quite dusk by this time, so I sent off a man to find Johnson, who had not yet turned up, and to tell him we were going to make a start homewards, but would wait where we were till he came.

Presently my messenger came running back and said the sahib was stalking a fresh herd he had spotted below in the plain, and would we come on as quickly as possible? As the route indicated was all on the way home, we agreed, and soon afterwards made out the figure of Johnson making his way, serpent fashion, towards some rocks some way below us. We could not, even from our elevated position, see what quarry he was after at first, but eventually we made out a string of camels being driven towards the camp. They were our patient baggage friends who had been turned out for a holiday amid the scrub, and who were now returning to their duties. "By Jove!" I said, "I believe Johnson has mistaken them in the dusk for deer. We must get down to him as quickly as we can, or he will be shooting somebody, to say nothing of a commissariat camel." It was just as I supposed—he was after the camels, and being on the low ground could only see their heads, which he mistook for a herd of antelope. Before we could get close enough to stop him we saw him raise his rifle and take a steady aim, and then "crack" he fired, luckily with no effect. Of course we all shouted at the top of our voices as we saw that he was reloading, and then commenced to run wildly down towards him.

At the sound of our voices he looked round, and seeing us careering madly over the rocks and broken ground, thought we had gone mad, and began to abuse us roundly for spoiling his sport, and losing a second shot at the deer.

"Deer!" quoth I, as soon as I got my breath. "Deer be hanged; they are our camels going home, and if you have not already shot one, you are more lucky than you deserve!"

Naturally he would not believe us at first, but on a more careful inspection he was at last convinced of his error, and pretty foolish he looked, begging us to keep it to ourselves. When we got into camp, however, we found that the camel-drivers had already spread the report of their being fired at, so the story soon leaked out, and in self-defence we had to give up the culprit's name, who, as may be supposed, got most unmercifully chaffed.

CHAPTER XI.

THE P. V. H. RACES.

"*Atra cura post equitem sedet*" may in some instances be true; but as in every case there are exceptions, I must be allowed to claim one for the Peshawar Vale Hunt Meeting, at the time about which I am writing. Certainly black care did not figure on the card on that occasion, for a cheerier meeting could not well be imagined. Everything contributed to make it a success. We had good entries, good weather, good going, and good sportsmen, and the two days' racing have always remained fixed in my mind as the most enjoyable at which I ever assisted. It was in the middle of the cold weather when the races came off, and precious cold it can be up there on occasions. We had been having some rare sport with the hounds, and more than half the animals who were to compete were almost in as good condition and training as if they had been regularly put through the mill. All they wanted was "winding up" by means of a few final gallops at full speed. I always held when I was in India, and I have never had any good reason given me yet for altering my opinion, that in a great number of instances horses are overtrained, and by overtrained I do not mean so much that they had too much work, but that the work was of too monotonous a character. The daily galloping round the course a certain number of times at a certain pace seemed after a time to weary them, and my experience proved that, for a steeplechaser, a day's hunting, or even a spin across country, did far more good than any amount of sweating on the racecourse. Of course I admit that a certain amount is necessary, but it was always overdone, and if I could manage it I invariably gave more than half the preparation as far away from home as possible—it must be remembered I am talking of some years ago, and *tempora mutantur*, I dare say—a proceeding which I found to work wonders.

I had one animal who would not train on a racecourse under any circumstances, no matter where he was. Directly he came anywhere near it he went perfectly mad, and shivered with excitement, taking so much out of himself that it was perfectly hopeless to attempt to do anything with him. He was a small horse, Peter by name, a well-known pigsticker, and one of the most magnificent fencers I ever rode, bold as they make them, and never making a mistake; and when I entered him for the Hunt Cup I looked upon it, bar accidents, as already won. One peculiarity about the beast I found rather profitable, which I may mention. His former master, from whom I bought him, had taught Master Peter to jump a walking-stick held out, as many times as he was asked to do it, and when he sold him he confided this trick to me. In fact, it went with the sale—a sort of "feature," as it were. I remember the first time I tried it outside the racquet court. I got on about three hundred rupees, for no one there knew anything about it, and one and all bet against the performance. I had stipulated for two shots, which were allowed; but there was no necessity, for at the first trial my friend hopped over without a minute's hesitation, and I walked off with £30 in my possession, quite happy. After that it used to be a regular standing dish when any strangers were present, and many an honest (or dishonest, if you like) rupee found its way out of their pockets into that of myself and my friends who were "in the know." However, this has nothing to do with the Hunt Races, so I will get on.

For some time before the meeting there was the regular excitement attending this particular class of sport, and every one in the station was actively engaged in preparing some sort of beast for one or other of the forthcoming events. Arabs, walers, country-breds, and tattoos were all hard at it, and the nearer the time drew towards the meeting the more horsey the conversation of the various owners became.

The big event was the Hunt Cup, a steeplechase over three miles and a half of fair hunting country, and, as I have said before, I had quite made up my mind that this was to be mine. It was for horses the property of, and regularly ridden by, members of the Peshawar Vale Hunt, so I had, I thought, a very fair line to go upon. I knew that I had the heels of most of them, and as far as the jumping went the rest were not in it with Peter, so that I had every reason to be sanguine. I also entered him for a flat race in case of accidents, and I had a very good country-bred with which I hoped to go near, for the Station Plate.

Oddly enough, Peter was not much fancied by the knowing division, and I managed to secure him in two lotteries for a very moderate sum. The first favourite was a slashing waler belonging to James' of the native cavalry, and there was a large section who were very keen about Richards' (the master's) chestnut; not that he had much pace, they said, but he could go all day and never fall down—two points which, in a steeplechase, are not bad things to rely on.

By the day of the races I had got both my nags as fit as they could well be, notwithstanding the difficulty of training my steeplechaser "on the course;" but, unfortunately for myself, I had caught a bad cold, which, accompanied by a touch of fever, pulled me down tremendously, and made me feel as weak as a rat. Tilson wanted me to give him the mount and stand down, but I did not see the fun of that, so elected to ride myself, giving him the ride on my country-bred, "Greypowder" by name, in the Station Plate.

The first race was a sort of preliminary canter—a hurdle race—which brought out a large field, among them being a horse belonging to the cantonment magistrate, a Mr. Brown, and at the eleventh hour he came to me and asked me to ride as his jockey had thrown him over. I told him I did not want to do too much, as I was not feeling well, and suggested his going elsewhere; but he would not take "no" for an answer, and at last I gave in.

"Where is the animal?" I asked; "and is he pretty fit?"

"My dear fellow," replied Brown, "he is bound to win. I have got him round the corner, as he is a bit nervous. All you have to do is to wait on them till you get to the last hurdle, and then come away and win."

"All right," I said; "but what about his jumping?"

"Well, I can't tell you much about that," answered Brown. "You see, I had him from a friend at Umballa, and he only arrived yesterday; but he tells me that he is a wonder. Anyhow, you will soon see."

Pleasant, I thought, especially if the method of gauging the beast's saltatory powers meant including a cropper at the first hurdle! However, there was no help for it, so I got his saddle and weighed, feeling very far from confident. The ceremony over, we went in quest of the "nervous" steed, and, to my surprise, I found a perfectly placid-looking animal of a milk-white hue, and evidently much out of condition, being walked about in rear of the stand. So far from exhibiting any signs of nervousness, like Mark Twain's celebrated horse, he appeared to me to be only anxious to find some convenient spot to lean against.

"But you don't expect me to ride that thing?" I ejaculated, directly I saw the brute. "Why, I don't believe he has had a gallop for a month."

Brown was very indignant at the depreciation of his racer, and offered to bet me anything that he won. Of course I declined, as I foresaw the consequences, for Brown would most certainly say that it was my fault. I had a great mind to refuse to go to the post; but sooner than have a row, as I had weighed, I at last got up and cantered past the stand. The appearance of my milk-white steed was a signal for a burst of laughter and a good deal of chaff, and then we went to the post. Fourteen runners faced the starter, and the flag dropped to an excellent start. We got over the first hurdle somehow—how, I never knew, and before we had got halfway to the next my friend was done, and began to blow like a grampus. Neither whip nor spur were of any avail, and consequently we arrived at the fence last of all. I drove him at it as hard as I could, but he only ran plump up against the hurdle, carrying it away, and getting considerably mixed up therein. Not an inch would he budge as long as the hurdle was round his legs. He did not even try and kick himself free, but stood stock still like a pig; and this was the animal that was so nervous he could not be saddled in a crowd!

At last I had to dismount and clear away the *débris* myself, by which time the race was finished, and then, burning with indignation, I rode back the shortest way to the stand, where I gave Mr. Brown such a piece of my mind as fairly astonished the worthy gentleman. Poor Brown! It was not his fault; he knew absolutely nothing about horses, and had been properly "had" by his friend at Umballa, for I heard afterwards he had given something over four hundred rupees for the brute on purpose to win that very race.

It was now getting time to weigh for the Hunt Cup, which I did with very different feelings, and was soon on the back of Peter, who was quite as keen to be off as his master. There were nine runners, among them being Ben Richards' old chestnut, and an animal called Curly Boy that I picked out as second best, and on which I determined to keep my eye. After a couple of false starts we were off, Ben Richards cutting out the pace as fast as he could, in which course he was right, for, as I have said, the old chestnut could go one pace all day. The first or second fence, I forget which, was in and out of an orchard, and, as bad luck would have it, in jumping out, a branch caught my off-side stirrup and whipped it clean away from the bar, leaving me with only one to ride the whole race with. I did not actually come off when the accident happened, but it was as near as they make them. As soon as I had steadied myself, I threw the other stirrup across the saddle bow, preferring to ride without any at all than be like a pig with one ear. I fancy most people will agree with me also, that it is far more tiring to ride with one only than with none at all.

We were all pretty close together till the third fence from the orchard, a nasty double, with a drop into a lane, and here three of us came a "buster," myself among the number. However, I was soon up again, and, though feeling somewhat shaken and rather pumped, was speeding alongside the chestnut, who was leading. Down we came to the water jump, five of us, all abreast and almost touching—a bound—a vision of water—a stumble—a heavy splash, and I found myself struggling back into the saddle, the only one over, the rest being well in the brook. Before I could pull him together, Peter was off like a sky-rocket, and three or four fields ahead of everything. The last fence, a low wall, came in view, and so cooked was I that I could do nothing more than sit on. Alas! my gallant steed made a slight mistake, and came on his head the other side in a bed of onions, rolling over with my left leg under him, and knocking all the wind out of both of us. Had he been able to get on his legs we should have won as it was, but it must have been quite two minutes before he attempted to move, which he did just as Curly Boy came over the fence. I scrambled on to his back the best way I could, and made play in the tracks of the leader. In another ten yards I should have caught him; but it was too late, and the verdict was against me by a short head. It was very provoking, as I am convinced if it had not been for the mishap in the orchard, and my being a bit off colour from my touch of fever, I should have won easily, as I should never have let my horse run himself out the way he did.

Of course the owner of Curly Boy was delighted, and thought his animal was something extraordinary, being perfectly prepared to run me a match over the same course any day I wished, for any sum. This I promptly accepted, and a match was made for a thousand rupees, half forfeit, to be run the following week.

I am glad to say that Tilson won me the Station Plate with Greypowder, which made up a little for my disappointment.

That night when we went down to the lotteries I found that for the Hunters' Flat Race, Peter was absolutely in no demand whatever, and in the first lottery I bought him for twenty rupees. Every one was after Curly Boy and a horse belonging to the R.H.A.; I forget the name. I could not make this out, till I found that Curly Boy's owner had been "gassing" tremendously about his nag, and that that old sinner McSweeny had been spreading rumours abroad that Peter was lame. "What did you do that for, you old coper?" I asked him, and his reply was characteristic. "Ah, well," he said, "I'm just thinking, my bonny boy, that it has been a wee bit disappointment for you this day, and there is no saying how much you may not be able to get back by means of a little judicious flattery." The idea of calling a deliberate statement anent the lameness of a perfectly sound animal a "little judicious flattery" struck me as exceedingly naïve. Of course it soon leaked out that my beast was all right, and in the second lottery I had consequently to pay a higher price to secure him. Besides the two lotteries, I had an even fifty with Curly Boy's owner that I beat him; so I stood to win a fairly decent sum on the morrow, if successful.

I was up betimes to see how Peter was, and found him none the worse for the previous day, so, having given him a breather before breakfast, I was quite content to let him be till wanted. After the morning meal I jumped on my tat and cantered off to the racecourse to have a look round, where I found a lot of sportsmen already assembled, among them being my friend Brown. He was evidently still very sore about his horse, and burning to have his revenge somehow; and when I saw him in deep confabulation with McSweeny, I knew there was something up. Presently the crafty Scot came up to me as if he had only that instant noticed my arrival, though I saw him spot me the moment I came on to the course.

"I have worked Brown up to a pitch; he will lay you two to one against your gee. Take him, and halves, mind; he is just foo about yesterday," he whispered. And then up came Brown himself. "I was just saying," said the undefeated medico as the gentleman approached, "that our friend here (pointing to myself) had much better let some one else ride for him to-day, after the way he lost you your race yesterday."

Brown bowed very stiffly to me, and, after a moment's hesitation, replied, "Of course, every one has a right to please themselves; but if he wants to win, I should say it would be better."

"There!" exclaimed McSweeny to me, "I told you so. if you ride I'll bet against you."

"How much, Mac?" I asked; "and what price?"

"I'll lay you a hundred rupees to fifty, if you like," was the answer—given, as I knew, simply to lead on the unsuspecting Brown; and it had the desired effect, for almost before I could say "done," he interrupted with, "Ah, I'll bet you an even five hundred too."

"Not likely," I said; "I am not quite such a fool as to take even money when I can get two to one. I'll take your five hundred to two hundred and fifty if you like, or double the amount."

"Thank you," he replied; "I'll bet you the five hundred (I think he called it wager) to half that amount on your side," and then he was going to walk away. McSweeny, however, had not done with him yet, for he stopped him at once and said, "How about the other matter?" "What other matter?" I inquired; and was informed that Brown wanted to make a match with me with his white horse against any one of mine, bar Peter, owners up, over six flights of hurdles, for two hundred and fifty rupees. This fetched me considerably, so I turned to Mr. Brown and asked him if it was true, and he with a somewhat grandiloquent air said "yes."

Now, the tattoo I was riding, though under thirteen hands, happened to be very fast and a capital fencer, and as I felt quite certain that Brown would never get over the first hurdle, or that if he did his horse would not, I determined to give him a lesson, and there and then I closed with him by saying, "Very well, I will run you this afternoon over six flights of hurdles, owners up, after the last race, if the stewards will allow it, and I will name my animal now—the one I am riding, viz.—the Market Gardener. Both McSweeny and Brown thought I was chaffing; but I soon undeceived them by tearing a scrap out of my betting book and reducing the terms to writing, signed them, and then handed them to the magistrate sahib for his autograph. I could see that he did not half like it, for he thought it an insult to pit a mere tat against his noble steed, but he had gone too far to draw back; and Ben Richards, who was secretary, coming up at that moment, I told him about it, and he promised to see the stewards and to get their permission, also to arrange to have the hurdles put up for us.

The joke went round the station like wildfire, and great was the chaff. Some of Brown's friends, who had been told wonderful tales of the white gee's prowess, took the matter up quite warmly, and backed their opinion freely, so that by the time the bell rang for the first race there was a heap of money on the match, and it became quite the feature of the meeting. As I was saddling

Peter for the Hunter's Flat Race I noticed Brown hovering about and looking rather anxious; and my syce told me he had been pumping him as to our chance of winning. Naturally, the worthy Ram Bux had made the magistrate quite happy by telling him that nothing else had a chance, and when I asked him if he wanted to bet any more he hurried off without giving me an answer.

We had no less than three false starts, which was annoying, because my mount, being especially eager, was not the easiest animal in the world to pull up, and I was afraid that he would take it all out of himself before we got to business. At the fourth attempt, however, the flag fell, and I jumped away with a clear lead of about two lengths. I made the pace a real hot one the whole journey, and before I got to the distance I had the whole lot settled, and coming away, won as I liked in the commonest of canters, fairly squandering the whole field. Such an exhibition of them did I make, that Curly Boy's owner paid half forfeit for our match there and then, and consequently I won about four hundred pounds, what with bets and lotteries, over the race, which I considered good business. Brown's face was a picture when I met him in the stand afterwards; and by the way he glared at McSweeny it was evident that he looked upon him in anything but the light of a true friend, or a useful turf adviser.

Directly after the last race was over, Ben Richards, as he had promised, got his men to work and had the hurdles up; and presently Brown emerged from the paddock mounted on his white horse, and for the first time in his life arrayed in all the glory of silk. There was a regular scream as I cantered by on my little tat, Tommy Atkins being peculiarly demonstrative. I heard afterwards that all our chaps had put their money on me to a man, which went some way to account for a large number of prisoners answering to the charge of "drunk," who eventually appeared in the orderly-room. We both got to the post together, and were off at the first attempt. Up to the hurdle all went well, but as my little beast curled himself over, I saw a dark object shoot by me and heard a crack behind. The dark object was Brown, and the crack was caused by the white horse stopping dead, and sliding into the hurdle. He evidently remembered the performance of the previous day, and was determined not to be fooled about a second time over any nasty jumps in which he might get his poor legs entangled. I immediately eased up the Market Gardener to make sure that Brown was not hurt, and having seen him scramble on again and thrash his old crock over the fallen hurdle, I started off again. At the second fence the dispenser of the law cut another voluntary, and as his horse did not go anywhere near the obstacle, it remained upright. As I passed the judge's box and turned to go into the paddock, I saw in the far distance the figures of man and beast still endeavouring to negotiate the hurdle; and as at every other attempt the two parted company, I may fairly claim to have had my revenge, and to have demonstrated the worthlessness of the white steed.

There was quite a scene with the unfortunate Brown when at last he was restored to his friends. He was livid with rage, and utterly blown and played out, while his personal appearance was not improved by the fact that in one of his involuntary transits through space he had, at the end of the described parabola, alighted on his nose, and caused that member to bleed violently all over his clothes. He swore that he had been swindled, and talked very big about the law and the penalties thereof, all of which was exceedingly ludicrous and caused immoderate laughter. Eventually he got so rabid and personal that he had to be removed and put outside to cool down—a process that took some hours to complete. However, by that time he was all right again, and he turned up at eight o'clock at the race dinner, which was held that night, a wiser if not a sadder man. I remember we had a very cheery evening of it, and did not separate till an early hour the following morning; and as I walked home with McSweeny the old rascal insisted on making up his accounts.

"Look here, ould mon," he said, after some abstruse calculations not unmixed with hiccoughs, "I'm just thinking—hic—dom the toddy—I'm just thinking that you'll ha to be paying me twa handred and fafty bawbees—hic—I mean rupees—the half of the siller ye pouched from the mon Brown."

"One hundred and fifty you mean, Mac," I retorted.

"Hoos that—hic—dom the toddy again," he exclaimed; "I just went ye halves."

"Yes," I said, "that's right enough; but you forget that you laid me a hundred rupees to fifty against my horse."

"Eh, that be dommed," he roared; "I did na mean that, I were codding the loony Brown for ye—na—na, twa handred—hic—and fifty."

"Not I, my friend, a bet's a bet, and one hundred and fifty it will have to be," I repeated; "but we will talk it over to-morrow, and now, good night," as I turned into my door, leaving him to go on, and I could hear him for some distance saying to himself, "Twa handred and fafty—bet be dommed—hic," till at last he rounded the corner and silence reigned supreme.

The next day he was at me again, but I stuck to my

guns, and refused to pay him more than a hundred and fifty rupees, to which he was at last bound to consent, though to this day I believe he is ready to swear that, notwithstanding all the trouble he took to make matters easy, he was diddled out of a ten-pound note.

CHAPTER XII.

A MIXED BAG.

I HAD not long arrived at a certain up-country station, celebrated for its sanctity and its "King Cob" manufacture, when I found myself relegated to the delights of a temporary residence under canvas in what was known as the musketry camp. The camp itself was situated about six miles from cantonments under a tope of mango trees, in immediate proximity to the ranges; and, barring the monotony of the proceedings, it was not half a bad billet, for after the day's practice was over—generally by about noon—and when the last squad of the "duffers," or third-class shots, had expended the requisite amount of ammunition in fruitless attempts to hit the target, the rest of the time was my own, and I could devote it to such kind of shikar as there was to be found anywhere within a reasonable distance.

There were two of us permanently quartered there as instructors during the musketry season, with a doctor, in case of accidents; and as each company, which came out in turn, brought two officers, our mess consisted of five, so that we were always sure of a rubber of whist in the evening, and could generally square matters amongst ourselves, so that two, if not three, of us were always able to get away for a day's sport. Occasionally, moreover, we used to fire very early on Saturday mornings, and, having finished our work by breakfast-time, four of us would start off on a short expedition till the following Monday, taking it in turns to leave either the doctor or one of the company officers in charge of the camp during our absence. I remember it was on one of these occasions, when the rest of the party had started out for a foray against the snipe, that I was left in charge, and having digested my dinner and lighted my second cheroot, I was thinking about turning in, when I was disturbed by a most extraordinary series of sighs or groans outside my tent. Thinking some one was hurt, I went outside and called my kitmutgar, who I could see huddled up over his hubble-bubble a short distance off. Directly he saw me, however, he fled; and no amount of persuasions or threats would induce him to answer my summons. I tried various other of my retainers, with a like result. No matter how much or how loudly I shouted, not a soul would respond or budge an inch, and all the time the sighing and moaning was going on with, if anything, increasing vehemence. At last I lost my temper, and on my bearer returning (Christian John), who I had sent somewhere to get me something or other, I asked him what the devil it all meant. Of course he knew nothing, but would go and see. Just as he was moving off there was a regular wail, like a banshee outside, and he turned pale and began to tremble.

"What the plague is that row, John?" I asked.

"Me not know, master, go see; think it is Shaitan," was his reply; but a second edition of the groan somewhat damped his ardour for "going to see," and he evidently wished himself anywhere but where he was. At last he summoned up courage to go off to investigate his brother-servants' behaviour, and the way he scudded across the space that separated my tent from the servants' quarters was a caution. After the lapse of about ten minutes he returned, accompanied by my bheestee (he dared not come alone), and informed me that it was the general opinion amongst the natives that it was Shaitan, or the devil, who was making the row, and that whenever that particular noise was heard, the first person who called attention to it would surely die. As I had undoubtedly been the individual who had been the first to notice it, I asked if they supposed I was to die, and was informed that "Sahib ko mallum," about equivalent to the "quien sabe" of the Spanish. I then ascertained that the devil had taken for the nonce the form of an owl, and that it was in that guise he was making all the bobbery. When I told John to get me my gun, which he did immediately, he begged and prayed me not to try and shoot it, for he said it would be fatal to me—"Master die for sure"—a fact that did not speak volumes for his Christianity. However, I was not to be deterred, and going outside, after some trouble, I at last detected the author of the mischief in a tree, and drawing a bead I brought the devil and all his works down at the first shot.

Never did I see men in such a funk as my servants were. After that not one of them would touch the owl, and, barring John, none would come near me that night again; and, from the conversation I overheard between them on the following morning, they were evidently much surprised to find me still in the land of the living. Indeed, I noticed that they watched me very closely for quite a week, expecting to see me drop down any moment, as a just retribution for such a bitter insult to Shaitan. As the time wore on, and I did not do so, they eventually decided either that I was too powerful for Shaitan to hurt, or too insignificant for him to take notice of (most probably the latter), and consequently took heart; but they would never admit for a moment that the bird I had slain was a common owl, or that I had not done a most outrageous and dangerous deed in shooting it.

Shortly after this little episode we arranged three days' sport, to commence on the Saturday and finish upon the Monday night, as there happened for some reason or another to be no musketry that day. The first day we agreed to shoot snipe and quail, of which there was a great number close to the camp, and sending a tent and paraphernalia on in the afternoon to a spot about fifteen miles away on the borders of a jungle, to ride out in the evening, and devote the following two days to a try after nilgai or blue bull.

Accordingly, on the Saturday morning very early, as soon as it was light, I commenced work, hoping to finish before breakfast; but owing to some delay I was disappointed, and consequently Howard, a subaltern, and myself had to remain to finish up, leaving the others to begin without us, and arranging to pick them up as soon as we had done. From having been permanently in the camp for some time, I knew all the best ground for miles round, and such was the selfishness of human nature, that I determined not to give the advanced guard the information, but to keep it till I could join in the fun, and so directed them to some snipe-ground in a contrary direction, arranging a trysting-spot at a ruined temple about a mile away. We could hear them banging away merrily all the time we were endeavouring to get Tommy Atkins on level terms with his rifle, and I am afraid that the checking of targets was carried out in a somewhat hasty manner in consequence. Anyhow, we got through quite an hour before I expected, and as neither of us had had much breakfast, I thought a second edition would not be a bad thing before starting, so sent off and ordered some just before we finished.

After changing into my shooting-kit, I went over to the mess-tent, where I found John having an altercation with my kitmutgar, and nothing ready. Of course I was very angry, and sitting down, told the kitmutgar to get it at once. To my astonishment he gave me a cheeky answer, and, without looking round, I gave a backhander, which caught the gentleman in the wind. Over he went, and lay huddled up without a move. I thought I had killed the man; and as all his fellow-servants trooped in and declared him dead, I confess I was in a mortal funk. "Here's a go," I said to Howard as he came in; "this chap was cheeky, and I gave him a backhander, and he seems to have died right off. You had better ride for the doctor and bring him along." And then turning to Christian John, I ordered him to clear the tent of the howling crowd. By this time the gentleman's family and "jat" (caste) were getting very demonstrative, and began to threaten me with the "kutwal" and the law. But John, who had his wits about him on that occasion, soon cleared them out, and for reasons best known to himself, sent for his crony, my bheestee. When that worthy arrived with his mussock, he looked for a moment or two at the recumbent form of the butler, and then declared he was "mut," or drunk as a lord. "Decko sahib," he said, as he prepared his skin for operations, and swish went the whole contents of the mussock over the blackguard. The cold water had the desired effect in a few seconds, and much to my relief the dead man got up as if he had been shot, staggering out of the tent drenched through, and vowing vengeance against the bheestee who had broken his caste.

As soon as this little drama was over, I gave John the necessary instructions about sending the gear on, and getting rid of the kitmutgar, and then Howard and I started off to the temple to join the others. When we got there we found them all assembled, and not best pleased at having been kept waiting; but my explanations and description of the murder so tickled everybody, that their anger gave place to hilarity. They had had some very good sport among the snipe already, having dropped on to some ground where they were as thick as peas; and so, as a change, I proposed to have a turn at the quail, which were close at hand. We walked down in line, about three yards apart, towards a sugar khate, but to my surprise we only got a brace. I was certain that the place was full of them, so could not quite make it out, and the others began to chaff me freely about my preserve. However, I was not going to be done, so I sent off to the camp for a long rope, a measuring chain, and my dog, and when the articles arrived I took the ground back again, making the guns walk about a yard or two behind the rope, which, held at each end, was dragged along the ground, two men following with the chain in a similar manner in rear.

This time it was a very different story, for, as I expected, the ground was alive with the little birds, who had laid like stones on the first occasion when we walked down, but who could not stand the rope dragging over them. Very pretty shooting we had for an hour, the only difficulty being to give the birds sufficient law. A quail is exceedingly easy to hit, as it flies perfectly straight, but being very difficult to put up, it will lie till the last moment and rise right under your feet, when you are very apt to fire in a hurry, and either miss altogether or blow the bird to atoms. However, we soon got what the Americans call the "hang of the thing," and by tiffin-time we had made quite a respectable bag. The only person not perfectly satisfied was my dog, who, not being much of a sporting character, considered his mission in life was to run in and eat everything we shot, and thereby managed to obtain for himself the best portion of the charge of Howard's second barrel, delivered at about thirty yards as he was making off with a quail he had killed with his first cartridge. This, as may be supposed, astonished Ponto considerably, so much so that he dropped the bird, and went for camp like the wind, evidently looking on shooting as poor sport, and taking no further interest in the proceedings of that day, or, indeed, so far as shooting went, any subsequent days, for I could never afterwards induce him to come within a hundred miles of a gun if he saw one.

After tiffin we had another "go" at snipe, and also got a few duck, and then went back to camp for an early dinner. We found the tent and things had gone all right in charge of John, who, by the way, had left word for me that the kitmutgar had gone into the station in order to obtain legal advice with a view of prosecuting myself and the bheestie for assault and damage—a fact which, as may be imagined, did not trouble me much. Dinner over, after a cigar and a peg, we mounted our steeds, and prepared to ride the fifteen miles to our shooting-camp. Unfortunately for me my tat was *hors de combat* from a wrench I had given him a day or two before, galloping after a jackal, and I only had one other animal out with me, a country-bred, which had been presented to me, a very good-looking beast, but the most wicked brute I ever rode, and a direct contradiction of the old proverb of "Never look a gift horse in the mouth," insomuch as had I looked I should never have accepted him, for his mouth was perfectly callous on both sides, and nothing short of a steam engine could stop him if he made up his mind to go, which he did on most occasions. The present one was of course no exception, and no sooner was I in the saddle than away he went as hard as ever he could tear, picking out a series of low boughs to gallop under, which gave me as much as I could do to avoid. To pull at him I knew was useless; the only possible thing was to sit on and hope for the best, which I did, feeling very much like the celebrated Mr. Gilpin, and like St. Paul, "wishing for daylight." Perhaps if I could, like that navigator, have "cast four anchors out of the stern," I might have brought up, but not having such articles about me I was obliged to go on. For two blessed miles did we tear before I could get half a chance, and when eventually we did stop, I was completely blown (I had just finished dinner when I started), and utterly at sea as to my whereabouts. Happily, the rest of the party had followed in my tracks, and after some little time come up with me, and the syces having put us right, we went on without further mishap, arriving at our tent about ten o'clock p.m. Having interviewed the shikarie of the place, and made arrangements for the next day, we had a peg round and turned in, being lulled to sleep by a chorus of jackals, who came out seemingly for the express purpose of serenading us.

We were up betimes in the morning, and had an early breakfast outside the tent—a performance which evidently afforded the villagers, who had assembled to look at us, intense amusement. Then we started off, headed by the shikarie, the rear being brought up by a very musical bullock hackery, which was to be used if required as a stalking-horse, for nilgai are somewhat after the manner of weasels, not to be easily caught asleep. For some time we went on in procession without seeing anything, but at last the keen eye of the shikarie spotted a herd, standing in some low stuff at the edge of the jungle with a convenient khate adjacent. They were luckily too far off to observe us and up wind, so the cavalcade was halted at once and the disposition of the force made. We drew lots who was to go with the hackery, which fell to me, and then the shikarie sent Howard away to the left with his son and prepared to take the other two, the doctor and the captain of Howard's company, Bond by name, off to the right himself, giving the driver of the hackery strict instructions what he was to do. The said instructions were to the effect that the bullocks were to be driven in an ever-diminishing circle towards the herd. Starting about ten minutes after the flanking parties had departed, I was to walk beside the cart or sit on the top if I liked, but once having commenced to move, we were on no account to stop for a moment, for if we did the animals would take fright at once and be off. Having made everything plain, away they went, and after waiting the prescribed time we followed suit. For the first mile I perched myself on the hackery, and got nearly jolted to death for my pains, but as we neared the quarry, who seemed to take no notice whatever of the vehicle, notwithstanding the ear-splitting music it made, I slipped off and walked beside it, keeping it between the nilgai and myself. Nearer and nearer we got, till at last we were within one hundred yards, and I dropped down full length behind a convenient little hillock on which I could rest my rifle, leaving the bullock cart to pursue the uneven tenor of its way. I found I had been a little too precipitate in my movements, for between my position and the bulls, of which there were three, some cows had placed themselves, so that I could not get a shot any way. I laid there for a short time, hoping that they would move, but not a bit of it. Directly a cow shifted a few yards and uncovered her male consort for a moment, he instinctively, as if he suspected danger, moved on too and again placed himself in security. Suddenly I heard the band cease, or in other words the hackery stopped, and instantly up went all the nilgais' heads, and they gathered themselves together for a bound. There was no time to be lost, and it was a case of *aut vaccis aut nullus*, and so I took a hurried aim and planted a bullet just behind my female friend's shoulder, as she was on the spring, and landed her head over heels. Up went the rest in the air and spread right and left. Crack from the left, crack from the right, and down came another beast, this time a bull, which fell to the bullet of the doctor, both Howard and Bond having made a clean miss. The natives then rushed in to perform the ceremony of the happy despatch by cutting the throats, but to our surprise the doctor's bull got up and made off as if nothing had happened, giving us nearly two miles tracking, but we reached the spot eventually where he had fallen again—this time stone dead. I then went back with the shikarie, who was very indignant, to inquire into the reason of the sudden stoppage of the hackery, and quite prepared to administer summary justice to the driver thereof. However, when we came up to the place, we found that it was not his fault, for the musical wheel had suddenly come off, and the article had promptly turned over, bringing the driver and one of the bullocks to ground at the same time.

After a prodigious amount of tinkering, we managed to get the machine in order, and having put the two nilgais on it we sent it back to our tent, where the skins were taken off and pegged out. I confess I was not best pleased at shooting a cow, but buoyed up with hope of better luck next time, I went on to stalk some others, of which the shikarie had had khubber. We had a long and weary tramp without success. Certainly we saw game, but getting within shot seemed to be an utter impossibility, try how we might; no matter what the nature of the ground, or how favourable for the operation; after a prolonged journey on one's stomach, or in some other equally uncomfortable position, on arriving at the place where one might reasonably expect to get a shot, the quarry were certain to have vanished into the air. At last we got so sick of constant failure that we gave it up as a bad job, and returned to our tent, from whence we sallied forth again after an interval, in quest of something for dinner, and in pursuit of which we were more lucky.

In the evening an indigo planter, who lived somewhere about eight miles off, having heard of our arrival, rode over to see us, and stopped to dinner, of course. A very cheery guest we found him, full of anecdotes, and a keen sportsman. I heard afterwards, by the way, that his timely presence saved us from being made fools of by our shikarie, who had arranged a tiger scare for his own glorification and our benefit. Excited villagers were to have rushed in during the evening meal, with shouts of "bhaag," and to declare their friend, and sometime brother, had been carried off, and that his blood cried for vengeance. Then we should, of course, have been turned out and led by the shikarie, having committed in our ignorance all sorts of folly in searching for the imaginary beast. When they saw, however, the arrival of the indigo planter, they were 'cute enough to recognize the fact that the game would not do, as he knew a bit too much.

The next day, instead of shooting or trying to shoot nilgai, we went over his factory and had a crack at some duck and snipe on a large jheel close by, and then, after an early dinner with him, we rode off back to the musketry camp, where I am glad to say I arrived, *this time* without having been run away with.

I am sorry to say on the Tuesday morning I was unfortunate enough to bag something fresh and unusual in the way of game, viz. an unoffending native, who was fool enough to cross the ranges just as I fired at the target at a long distance. The bullet struck him somewhere about the right shoulder, and though it did not kill him it rendered him a sadder and wiser man. Naturally the incident was put down to the appearance of Shaitan on the tree by my servants, though they could not quite explain what the wretched man had to do with my wickedness in slaughtering Shaitan or the owl. Anyway the kitmutgar thought he could make capital out of it to bolster up his own case, and did his best to make me out a murderer, in which I am glad to say he did not succeed.

It must, however, be admitted that my bag was somewhat varied in a short time, consisting of duck, snipe, quail, nilgai, a native, and last but not least Shaitan himself, who, though it is some years ago, has hitherto been unable to retaliate or wreak his vengeance for the insult he received.

CHAPTER XIII.

A SONEPORE MEETING.

ONE of the cheeriest gatherings I ever remember to have been present at in any country is that of the Sonepore Race Meeting, held annually under the delicious shade of its grand old tope of mango trees. I do not mean that the actual racecourse itself is under the trees, but the various camps are pitched there, wherein, during the intervals of racing and dancing, high revel is held. Sonepore is a sort of Indian Goodwood, only more so, that is to say, it was in the days of which I am speaking, and for one week it is a case of "to your tents, O Israel!" every one vieing with each other in the art of exercising hospitality. And what a pretty sight it was in the evening when the lamps were lighted in the great shamianas and dining-tents, and the whole place rang with laughter and merriment from the different camps! What practical joking, too, went on, and what rivalry between the various parties! It was a week of pure unadulterated enjoyment which, if I live to the age of Methuselah, I shall never forget, and which, alas! I fear I shall never go through again. Yet though the heyday of the blood may have grown tame, and many years have gone by since as a youngster I threw myself into all the fun of the fair, I firmly believe that, given the chance, I should still take as great a delight in it all as ever, and by the end of the second day have become a boy again.

It was in the year 18— that I received an invitation from a well-known local magistrate, who we will call Desmond, to make one of his party for the races, and the same post brought a similar epistle to a friend of mine, a certain Captain Hall. At first I remember I was for refusing, not knowing what was before me, but Hall dissuaded me from taking such a foolish step, and accordingly we both wrote to accept the invitation, and straightway applied for leave of absence, which was granted. As our kind host had informed us that we need bring nothing with us except a few rupees to gamble with and our best digestions, there was not much to arrange in the way of luggage, and a portmanteau, apiece containing our kits, together with the inevitable rezais, completed our impedimenta. In addition to these two articles I took my own saddle, as I thought very possibly I should get a mount, being at that time a light weight. Of course we had a bottle of brandy and some sodawater with us in order to stimulate and refresh the inner man, to say nothing of a box of No. 1 Manillas, wherewith to sooth our nerves in the event of any undue excitement.

Everything being propitious, we started in the best of spirits, and beyond losing my ticket for some time, and thereby causing a semi-fraças with the authorities at the station, who wanted me to pay over again, we had no adventure *en route*, and arrived at the camp about an hour before dinner on the first day of the meeting. Our host met us a short distance out, and personally conducted us to our tent, where my bearer soon had things unpacked and our kits ready.

After a wash and brush-up and a tumble into evening

clothes, we walked across to the drawing-room tent, and were introduced in due form to the assembled guests. Most of them I knew before, and with those I did not know we soon made friends, so that in about ten minutes we were all as thick as thieves. We found that with one exception, or I should say two exceptions, we were the last comers, the laggards being what was known as a "competition-wallah" and his wife. He had only been married a few weeks, Desmond told me, and was horribly jealous, so we were warned that when he did arrive we were not, under pain of death, to evince the smallest disposition to flirt with the lady, and of course we promised to be on our best behaviour.

By the time that confidences had been exchanged, the gong went for dinner, and, having been told off to our respective partners, we adjourned to the mess tent and sat down. About the middle of dinner, when the champagne corks had been firing a *feu de joie* for some time, the competition-wallah and his bride arrived, his name being Galton. I think, bar none, he was about the ugliest man I ever clapped my eyes on, while his wife was exactly the reverse, being very young, very unsophisticated, rather shy at first, and excessively good-looking. As bad luck would have it, she was popped down in the only vacant place at the table, which happened to be next to myself, while her husband found a seat almost exactly opposite. Of course I did my best to make myself agreeable, and we were soon the best of friends, which, however, did not seem at all pleasing to her spouse, for throughout the meal he did nothing but glare at me and look pistols and coffee between every mouthful. I remember she informed me that she was just nineteen, had lived all her life at Highgate, and thought India a paradise; and then, suddenly catching her husband's eye, said, "Oh, but I must not talk so much to you; George" (the ogre's name) "does not like it." This put me on my mettle, as may be supposed, and forgetting all the warnings of mine host, and at the risk of being accused of rudeness to the lady who I had escorted into dinner, I laid myself out, from pure devilment, to flirt desperately with the ogre's wife, and I am fain to confess that I found her a very apt pupil. The more I talked nonsense the more irate Mr. Galton became, till at last he could hardly contain his wrath, and by the time the ladies left us to our cigars he was as sulky as a bear and would scarcely speak a word to a soul, more especially to myself.

I am sorry to say that Hall and I heard him rating his bride soundly on her behaviour after we had all retired for the night, their tent being in close proximity to ours, so much so that Hall said to me: "I tell you what it is; if you go playing the fool, you will have a row with that ass, and he will make that unfortunate girl's life a burden to her. How the deuce she ever married such a chimpanzee I can't think." This, however, by the way.

That night, there being nothing on, we retired early, and after the conversation I had just alluded to, Hall and myself were soon fast asleep. It seemed to me as if I had only been in bed about ten minutes when bang, bang, bang, on a big drum, and then the sound of a military march just outside our canvas walls commenced.

"What the devil's up?" said Hall.

"I don't know," I replied. "Another mutiny I should think," and then bang, bang, tum, tum, tum, and a full blaze of brass went down the street. "Half-past five," I groaned looking at my watch, "that's *reveille,*" and then we both blessed the institution fervently, and prepared to tumble out for chota hazri, at six-thirty.

It may be imagined how one did anathematize the band in the morning after the ball, when one had got back to one's tent at about four a.m. and had scarcely turned round before they struck up. In fact there was a round robin signed after the first morning, and we obtained another hour's grace on these special occasions, though even that was a trial which induced and produced many a big, big D. Chota hazri over, we went down to the course and strolled in and out the subscription or assembly rooms, watched the horses gallop, or took a spin one's self until it was time to return for breakfast, after which everybody was left to their own devices till the afternoon, when the riding parties, etc., were organized.

On the first morning I had seen the entries, and found that a friend had entered his horse for the next day, and at noon I received a letter asking me to ride, as he did not expect to be there in time. This was a signal for some of the ladies to ask me to give their animals a canter before they rode themselves, as they were afraid they might be too fresh, and they did not want to tire themselves before the ball which was to take place that evening. (On the first day the lotteries are or were held in the afternoon and the ball in the evening, after which it is alternately evenings of lotteries and ball; at least, I think this was the *regime*). Our host had undertaken to provide all those who had not brought their own nags with a mount, but on totalling up it was found that there was one short for the ladies; at least, the horse was there, but it was a waler who had never had a side-saddle on, and Desmond did not consider it safe. In a weak moment I volunteered to try it and break it into a habit, and accordingly I was promptly arrayed in an old skirt, amid great chaff and laughter, while the waler was saddled with a lady's saddle. All being ready, I was hoisted up, when to my horror I found that I had no third pummel and felt very much like a parched pea on a drum in consequence. However, as my steed seemed not to mind the habit a bit, I took heart of grace and rode gaily off on to the course. Artful beast! No sooner had I arrived at the mile distance, and well away from all assistance, than he began to buck in the most determined manner, and I found myself flying here, there and everywhere. I saved myself from going over his head by clutching the saddle fore and aft, and, after two or three narrow escapes, I managed to chuck his head up and returned to camp quicker than I came out, in order to get my saddle substituted for one with a third crutch. As soon as this was done I was all right, as I found I could sit his bucking with the greatest ease, and after a desperate fight, lasting over half an hour, I eventually subdued him completely, and brought the beast back with great *éclat,* a perfect lady's hack. Indeed, he was never known to buck again, though I am grieved to say that the habit skirt suffered severely in the encounter, and a pin or two with which it was fastened in some mysterious manner, known only to women, round my waist, contrived to insert themselves some distance into various parts of my body, chiefly into that portion which by rights should have been upon the saddle. Still, I had vanquished the fiery untamed, and felt that I richly deserved the iced peg which was presented to me as a reward for my prowess, on my return to camp.

As soon as the lotteries were over—at which *séance,* by the way, I noticed Hall made a good deal of running outside the rooms with Mrs. Galton, instead of coming in to attend to business—we adjourned for an early dinner, at which the ladies appeared in what would nowadays be called tea-gowns, as they preferred to dress for the ball afterwards. When I had made myself beautiful for ever, and the evening meal was over, I walked across to the drawing-room tent, and found the sole occupant of the same to consist of young Mrs. Galton, who was in dire distress at having caught her ball-dress in a tent-peg, and torn it in what a yachtsman would call "the after leach." Naturally, I offered to help her, and was actively engaged in sewing up the rent to the best of my ability, when a gruff voice shouted out behind me, "Helen, come here at once," and at the same time I heard a suppressed titter. On looking round, I perceived that the voice proceeded from the ogre, who was pale with jealous rage, while the tittering came from the rest of the party, who had assembled unperceived by me. I can quite imagine that to the uninitiated my position must have seemed, to say the least of it, peculiar, for I was on my knees busily engaged in repairing the damage, while the lady was seated on a low ottoman, and, in her anxiety to see how the work was progressing, I am afraid our heads were often in very close proximity. Still *Honi soit qui mal y pense,* and I can safely say I was never further from flirting than I was on that occasion. However, the ogre was evidently of a different opinion, and swore he would not let his wife go to the ball, at the same time looking murder and sudden death at me. Desmond at last managed to pacify him, and on our way to the ball begged me to steer clear of the lady in order to avoid a row. This I did my best to do, and I only asked her to dance once, when, poor soul, with tears in her eyes, she said her husband had ordered her to dance no round dances with anybody but himself. He kept hovering about her all the evening, keeping one eye fixed on me the while, and paying repeated visits to the refreshment department to keep up his spirits, till at last, like the pitcher, he went to the well (or bar) once too often, and got broken, or, in other words, tight. I had missed him for about a quarter of an hour, and was in the middle of a set of lancers, in which Desmond and Mrs. G. were my *vis-à-vis,* when suddenly he staggered into the middle of the set, and, with an oath, seized his unfortunate wife and dragged her off home there and then, returning himself in half an hour's time more drunk than ever to demand satisfaction from your humble servant.

Desmond, of course, was furious, and we all did our best to pacify the idiot; but it was no go, so at last we had to take him bodily outside. No sooner did he get there than he made a sudden rush at me, and in self-defence I was obliged to let him have it straight from the shoulder, and catching him in the chest—I purposely avoided hitting him in the face—I obtained what would be called in the parlance of the ring, "the first knock down blow," and then he was carried away to bed.

The following morning, after an interview with Desmond, he wrote me an apology, and then took himself and his bride away from the camp, and I have never set eyes on them again from that day to this. Poor little girl, I have often pitied her, for through no fault of hers she lost all her fun, and must have realized what a terrible mistake she had made in the matrimonial lottery when she consented to become the wife of a man like Galton.

Next day I confess I did not feel particularly fit to ride, for late hours and unlimited champagne are not the best of preparations; but a sharp spin early in the morning and a cold tub put me all square, and after breakfast I was as well as I could wish. The animal I had to ride was an awkward brute, who would win the Derby one day and be beaten by a cart-horse on the next, and one never knew what sort of a temper he was going to be in. As he had been run up pretty high in the lotteries, and I had had to give a long price for him, I did not quite like it; for I thought, if I was beaten, my absent friend would say it was my fault. Happily it was one of the brute's good days, and he ran like an angel, winning his race after a desperate set-to, by half a length.

There was great rivalry between our camp and that of the Commissioner Sahib over the race, for a jockey out of his camp was riding the first favourite, and they were rather inclined to scoff. But all our party were on to a man, ladies as well, supporting, not the horse, but the rider, and consequently there was great excitement when it came to such a close finish. I received quite an ovation as I rode in to weigh after the race; and that day and the next we flew a flag of my colours, which one of our ladies had made, on a pole in front of our shamiana, in defiance. The enemy tried to capture it during dinner the first night, and came over *en masse*, but our servants having given us notice of the invasion, we quickly rallied round the standard, and the invaders were forced to beat a retreat amidst a shower of oranges and other fruits, whilst we pursued them right into their own territory, both sides laughing and shouting like the pack of school children that we were.

At the next day's racing there was a deuce of a squabble between a brother officer of mine and a well-known officer of the past, whose *metier* was cards or a *good* bet. It appears that he had laid my pal three hundred rupees that he could carry him a certain distance in a certain time, and when it came to business he got out by saying he would carry the man, but no clothes, and that the rider must strip stark naked, and in that plight be carried past the stand.

Champion, the name of the taker of the bet and the rider, was not going to be done like that, and, without a moment's hesitation, off went his garments one after the other, shouting as he stood in the dressing-room *in puris naturalibus*, "Now then, I am ready for you, come on."

However, the gallant card-player would not come to time, nor would he pay forfeit, and consequently there were words. Champion paid him out in the ball-room afterwards, where he discovered him asleep, and placed a lighted piece of paper across his patent-leather shoe with great results. Anything more painful than when the fire comes to the patent leather I don't know.

That same evening, by the way, I am sorry to say, Champion was so elated with his success that he "refreshed" himself too freely, and got into a sentimental maudlin state, fixing himself on to one girl whom we both knew very well. About the end of the evening Hall and I were talking together, when I saw this same young lady suddenly burst away from Champion and go for her chaperone. As she passed us I stopped her and said, "What is the matter, miss?" to which she replied, "Oh, I don't know. I think Mr. Champion is going mad;" and then some ladies of our party took her off.

Presently from the middle of the group I heard great sounds of merriment, and on Hall and self going over to inquire what it was about, we were told that the reason Miss —— thought Champion was mad was that he had proposed to her three times, or to put it in the girl's own words, "He has asked me to marry him three times to-night on separate occasions, and I have said 'yes' every time. The last time I told him that I had given him an answer before, and he only laughed. I don't understand it." How we did roar! And to make it more ludicrous, we were joined in the middle by Champion himself, who laughed louder than any of us, though he did not know what at. We took him between us to his abode, and half-way home he insisted on sitting down and confiding to us—that "a girlsh wants to marry me—hic—told me so, but she won't—hic—nor a fool—goo' night;" that was the last word he spoke, and next day I advised him strongly to clear out, which he did, and left Miss —— lamenting.

CHAPTER XIV.

A HAWKING EXPEDITION.

It is with some diffidence that I attempt to recall to my mind the few days' experience of hawking that I enjoyed in India, for I confess that, for some reason or another, I never entered very heartily into the sport, and consequently am obliged to own that I knew very little about the subject so far as the practical working of the same is concerned. However, I managed to spend three or four very cheery days on the only occasion on which I had occasion of joining in the fun, so, if my readers will pardon my want of knowledge concerning the technical details, I will endeavour to describe them.

It was in the N.-W. Provinces where we were quartered, not a hundred miles from Peshawar and the Khyber Pass, when we got a pressing invitation from some friends in the frontier cavalry to come out and join them for a few days' hawking. I was sitting in the mess one morning after breakfast, doing my best to make a fool of a No. 1 Manilla, when Tilson came in with the letter and said—

"Look here, old man, are you game to make one of a party to go out hawking?"

"What's the fun of that?" I asked. "I know nothing about it, and don't want to. I have always heard it is great rot."

"Nothing of the sort; it's splendid sport," replied the

unblushing Tilson. I say unblushing, for he knew no more about it than I did, which was not saying much; and I don't believe he ever read a book on the subject. Nevertheless, he was very indignant when I told him so, and insisted on it that he was quite an authority. "Besides," he argued, "we shall have a real good time of it with these frontier chaps, you know, so you had better ask for leave and come. McSweeny is coming, and Johnson, if he can get away."

"That's another thing altogether," I rejoined. "You never told me anything about the frontier chaps. I am on for that right enough, for I can win my expenses at black pool there, but if you expect me to ride about the country with a nasty pecking bird on my fingers, and to swing a bit of meat and feathers at the end of a string round my head all the time, you are vastly mistaken. Fancy old McSweeny dashing about in long boots and a hat and feathers with a great fowl on his arm!" (I had derived my ideas of the sport from old pictures.) "Hang it; I'd go any distance to see that, so you can put me down as one, and I'll go and get leave;" which I promptly did and was booked.

It was about a twenty-four hours' journey to reach the quarters of our hosts, for which we should have to lay a dâk, consequently we decided to send on our nags with their attendant syces, and to write and say that we ourselves would turn up in the course of a week, probably almost as soon as the horses. The next thing was to arrange with the baboo about the transport of our persons and paraphernalia, and a deuce of a business it was, for, being off the general line, there was a difficulty about the relays, and the frontier being in a somewhat unsettled state, the astute native sought to make capital out of the fact, and asked us about three or four times the proper fare for the job. For a long time he held out for his terms against all our remonstrances, till at last I suggested that we should give up the trip altogether, and began to walk away. Then he came down by one-half at a bound, but, seeing that my ruse was successful, I turned a deaf ear and continued my retrograde movement. Every hundred yards I went, or rather that we went, for every one followed my lead, took something off the price, till at last the proper tariff was reached, and we promptly closed, taking care to get it put down in writing with all the conditions of relays, safety, and speed set out in the aforesaid document.

Having settled this matter, and given our orders for the time and place that the gharrie was to be in in three days' time, we returned to the mess, and having regaled the inner man, spent the next few hours before dinner in looking out the necessary kit and giving our respective bearers their instructions concerning the packing thereof. As the distance itself was not so very great that we had to traverse, but on account of the roads, or rather the want of them, the dâk would have necessarily to travel slow, we calculated that we had allowed ample time for our syces with their charges to arrive before us; so we did not trouble ourselves much on that score, but devoted the intervening three days to the study of the sport on which we were about to embark.

Johnson, from somewhere or another, managed to fish out an old work on hawking, and we were not long before we had all of us got considerably mixed as to the relative merits of peregrines, merlins, and luggars, to say nothing of the baz and shikra or sikra hawks. We mastered the intricacies of jerseys, hoods, and lures pretty well, but nowhere did it say in that book what the proper dress of the hawkist should be. I insisted that the only orthodox and recognized turn-out must be long boots and a hat with feathers, and pointed to a plate at the commencemencement of the work on which we were engaged, where a party was depicted, *tempus* Charles II., in the act of starting for the chase, to corroborate my theory. So closely and persistently did I adhere to this idea, that I very nearly persuaded McSweeny to invest in the requisite attire. Indeed, I have every reason to believe that he took with him, carefully concealed in the bottom of his portmanteau, a hat which he had had manufactured in the bazaar, closely resembling one of those which figured in the frontispiece of the book. At last the time came for the start, and, after the usual delay and shouting, to say nothing of bad language and blaspheming, we were off, with Christian John, to act as body-servant to the four of us, on the box, and ourselves, viz. Tilson, Johnson, McSweeny, and your humble servant inside.

I have been a good many miles in a dâk in my time, both in a gharrie and in a post car, but I don't think I ever remember passing such a thoroughly miserable time as I did on this occasion. In the first place there was, after the first ten miles, scarcely any road worthy of the name, and we were flying about like parched peas on a drum. Secondly, we were such a tight fit inside that any idea of sleeping, except in snatches, was out of the question. (We had arranged for a double dâk of two gharries, but at the last moment the baboo came and told us that he could not get horses for love or money, so we were obliged to put up with one at a reduced fare.) And, thirdly, our Jehu was not well up in his route, and was continually getting off the track, and having to make a cast either backwards or forwards to hit off the line, besides being in a mortal funk the whole of the journey for fear of robbers and other "budmashes." About half way, to complete our joy, we came to a sudden standstill in the middle of a stage, and, on inquiring the why and wherefore, were informed that Christian John was "bhote bhemar" with cramp and colic, brought on by a mixture of constrained position, the fearful jolting, and some stuff which he had drunk at one of the halting-places. Luckily we had McSweeny with us, and his medical ardour burned with a fierce flame, for in a moment he was out of the door and hard at work on the sufferer.

"Come here, all you chaps, and help me to rub," he shouted in a few seconds; and out we all got to aid him.

We found poor John twisted up like a corkscrew and yelling with pain, and the more we rubbed the louder he howled.

"Let me die, sahib, let me die; I very bad, oh dear, o-o-oh! Doctor sahib, I die," he moaned, till McSweeny fairly lost his temper, and said—

"You black deevil, it's na deeing that ye are; it's just making a dommed fule o' yersel' that you're been wi' yer hubble-bubble and a' that; gin yer na, stop yer greeting; I'll just flay ye in wee bit pieces, I will." And then, having poured about half a tumbler of raw brandy down his throat, which, I must confess John seemed, notwithstanding his approaching end, to thoroughly appreciate, he got him up on end and began to shake him like a terrier would a rat, till the unfortunate man bellowed out, "All good, now, sahib, all good; we go on," and bounded on to the box again quite cured, while we all resumed our places in the interior of the car.

When we had refreshed ourselves with a peg round, after our exertions, during the imbibing of which McSweeny said with a chuckle, "I'm just thinking that that treatment for colic will not be found in the pharmacopœia," we made a fresh start, and eventually after many weary hours arrived in a somewhat dilapidated condition, though happily safe and sound, at our destination, where we were met by a bevy of our hosts, who had been for some time on the look out for our arrival.

A wash and brush up, accompanied by a tub, put us all straight again, and the information that our nags had arrived all right the previous day was also satisfactory, and we sat down to a late tiffin with appetites of three hundred horse-power. Having literally filled ourselves quite full with the good things provided for our delectation, and washed them down with a bottle or two of excellent champagne, we all four of us turned in and slept the sleep of the just till it was time to dress for dinner.

Punctually at seven o'clock I was awoke by Christian John, who, although he had quite recovered from his recent attack of colic, evidently from his manner had something on his mind which he did not like.

"What's the matter with you, John?" I asked; "you look as sour as an unripe lime."

"I not sour, sahib," he replied, "but people tell me bad things;" and on my further questioning him, he informed me that the servants had told him that it was very dangerous to go hawking or even riding about outside the radius of about two miles, because the hill-men would shoot at anybody they saw. He was not certain whether I should take him out with me for shikar, and consequently was in a regular stew.

"Hill-men be hanged!" I said; "if they did shoot they would not hit anybody; you're getting to be a regular old woman." And then I relieved his mind by telling him that it would not affect him anyway, as I should certainly not take him out with me. On receipt of this piece of news he cheered up considerably, and was quite brisk in putting my things out for dinner—a proceeding which rather "fetched," as I considered he might have shown more anxiety for the life of a master who had been always good to him. Accordingly, I determined to try and damp his satisfaction a little and said—

"John, I shall not want you myself, but I can't answer for the others; perhaps Dr. McSweeny may be glad of your company."

"I not Dr. Sahib's servant. If master not want, I not go," replied John. "I got to look after master's things. If master say go and give order, I go; if I get kill it is kismet, but for Dr. Sahib I not go out to get kill."

The last part of his remark was said with such withering scorn and with so much emphasis, that is was quite clear that he had not forgotten or forgiven the rude shaking he got *en route;* and as he certainly had right on his side, I let the matter drop, and having dressed, went over to the mess, where I found everybody assembled for dinner; and a right cheery meal it was, full of fun and chaff, and plenty of iced champagne that maketh glad the heart of man. Between them our hosts managed to fill up both Tilson and McSweeny to the brim, and by the time we adjourned to the billiard-room, they were in a state that may be described as exceedingly happy. They were not the only ones, however, for the black pool of some of the cavalry boys was quite as eccentric, and I soon found myself amassing quite a fortune. Eventually McSweeny went to sleep between his strokes, and it was found impossible to wake him; the only reply any one being able to get out of him, when he was told that it was his turn to play, being, "Na, na; I'll ha' na muir; I'll just go to bed the noo. Gude nicht, gude nicht." So we agreed that it was time to knock off, as we had to make an early start on the following morning, and after a small brandy and soda, we carried the sleepy medico to his couch and then separated for the night.

The next day I was up betimes, and had inspected my nags before chota hazri was announced, after which meal we were under orders to assemble for the day's performance, the scene where the hawking was to take place being some seven or eight miles away under the shadow of the hills.

I found that Christian John's report of what one might expect was not very much exaggerated, for I was told that it was a hundred to one that the hill-men could have a crack at us sooner or later, before we had finished our sport, but that, as they never managed to hit anything, it was looked upon rather as part of the entertainment than anything else, and added somewhat to the excitement of the proceedings. Chota hazri over, eight of us fell in, and lunch was sent on (under an escort I observed) to a spot which had been selected beforehand. We then rode off, accompanied by a fairly numerous retinue of falconers, etc., with the necessary birds.

On arriving at the meet the head falconer was summoned, and a preliminary flight was arranged at some crows, and following that at a crane which was sighted standing on one leg by the side of a marshy and reed-grown pool. To me, who had never seen anything of the sort before, it was a wonderful sight to witness the manœuvres of the hawk and its quarry to outwit each other, especially in the case of the crane. Both endeavoured to get above the other, but the hawk always managed to gain the upper hand, and prepared to drop like a bullet on its victim. However, just as the fatal blow was about to be struck, the crane managed to twist out of the way and down came the hawk yards below it towards the earth, having missed his aim. Then, with an upward sweep, he was after the game again, and finally struck home and brought the crane to the ground, where it was captured by the falconer. This, however, was looked upon as very poor sport, and it was not till a herd of antelope were viewed that any excitement was apparent. Directly this took place, the fun began. Two of the larger hawks were immediately loosed, and on spotting the deer they went like an arrow from a bow. Instinctively the antelope seemed to recognize what had happened, and were off full tilt with a bound, travelling at such a pace that it was all we could do, riding our hardest, to keep them in sight, the two hawks meanwhile following over the animal which they had selected. It was no easy matter to ride straight with one's eyes and head in the air, and required a certain amount of confidence to travel over the country at breakneck speed, without looking where one was going to, but somehow one soon got into it, and I was getting on splendidly when I suddenly found myself flying through the air with my gallant steed turning somersaults in my rear. He had put his foot in a hole and had tumbled head over heels before I knew what had happened. However, there was no damage done beyond a little shaking, and I was better off than McSweeny, who, in his excitement, rode straight into a nullah full of water, and was precious nearly drowned before he could be extricated from underneath his horse. By the time this had been done, one of the hawks had made his swoop, and had attacked the deer in the region of the eyes, and in another half mile the capture was effected. I should say that the course or flight was about three miles from start to finish, and as we had been going at racing speed most of the way, it was a very pretty bit of sport.

After three or four more flights we came to where our

lunch was laid out, and I can answer for it that, if every one was as hungry as I was myself, the sight of the good things was a very welcome one. About the middle of the meal we were interrupted by the sounds of "ping-whip," "ping-whip," "ping-whip," and the escort got hurriedly under arms.

"What's all that falling about?" I asked innocently of one of our hosts.

"Bullets," he replied. "Some of these infernal budmashes of hill-men, I wish we could catch them;" and then, suddenly pointing to a low hill, about four hundred yards off, he exclaimed, "Look there; there are a dozen or more of them."

Following the direction of his finger, I saw some wild-looking figures running about on the brow of the hill, each with a long matchlock in his hand, and presently a little puff of smoke and the peculiar "whip" of a bullet as it went into the earth close to us showed that one or the other of them had indulged in a pot shot.

As we did not see the force of sitting still and offering ourselves as animated targets for the delectation and practice of the matchlock men, we packed up our traps as quickly as we could and retreated into a nullah out of sight, where we held a council of war. McSweeny and Tilson were all for carrying the hill with a rush, but our hosts would not hear of it, for they said that we could not say how many of them there might be, and, moreover, if anybody got shot, that there would be a pretty little row and an end to all sport in the future.

After a lengthy discussion and argument on the *pros* and *cons*, it was eventually decided that we should send to the rear a certain number of our escort with some three or four sahibs, mounted, together with the falconers, etc., to make it appear that we had all retired, and that the remainder of us would line the nullah, and wait the development of events. If we found that the hill-men were not in force, we would then all rejoin and drive them off, whereas, if on their coming out of their stronghold we found them to be too strong for us, we would fire one volley and make tracks home as rapidly as we could, picking up the others *en route*.

For about ten or fifteen minutes after the departure of our advanced guard, who, by the way, were treated to a brisk fire until they were out of range, nothing occurred, and then slowly one by one the enemy emerged and gathered in the plains till they mustered about two-and-twenty, half of whom were armed with matchlocks. For a few minutes they held a consultation, and then the musket men slowly advanced. I forgot to mention that the signal for the recall of the party we had sent off was to be three shots fired in the air, and as the enemy approached to within about one hundred yards, the leader of the hawking expedition drew his revolver and gave the three shots in rapid succession, and then told us and the men of the escort who had remained to fire a volley all together, and then, without waiting to see the result, to jump on our nags and charge. Bang went all the guns and revolvers, and before the smoke had cleared away we were up in the saddle, and, having been joined by the rest, were all galloping towards the hill, to which bourne the budmashes were flying for their lives, all excepting two who had been hit in the legs, and were consequently, for running purposes, rather out of it. We managed to capture two others, also five matchlocks, which had been hurriedly thrown away, and had the satisfaction of seeing the rest of the gang going, as if the devil had kicked them for miles, till they were eventually lost to sight. Having called McSweeny's professional services in to the two wounded men, who were both found to have only received a flesh wound through the calf of the leg, and which he stated, "would do the dommed savages no that much harm," we tied all four prisoners together and sent them in to quarters, and then went ourselves to try for another deer. Whether the firing had driven them away or not I cannot say; but though we rode for miles we never managed to catch sight of one, so after a couple of flights at some crows, we decided to give it up and make for home, where we arrived just in time to dress for dinner. Of course the story of our adventure had preceded us, and Christian John pretended extravagant joy at my safe return, at the same time taking great credit to himself for the accuracy of his prophecies. "I tell master bad men shoot," he said. "I say true, not lie, though master not believe, all same." To which I replied, "Quite right, John; but I also told you that bad man would not hit; how about that, eh?" and so we were both mutually satisfied.

CHAPTER XV.

AN UNLUCKY SHOT.

SOME few chapters back I gave an account of how I very nearly, through an unpremeditated act of violence, had to stand a trial for wilful murder, or rather should have had to stand it, if the victim of my wrath had only done what (in the opinion of his friends and relations) was the right thing, and died, instead of merely disgracing himself and his caste by being proved "mut," or blind drunk.

I confess that that little episode taught me two salutary lessons, one of which was—never, under any pretence, nor even by accident, to lay violent hands on a native; the other being that nothing would afford the pious Hindu or the equally sanctified Mussulman so much gratification as the rendering up to justice of one of what they are pleased to call their white oppressors. The extreme vindictiveness and eager look of gratulation that was visible on every countenance gathered round my prostrate khitmutgar, coupled with the extreme and equally apparent disappointment that succeeded when that worthy arose and staggered away, showed me too plainly that one and all would have gladly assisted at my funeral rites, provided that they had been carried out with the aid of a piece of cord and a hangman's knot. Shortly afterwards I had further proof of this fact, as also to what lengths the mild and placid native will go in order to fabricate evidence against, and secure the conviction of, a white man.

We had one day been out pigsticking in camp—a large party—and were riding back to cantonments in the cool of the evening, some six or seven of us all together. McSweeny, the doctor, the Magistrate Sahib, and myself were a little in advance of the rest, and had just turned the corner leading to a large village, when our attention was attracted by the most infernal shindy outside one of the chief houses of the place. There was a large crowd surging backwards and forwards, all shouting at the top of their voices, a red turban or two here and there showing the presence of the police. In the distance one might have almost imagined one's self at an Irish fair, or an eviction may be, as every one's attention was evidently directed to something in the doorway of the house.

"What the deuce is the matter, I wonder?" said the magistrate to me.

"A wee bit bother," said the medico; and then we all three stuck our spurs in and dashed on.

Making our way through the crowd without ceremony, and to the actual discomfort of more than one demonstrator who got in the road, we at last came up to the doorway, when what was my astonishment to see two men of my regiment, bound hand and foot, covered with dust and blood, and evidently being subjected to very severe treatment. They were both excellent characters, sober, quiet men, and great favourites in the regiment; so I could not make it out at all. The presence of the Magistrate Sahib, however, acted like a charm, and in a minute the noisy crew were silent, and we obtained a hearing. In answer to our inquiries, we were informed that the two soldiers had fallen on an inoffensive villager, and, because he would not give them water, they had deliberately shot him where he stood. Moreover, they were both mad drunk, it was added, and if the people had not taken away their guns and tied them up, the whole village would have been murdered.

"Bring me the guns," said the magistrate; and they were brought, both being loaded. He said nothing about this, but turning to the head man, asked who had seen the deed done. Whereupon three or four villainous-looking men came forward and deposed that they had been present when the shot was fired, and had immediately given the alarm and fallen on the two men, and, with the aid of the rest of the village, had taken away their weapons and bound them.

"How long after the shot was fired did you take the guns away?" was the next question.

"At once, protector of the poor," etc., was the answer.

Here McSweeny, who had been taking everything down in his pocket-book, interposed, and asked if it would not be well to see the corpse, a request which was at once acceded to; and the jemadar of police having come up, he was ordered to clear the ground, and lead the way to where the victim of the white man's brutality was lying. Dead enough he was, there was no doubt of that, and he was lying on his back just by his open doorway, with a lotah of water by his side, a pool of blood filtering into the dust from his head. Without a word, McSweeny, who was no fool in emergencies, jumped off his horse and made a careful examination of the body, jotting down notes in his pocket-book. I noticed also that he took something out of the dead man's hand, and wrapping it up in paper put it in his pocket. As soon as he had done he came up to the magistrate and whispered something in his ear, which seemed to astonish him somewhat, as he called the jemadar over, and giving him some directions, sent him away. He then turned to the men who had testified that they had seen the shot fired, and asked them carelessly if it was here that the man had been killed, to which they gave an affirmative answer, and on being told to describe the scene, went through it in pantomime; one ruffian playing the part of the murdered man, and the other two those of the murderers, while a forester gave a glowing description of the whole.

We then retraced our steps and interrogated the soldiers, and here we had a very different tale. Jones, the elder of the two, said—

"We had been out shooting, sir, and were coming back through the jungle as it was getting dark, when my chum shot at a flying fox, which he killed, at least it fell, though we could not find it, and after hunting about for some time, I says, 'Come on, Bill, we shall be late.' We had got about three-parts of the way through the village, when all of a sudden the niggers came running after us—shouting and yelling—with bamboos and stones and things, and before we knew what was what, we were knocked down, tied hand and foot, and dragged in here. Then they brings a dead nigger out of the jungle, and sets him up where you see him, and, as far as I could make out, wants to swear as we shot him. I believe, if you had not come up, sir, they would have made short work of Bill and me. As it is, I feel as sore all over as I don't know what. Regular budmashes they is, and no mistake."

All this was said with such a simple air of injured innocence, and was corroborated in every particular by

Bill, that I was quite certain that there was some foul play somewhere at work.

"What did you do after you shot the flying fox?" asked the magistrate of Bill. "Did you fire at anything else?"

"No, sir," replied the man. "I hunts about for some time, and then I loads my gun" (they were muzzle-loaders), "and I comes after Jones here, who was getting impatient to get back to barracks."

"That will do, men," said the magistrate. "I am afraid you will have to go into cantonments as prisoners till this is cleared up, and I shall hand you over to the regiment. There will have to be an inquiry."

"But, sir, we've done nothing wrong," ejaculated Jones. "We never shot no niggers. Why should we be made prisoners?"

"I don't believe either of you shot the man on purpose, but I believe you shot him by accident, and I must find out how. Besides, I can't let you go free," said the magistrate. "I am sure you will both go in quietly, and you may be certain I will do my best for you."

"Very well, sir, we will go quiet enough," replied Jones; "but don't handcuff us, sir;" and I am glad to say this was not done.

We all moved off together, with a detachment of police guarding the two men, after orders had been given that nothing was to be touched till after the inquiry and inquest.

Doubtless all this would seem a very strange proceeding to English ideas, where the first thing is to warn a prisoner that anything he says will be used against him; but the Indian magistrate has to play, or had to play, many parts, and was necessarily constrained to act more after the fashion of the French *Juge d'Instruction.* So in reality there was nothing out of the ordinary course in attempting to get at the real truth before the matter appeared in court.

Before the examination was over, we had been joined by the whole of the rest of the pigsticking party, and naturally the sole topic of conversation during the ride home was about the murder. McSweeny, however, would not say a word, and when asked his opinion of the matter, simply answered—

"The man's just dead, ye know."

"Yes, we know that," every one said; "but how did he die, and who killed him?"

"I'm na that prophet to tell ye," was all the worthy medico would vouchsafe, though I could see from his manner that he had a lot up his sleeve that he would not divulge.

That night Jones and his chum Bill were consigned to the guard-room, and a court of inquiry was ordered to assemble the following day, at which I had to attend in an official capacity as watching the case on the prisoners' behalf. Without going into the story and recapitulating the evidence, it will be sufficient to say that, after nearly a week's careful deliberation, the court came to the conclusion that the men were innocent, and they were liberated, to the great joy of their comrades.

Of course we all thought that the affair was ended. Judge of our surprise, therefore, when they were suddenly rearrested on the charge of wilful murder by the civil power. Why this was done I cannot imagine, but I always had a suspicion that, the part of the country where we were not being in a particularly loyal humour, it was a sort of sop to Cerberus to prevent dissatisfaction. Anyhow, it was a cruel and unjust proceeding on the part of the authorities, and caused a deal of bad feeling and plenty of official correspondence.

The first fight we had was when the civil power applied for the evidence of the court of inquiry, which was promptly refused, as it would be required for the defence; and though we were threatened with judge's orders, criminal codes—racks, chains, and dungeons—we stuck to our point and carried the day. The officers of the regiment all subscribed, as did in fact the whole corps, and the best counsel in the country was retained for the defence, while I for the second time was told off to watch the case and assist him.

The court was crowded with natives of all shapes, colours, sizes, and denominations; and as the witnesses for the prosecution gradually unfolded their tale, there was a distinct murmur of admiration amongst them, for they evidently thought that they had at last scored one too many for the white Shaitan logue. Our barrister scarcely cross-examined, merely making each individual repeat his statement, which they did with considerable variation, though all of them swore that their brother had been shot standing up with his face to the foe.

When it came to the defence, the first witness put into the box was my friend the magistrate, who detailed his knowledge of what had occurred.

"Have you any reason to believe that the man was not shot where he was found?" was the next question.

"I have," was the reply. "He was shot in the jungle, quite four hundred yards from where we saw the body."

"Where was he shot—I mean, in what part of the body?" followed.

"In the back and base of the skull," said the magistrate.

This caused a considerable flutter in the native dovecot; and then McSweeny was called. I confess I was astonished at his evidence. He produced first an accurate plan and drawing of the body with all the wounds, gave it as his opinion that the shot must have been fired from a distance of quite forty yards, and then produced the article which I had seen him take from the dead man's hand.

"What have you there?" asked our counsel.

"A wee bit black earth and some grass, which I just took away from his hand," answered the medico. "He had gripped it when he fell, and I'm thinking the jemadar can find the sister bit the noo."

The magistrate was recalled to speak to seeing the earth taken out of the dead man's hand; and then the jemadar proved finding the spot where he was killed, with the same earth, the same grass, and the marks of blood.

And so matters went on till the prosecution saw that they had not the shadow of a case. Never did I see blank consternation so visibly depicted on any countenances before as on those of the assembled crowd, who had come to see the white men done to death. On the verdict of acquittal they looked as if they were quite ready to cut their own throats, or anybody else's, if they got the chance.

It was quite clear, as indeed it had been at the inquiry, without McSweeny's evidence, how the accident had happened. The native had been in the jungle when Bill shot at the flying fox, and had been killed accidentally, without either of the men knowing what had occurred. When the body was found, which it was almost immediately afterwards, the budmashes thought to make capital out of it, and had dragged the corpse into the village, arranged the dramatic situation, and fallen on the two white soldiers, whom they had ill-treated, bound, and accused of murder. If it had not been for McSweeny's cuteness, and the stupidity of the witnesses in swearing that they took the guns away at once, and that the man was shot facing the murderers, it might have gone very hard with Jones and his chum, and I am not at all sure they would not have had to pay the extreme penalty for their day's sport.

As it was, everything turned out all right, and I am glad to say that the lying witnesses and the head man of the village were promptly arrested and tried, and, what is more, received a heavy and well-deserved punishment for their perjury and attempt to swear away the lives of innocent men. We had, however, to send both the men back to England to the depôt, for so bitter was the disappointment and the feeling against them amongst the native population, that their lives were not safe, and it led to an order being issued against men being allowed to go out shooting. There is no doubt the men were glad to get away, for the anxiety had told on them terribly; and even if they had remained with us, I do not believe anything would have induced either of them to have gone out for a day's sport a second time.

Both have left the service now some time, and years after the event, I was shooting in one of the home counties on one occasion, when a covey of partridges got up behind the line (we were walking the birds up); I turned round to shoot, when, just as I was going to pull, I saw one of the beaters, who had lagged behind, just in the line of fire. Luckily I saw him in time, and stopped, so no accident happened; but an under-keeper, who I had not noticed before (it was his beat, and he had only just found us), came up, and, touching his hat, said, "Beg pardon, sir, I thought it was a case of the flying fox again; it gave me quite a turn." It was Jones's chum Bill, who, true to his natural instincts of sport, had taken his discharge and got a berth as an under-keeper, and who was as pleased to see me as I was to see him doing so well. The head-keeper told me afterwards that he was a first-rate man in every way; the only fault he had to find with him being his extreme aversion to carrying a gun. "I can't rightly make him out," he said; "he is as good a shot as needs be, but it's all I can do to get him to shoot vermin, or a rabbit, even; he seems quite scared of a gun, like." I found that his story was not known, and so I kept his secret; but I was not astonished at his antipathy to firearms, considering that on one occasion they nearly brought his head into a noose.

I am afraid that I have laid myself open to the objection being made that the above narrative is scarcely Indian sport, for a native hardly comes under the head of big game, nor can a trial for murder be called sport; but as it is a literal fact, and shows pretty clearly one of the dangers that every sportsman runs, or is open to, I must claim indulgence, and I sincerely hope that a like mishap may never occur to any of my readers.

CHAPTER XVI.

MY FIRST TIGER.

I HAD been some little time in India before I had the chance of having a shot at, or a try for, the animal known as the Bengal tiger, or more familiarly nicknamed "Stripes." Of course, like all youngsters and fresh comers, I had dreamed of the sport, read of it, talked of it, and thoroughly made up my mind that to return to England without having slain at least one tiger, or assisted at all events at his obsequies, would be beneath contempt. Even in those days England and India were getting far too close to each other for any would-be sportsman to foist on his acquaintances fables of his deeds of daring. It would not wash. Just as he had finished a snake or tiger or yarn that bid fair to take the roof off the house, and had set most of his audience wondering if such things could be, it was a hundred to one that some friend, more enlightened than the rest, would commence to cross-examine, and, from a knowledge of the country, would contrive in ten minutes to prove the narrator a boasting liar. It was all very well when India was almost an unknown country, and the getting there and back a serious consideration. Then men, whose business or duty took them across the seas to the gorgeous East, could on their return lie about shikar to their heart's content, and, judging from some of the old stories I have heard, *did* most unblushingly; but at the time I am speaking of that was played out, and one had rather to understate one's experiences than over-colour, if one wished to be credited at all.

To a certain extent, therefore, knowing all this, I was particularly anxious to have a "go" at a tiger, and, if possible, secure a skin as a trophy, so that there might be no mistake on the subject when I did get back to my native heath. Consequently I was in the seventh heaven of delight when the post brought me one morning a letter from my friend, the Commissioner Sahib, asking me to join a party for three weeks' tiger shooting. He informed me, moreover, that we were very certain of having some sport, for the first week at all events, for the Rajah of B. had given instructions for a big shoot on that occasion, and was coming out himself *in propria personâ*. A further inducement also for a subaltern officer was that, beyond my baccy and ammunition, rezai and resolution, everything would be "all found." The only difficulty I foresaw was the momentous one of obtaining leave. We were somewhat short-handed at the time, and I was not at all certain how my colonel would look on my application. However, "nothing venture nothing have," I argued, and so, having squared a brother officer to be answerable for my duty during my absence, I went off and firmly put in my request. The first question I was asked was: "Where are you going at this time of year?" And when I said, "Tiger shooting," the colonel said, "You know nothing about tiger shooting; you will only get into a mess, and most likely get chawed up, if you don't get sunstroke." Nevertheless, after a certain amount of argument, and the pointing out on my part that everything must have a beginning, tiger shooting included, he gave way, and forwarded my application, which, in due course, was granted, and I prepared myself for the fray. I had two good rifles, an Express and a bone-crusher, both of which I could thoroughly rely on, and these, together with my 12 smoothbore, completed my battery, which Christian John had orders to see properly packed up, and they were placed under his immediate charge, for, of course, he was told to accompany me. I was sorry that none of the other chaps could come too, as it was the first time I had been away without one or two of them. McSweeny was particularly caustic on the subject, and I could see that under the advice he volunteered there was a substratum of disappointment that he was not to be of the party. "Ye will just see," he said, "that you're no grabbit by the animal, and that you'll no be makin' a fule o' yoursel'; and you'll no bide in the sun wi' nair a wee bit hat on yer head, for ye ken I shanna be wi' ye to tek that care of ye that I always ha' done. I'm thinkin' freely that the colonel is daft to let ye go, but it canna be helpit the noo;" and then the good-natured old medico went off and put me up some quinine and other remedies, which he insisted should form part of my travelling equipage.

I had a long railway journey to commence with, and then a twelve hours' dâk before I reached the trysting-place where everybody was to meet, and I was rather puzzled how I was going to manage the latter portion of my journey, for I could get no information at the station as to whom to write to lay the dâk, and the country was a *terra nova* to me entirely. However, just before starting, I received a telegram from my host, the Commissioner Sahib, saying that he would meet me on a certain date at the railway station at the other end, and that he would see all about the dâk, so that we could go on together. This relieved my mind considerably, as may be supposed, and at the appointed time Christian John and myself took our places in the train and steamed off full of ardour and expectation (at least I can answer for myself; I don't fancy John cared much about tigers) for the land of sport and glory. It was night, or rather evening, when I started, and I did not get to the junction, where I had to change, till seven a.m., so after an iced peg, and telling John to arrange for some chota hazri early, I unrolled my rezai, got into my sleeping kit, and was soon in the arms of Morpheus, where, strange to say, and contrary to my usual custom, I remained fast as a church till the following morning. I had time at the junction to get a bath and a wash and brush up, and two hours after I managed to make a breakfast at the station where we stopped for the purpose, that would not have disgraced Gog and Magog of ancient history. True to his word, at the end of the journey, the first person I saw on the platform was my host beaming with smiles and welcome. "Here you are!" he exclaimed, directly he saw me. "That's capital. I have arranged the dâk; we start this evening. And now come over to the bungalow. I have ordered dinner, and there is some champagne in ice." (It was about six p.m. when I arrived.) "I dare say you could do some now." You may guess what my answer was—at least any one who has had experience of an eighteen or twenty hours' journey on an Indian railway, with its concomitant of dust and heat, will not require to guess very much or to hesitate as to what reply they would make to the offer of iced simpkin at the end of the trajet. I know it did not take me long to decide myself, and five minutes after entering the bungalow, I was well into a tankard brimming with champagne and a dash of soda-water added thereto.

After an excellent dinner, provided and served up by the Commissioner Sahib's own cook, the gharrie came round, and having arranged our bedding, packed the impedimenta on board, and lighted our cheroots, we embarked, and amid much noise and shouting, cracking of whips, and native blasphemy, we dashed off *en route* for the trysting-place and the tigers. Looking back now, after a varied experience of dâks, I can safely say that that journey was one of the most comfortable that I ever took. Whether it was because they had a burrah sahib inside, and therefore took more care, I cannot say, but the fact remains that we rolled along as smoothly as possible, and on the completion of our baccy we both fell fast asleep, and neither of us woke except, perhaps, for a few seconds at a time, when some unavoidable jerk brought us temporarily back to things mundane, till the sun was climbing the heavens the following morning, and we were within a couple of hours or so of our journey's end. We pulled up for a short time at the next change, in order to allow time for the brewing of some coffee or tea, I forget which, and then on we went, arriving at the camp just in time for breakfast proper, after the necessary tub, of which we both stood in much need.

The camp itself was pitched in a pretty sort of glen in close proximity to the jungle, and was shaded by large overspreading trees, whilst away to the rear of the big shamiana a goodly troop of elephants could be discovered through the foliage enjoying life in their own ponderous way. Our arrival was announced by the simultaneous barking of many dogs—(I did not see any fat bulls, but there were plenty of the other animal about me), and as our gharrie drew up, our host—for the first week the Rajah of B.—emerged from his tent, somewhat gorgeously arrayed, I thought, for a sporting gent, to welcome his friend the commissioner, and my humble self. Very cordial, too, was his greeting, and after a chat we adjourned to hazri, where we found some of the rest of the party, six in number, assembled. I only knew one man amongst them, and he had come out from England with me, an old shikari, Goff of the Central Indian Horse. Of course the commissioner knew every one, but it did not take long before we were all as thick as thieves and as cheery as sandboys.

There were two more sportsmen expected, and during the course of the day they turned up, making our party up to ten, without counting our host, the rajah. One of the late arrivals was the most peppery old Curry Bhât I ever saw—a certain Colonel Thorpe, a good-natured, kind-hearted old soul in his way, so long as everything went well; but from long residence in the East his liver was none of the best, the least thing putting him out, and when that calamity occurred he literally breathed brimstone and bad language, and surrounded himself with a perfectly impenetrable wall of blasphemy. Nobody, however, seemed to mind him, and as he served to keep us all amused, one very soon began quite to look forward to his explosions. My first introduction to him was not a propitious one, and caused a really legitimate outburst on his part. It was just before dinner, and I was in my tent, which I occupied with Mr. Commissioner Sahib. Christian John having omitted to empty the washing-basin, I had just been giving him beans, and told him to take the thing away, empty it, and bring some clean water. Like all servants, to save trouble, he just went outside the tent, and, without looking, emptied the chillumchee swish just as old Curry Bhât was passing! Bang went all the dirty water over him, and then the band began to play. I ran out to see what on earth had happened, and just arrived outside in time so see John's flowing draperies disappearing in the distance, with the colonel in full pursuit. They must have gone a mile full tilt before my Christian bearer dodged and came flying back to me, and, rushing into the tent, crawled under the charpoy, crying, "He kill me, master; he Shaitan, he bad man, use bad word; save me!"

A few seconds later the colonel arrived, very much blown, but pouring out oaths incessant, and seeing me standing in the doorway of the tent, backed by my friend the commissioner, pulled up, and turned the vials of his wrath upon me.

"Is that d—d black hound your servant, sir? By heavens he's wet me through! * * *" (N.B.—The reader must fill in the stars for himself.) "I'll kill him, I'll kill the * * *" And then, as the sense of the ludicrous struck me, and a smile came to my face: "Who the devil are you, sir, to laugh at me? By gad, sir, I'll have you know I'm not to be laughed at by a young whipper-snapper, I'll——"

What more he would have said I can't say, but happily the commissioner stepped out and introduced me in due form, apologizing for the accident, and then we all three suddenly burst into a roar of laughter, during which John beat a retreat, and our friendship was begun. I noticed, however, that John gave him a very wide berth all through the shoot, and on more than one occasion he confided to me that "Colonel plenty bad man, kill all his servant, no man stop, he Shaitan."

The following day the shoot was ordered, and early in the morning we were under way for the first beat, and I found myself seated in a howdah, with the commissioner, Goff, and old Curry Bhât, being on my right and left, the rajah occupying the centre and direction of the line. Of course we had all strict injunctions to fire at nothing under pain of death, save and except Mr. Stripes, and my companion gave me all the information concerning the etiquette of the sport. We were proceeding very comfortably, somewhat to my mind like a ship in a heavy sea, when suddenly three of the elephants stopped dead round a thick patch of jungle. "Look out, there is a tiger here!" whispered the commissioner; and look out I did, "all of a tremor like," with excitement. All of a sunden there was a rush, a trumpeting of the elephant, and I saw a yellow ball fly out of the bush, straight at my face, it seemed to me, and there was Master Stripes just below the howdah on the elephant's shoulder, and the elephant going through the jungle with a fair wind about ten knots. I confess I never thought of the danger of shooting the elephant—I was too excited for that, so I bent over the howdah where I could just see my gentleman; and at the risk of being pitched out, I got a bead on the tiger, and slapped in both bullets at close quarters. He bounded off with a roar that increased our pace another two knots, and then the mahout managed to bring the ship too, and to my great delight there was the tiger, giving a last kick where he had dropped when he jumped off. It was a great piece of luck for me, as I had now my much-coveted skin to prove the truth of my stories when necessary. Curry Bhât was somewhat inclined to feel aggrieved that no one else had had a shot, and said it was not sport; but as his elephant had bolted the instant the tiger appeared, and he had been within an ace of having his brains dashed out on several occasions, it would not have affected him much. The only thing every one seemed to consider odd was that the tiger had charged without having been wounded or fired at, but the fact remained, and there was no accounting for his taste. We found our elephant was little hurt, and after a certain amount of remedial measures we went on. The next excitement was a drive where we were posted, and three tigers were afoot, one breaking back through the beaters, happily without killing any one. The rajah killed one, and Curry Bhât and Goff divided a claim to a second. I don't suppose to this day it is settled whose is the skin, but I remember there was an exceedingly animated dispute over it.

That night, notwithstanding that I was very tired and exceeding hot, I did ample justice to dinner, and, after a certain amount of simpkin, began to look on myself as a regular tiger-slayer, and went to bed as happy as a king, and as proud as the historical peacock. The next day proved a blank, and we shifted camp to the other side of a small jungle, where there was khubber of a man-eater. It was proposed that some of us should sit up in a machan the first night, but Curry Bhât gave such a dismal account of his experiences of that game—how he had sat for hours, and had been nearly eaten alive by mosquitoes, and had gone to sleep at the critical moment, only waking to find his chance gone, and himself so cramped that he could not move—that our ardour was considerably damped, and no one would volunteer; so the project was abandoned.

The following day we started a fresh beat over the new ground, and here in crossing a stream our elephant nearly got bogged, an experience I never want to repeat, for it was a case of leaving the ship the best way we could in the quickest possible manner, otherwise if the animal had managed to get at us he would inevitably have whipped us off with his trunk, and popped us under his feet as a possible means of support. I admit the exit was not a dignified one, and we both got wet and muddy in the operation, but it was better than acting as a temporary foundation, and I was right glad to find myself safe on *terra firma*. After some little time our beast managed to get out all right, and, finding a harder bottom lower down, we crossed in safety. We got one tigress that day, but saw no sign of the man-eating gentleman. I will not attempt to describe our subsequent days' shikar, for so much has been written on the subject of tiger shooting by far abler pens than mine, that my description would be but nothing worth. Besides, it was my first initiation into the sport, and I was only a novice. I know we had varying luck, and, for the first three days after the rajah left, never fired a shot. Personally, I did not get another skin on that trip, but I enjoyed it all immensely, and among the trophies I have, I value that tiger skin above all the rest.

CHAPTER XVII.

A CARD PARTY AND A CATASTROPHE.

WHEN I was in the City of Palaces, Calcutta, to wit, it used to be our custom two or three times a week to meet at dinner at some friend's house, resident a little way out of town, and when the cloth was off the table and the cheroots in full blast, to indulge in a rubber of whist or a mild game of loo. Many a pleasant night have I had of it in the various bungalows round—"detached villa residences, with spacious grounds and stabling, situate within half an hour's drive of the city," I suppose is the description that would be put upon them by the enterprising London house agent. Sometimes matters used to be kept up till a late hour, or rather an early hour in the morning, and occasionally, I am bound to confess, that the course steered home was not always of the straightest. In fact, more than once we had to pick up the pieces, and to send the buggy to the coach-builders the following day for repairs. However, with the exception of one broken leg, nothing serious ever happened, and as our friends, the merchants and civilians, generally, were all the best of fellows, we were wont to enjoy ourselves immensely. One particular occasion I have vividly impressed on my memory though, as I had as narrow a squeak for my life as ever I want to. It was after the first day of a cricket match—Public Schools *against*

The World—if my memory does not fail me, and we had had a real doing all day in the sun, and consequently had put away a fair share of gin and tonic, etc., etc. Stumps were drawn at six p.m., and five of us dashed home to Fort William to have a cold tub and shift before dining with Cook, a rich merchant who lived in a charming bungalow with an enormous garden and compound, about three or four miles out. Cook himself was captain of the public school team, and the last thing he said as we left the pavilion was, "Don't you chaps be late, and bring plenty of rupees with you, for I have a lot of fellows coming, and we will have a loo after dinner." The five of us were Tilson, Gordon, Champion, our Irish assistant-surgeon, O'Grady, and myself. McSweeny could not come, for some reason or another, and I don't think he altogether fancied playing loo, as he used to say, "It's all dommed luck ye ken, just as ye air mixing a wee bit peg and fashing yerself about the soda, ye mak a fule's mistake and looed ye air. Na, it's na bonny enough for me."

O'Grady, on the other hand, like so many of his compatriots, was a keen card player, and a gambler at heart to boot. And although, whether it was whist or any other game, he always talked to his cards and let everybody know exactly what he had got in his hand, somehow he used, as a general rule, to come out on the right side, and to get up from the table with more rupees in his pocket than he sat down with. I remember once his sitting down to play écarté with a French count who was travelling in India, and who had drifted to the station where we happened to be. The Frenchman was really a fine player, but O'Grady bothered him so with his running comments on the game, and the calm way in which he kept on turning up the king, that *perfide*

Albion, or perhaps, it would be more strictly correct to say *Irlande*, knocked him into a cocked hat and won quite a nice little sum of money, much to the count's disgust.

Well, having dressed ourselves, we hired two "ticca gharries," those abominations composed of rotten wood and string—principally the latter—and proceeded to drive out to our dinner. After two or three breaks down, which in each case necessitated the further application of string, produced by the coachman from some mysterious hiding-place, we at last arrived safe and sound; and, what was more to the purpose in our host's eyes, in pretty good time, being only a quarter of an hour late.

Indeed, we were not the last, for there still remained to come a well-known legal luminary and an equally well-known sporting divine, who afterwards, by the way, won great distinction and a V.C. in the field. We found, as our host had told us there would be, a large party assembled, who one and all, directly they saw him, began to chaff O'Grady and to abuse Cook for asking a man so proverbially lucky as him to win their money.

"Is it the money you're thinking about, ye blackguards?" said O'Grady, when he heard them. "Bedad, it's moighty little that I'm troubled with that same myself. Pwhat's a rupee or two to the likes of you. It's myself that has to sweat the life out of me for an ungrateful country for just nothing at all, when you gentlemen have only got to sit in a toidy cool office and dhrink pegs all day. Sorra the one of ye does a shtroke of work except to kick the punkahwallah now and again and drawing pay that would keep a prince all the toime. And after all this, by jabbers, ye grudge me the chance of taking a paltry rupee or two, because I'm a better hand at the cards. Money, pah, I'd scorn it!"

Of course everybody roared at this sally, no one louder than O'Grady himself; and the two truants having arrived, we all trooped in to dinner. And what a dinner it was! Everything cooked to perfection; and the champagne, iced to a turn, flowed like water; while the "feast of reason and the flow of soul" kept everybody up to concert pitch.

O'Grady and the parson told stories against each other till everybody was fit to fall off their chairs from laughing. After every yarn of the divine's, O'Grady would shake his head and look horrified, saying, "Bedad, and you a clergyman, too? and we are to just swallow that for gospel truth! Mother av Moses, I should never have thought it of you!" And then he would proceed, with the gravest face in the world and without moving a muscle, to tell some outrageous cracker himself that fairly took the roof off—inventing the story as he went on, and ending up always with "and there's the truth, as sure as my name's O'Grady."

When the cheroots and coffee came, which come they did at last, we all adjourned to the verandah, while the servants prepared the board of green cloth, and then, when they informed Cook that everything was in readiness, we returned and set to work to play loo in earnest. Luckily the stakes were not large, and it was limited, or some of us would have fared badly, for, towards the small hours, the iced pegs on the top of the champagne began to take effect, and the play was getting somewhat erratic. Of course O'Grady was winning hand over fist. The more he drank the better he played, and he could do nothing wrong if he tried, and by the time grilled bones appeared, he had amassed a pile of rupees and chits.

I also had been pretty lucky, and had got my share of plunder, so consequently I felt at peace with the world and mankind in general. Tilson, on the other hand, had lost, and what is more, with his money he had lost his temper, and was inclined to be quarrelsome.

One of the other guests, a broker, was in the same state, and the two laid themselves out to make matters pleasant for each other, so that the announcement of bones came at a welcome moment, and in all probability saved a jolly row between the belligerents.

After supper we played for another hour, and then the party broke up. Most of them wanted to go on, but Cook, with an eye to the next day's cricket, was firm and said "no." So everybody had to give in, and in a short time the compound resounded with the shouts of owners and syces for their various conveyances. Our party was the last to leave except the parson and his friend, and maybe two others.

Tilson, who by this time was sleeping, got inside the first gharry and coiled himself down promptly, I following him, expecting O'Grady to come next to me; but the madman did not see it at all, and with a wild yell he jumped on to the box, turned the driver on to the roof, and, whipping up the tats, went off at full gallop. "We shall never get through the gates safe," I thought; and I tried to get out, only to be shoved back again by the watchful Irishman, who seemed to have an eye all over everything. Presently we went off the road, and tore full split down a hill over the grass. I had just time to shake Tilson into a semi-wakeful condition, when souse went the whole conveyance, ponies, gharry, O'Grady, coachman, and ourselves, into a deep tank at the bottom of the compound. We all went under water for a moment or two, and then the gharry rose. O'Grady and the gharrywan swam ashore promptly, but Tilson and I were regularly boxed in, and could not get out, for both the doors were fast jammed. Happily, the plunge into cold water had sobered Tilson, and by a united heave we burst the upper door right out just in time. Had we not managed to effect this, we must both of us have been drowned to a certainty; as it was we had swallowed a gallon or two of water, and felt far from lively. All we had to fear now was a kick from the ponies, who were struggling madly as they felt the gharry dragging them down. However, we both got off safe, and landed on *terra firma* after a short swim. Here we found Cook and the rest assembled, and O'Grady in a dire fright at what he had done. He was crying like a child, thinking that Tilson and I had gone, for we had burst open the side away from him, and he had not seen us get out. When he saw us safe, he was like a maniac or a reprieved murderer, and danced about like a fool.

Then came the question—How were the ponies to be saved? They were gradually sinking deeper and deeper, and their struggles, poor things, were getting fainter and fainter every moment. It was evident that in a few minutes they would be dragged under and drowned, unless they could be got clear. Of course, the only time that the rope traces were wanted to break, they held; at any other time they would have cracked up long before, but on this occasion they absolutely refused to go. While we were all debating what was to be done, the parson, who had run off to the bungalow, and roused up every nokah in the place, suddenly appeared again at the side of the tank with a coil of rope and a long knife in his hands, and then, throwing off his clothes, he plunged in and swam out to the gharry.

Over this he crawled, and then dropping on to the backs of the tats, with a few well-directed cuts he severed the traces, harness, etc., and the poor brutes scrambled ashore, where they stood shivering with cold and fright. It was a gallant action performed by a brave man, for had he slipped or got entangled among the nags, his life would not have been worth five minutes' purchase. As soon as he had done with the animals, he attached the rope which he had taken out to the gharry, and then brought the end ashore with him. Having done this, he tied a long and stout bamboo pole crossways to it, and everybody then tailed on to the rope, two of Cook's carriage-horses being hitched on to the pole. We soon had the four-wheeler ashore again with this united force, and though it was minus one side I do not think it was much the worse for the immersion, and certainly it was infinitely cleaner. Naturally the gharry-wan, as soon as he saw everything fairly secure, began to open his mouth and to demand untold wealth from all and singular, in compensation for the damage done; but as O'Grady threatened to throw him into the tank again if he did not hold his row, he eventually thought discretion the better part of valour and subsided.

The next thing for consideration was how we were to get home, for to drive three or four miles in one's wet clothes in a soaked gharry meant a certain attack of fever, which I for one did not see the fun of risking. Cook offered to put us up, but as both self and O'Grady were bound to be in Fort William early that morning (it was now nearly 3.30 a.m.) we could not avail ourselves of his hospitality. However, we borrowed a change of clothing, and then three of us got into Cook's buggy, which, needless to say, I did not allow the Irishman to drive, and by that means we arrived home safe and without further mishap. Before turning in for a couple of hours, I asked O'Grady how he came to make such an ass of himself, and he tried to make me believe that the tats ran away with him, a story that would not go down at any price.

The following day Nemesis overtook him, for the master and owner of the ramschackle turn-out appeared, accompanied by a small crowd of hangers on, and insisted on payment for damages and detention; which, after a lengthy and heated discussion, the Hibernian medico was forced to pay, arriving at a sort of one-sided compromise, in which, of course, the native got much the best of it. O'Grady's punishment, moreover, did not end here, for on turning out the pockets of his soaked kit he found that, besides losing a fair amount of rupees in the struggle, the water had reduced some of his chits to a pulp, and obliterated the signature of many others. "And that is phwat ye call luck, bedad!" he moaned. "After setting up half the night, and whasting all my beauhty sleep, to have me hard-earned gains whiped out by a trifle of dhirty water. It's not fair at all, at all." Tilson and I had to remind him in forcible language that it was entirely owing to his own d—d folly that the misfortune had happened. But it took us all our time to convince him; and he did not show proper contrition until I pointed out that he might think himself exceedingly lucky that he had not got to stand a trial for the manslaughter of Tilson and the gharrywan, to say nothing of myself.

CHAPTER XVIII.

OUR TRIP TO THE SUNDERBUNDS.

SOMEHOW or another the river Hooghly always seemed to have a particular spite against me, for on three distinct and separate occasions I was within measurable distance of solving the mystery of the "great beyond" when on the "bosom of its rolling flood." The first time I made acquaintance with it, I, in company with the rest of the regiment, arrived in Diamond Harbour at the commencement of a cyclone. It was the first trip to the East of one of H.M. troopships, and before we got into harbour we had a pretty job to find our way, one of the light vessels having gone wrong. What with that, the pilot brigs being also absent, and the state of the glass, there was little doubt in the minds of any one that we were in for something out of the ordinary run. The captain of the trooper wanted to steam straight up to Calcutta there and then, but the authorities, with visions of the James and Mary and other dangers, decided that we were too big a job, and ordered us to embark (or disembark, I do not know which is right) into flats in order to be towed up to our destination at Fort William. I remember none of the natives liked the job, and the warnings of the impending storm were very manifest long before we arrived. But notwithstanding all this, the brigade-major at Calcutta, with that perspicuity which is so often part and parcel of a staff uniform, issued instructions that we were to remain on board the flats for the night. Happily our colonel had been in India before, and, what is more, had also experienced a cyclone in all its glory, and consequently refused absolutely to obey. The brigade-major fumed and fussed, gesticulated and swore, and pointed out all sorts of general orders, etc., but to no purpose, for our chief settled the matter by sending me off to the general with a note, and thereby getting the order to land at once.

It was no joke getting back, for the wind had begun to rise, and we could scarcely make way against it. Half-way to the flats one of the oars broke, and the rower catching a crab nearly sent me into the water, from which it would have been a hundred to one I should never have got out, though one of our men did fall overboard, and was saved by a miracle. Five minutes after we had got the last of the baggage-guard ashore, the cyclone burst, and how we got the waggons with the kit into the fort is more than I can say. I never knew how it could rain and blow till that night; the whole of the barracks rocked like poplar trees, and great pieces of the church were blown down, while adjutant birds and hawks were dashed about like shuttlecocks and killed in hundreds. In the morning not a vestige of the flats were to be seen, and the steamer which towed us was high and dry on the bank with a broken back; so if we had obeyed the brigade order we should have been gone coons.

The second time I was nearly done for was at Garden Reach, where I had gone to see a friend off to England by the P. and O. They were swinging the vessel in the stream, and had a great hawser fast aft, about as thick as a man's thigh, and on the shore end of this were standing and crouching a crowd of natives, to keep it down, I presume. I was on the quarter-deck watching the operation, when suddenly, with a report like a cannon, the hawser parted, and the two ends curled straight up in the air like a gigantic snake. The in-board end came with a rattle, and swishing past me within a foot, nearly knocking me down with the wind of it, crashed into the bulwarks and deck-gear, cutting a tindal almost in two, and killing two other lascars as well. The people ashore fared no better, for there were three killed and six or seven fearfully injured. How the beastly thing missed me I can't think; but it was a great deal too narrow a shave to be pleasant I remember, and for a long time I never could go near a warp without feeling in a dire funk.

The third time (they say there is luck in odd numbers) I was on a board to condemn some commissariat stores, and, amongst other things, we had to inspect some beer which was on a species of raft alongside. Without thinking, I jumped off the bank on to this floating platform, and, to my horror, the infernal thing opened and through I went, the raft closing over my head at once. It was a mercy I could swim, and also that I was not hurt in going through, for I kept my head and allowed the current, which was running like a sluice, to carry me clear, and then I managed to get out of the undertow and into a native boat, much to everybody's surprise. I am thankful to say the beer was condemned, and the platform or raft as well, which was some little consolation, although it did not pay me for my damaged uniform and nerves.

After all these mishaps, one would have thought that any one with a grain of sense in their heads would have steered clear of such a dangerous enemy as the Hooghly.

But I was young and foolish in those days, and not given to pay much attention to omens or warnings of any sort, and so, having read a great deal of the magnificent sport to be had in the Sunderbunds, a party of us made up our minds to go and have a try. Everybody told us that it was madness, and that we should never come back; but opposition only made us more keen, and we talked nothing but big game and tiger, and what we were going to do, for weeks. It was only after finding that we could not do the job under three weeks, and that the X's would be more than our subaltern pockets could stand, that we reluctantly gave up the idea of the wholesale slaughter (by anticipation) of stripes, and said, in a lofty way, that we would "put off the expedition till the following season."

It was about a fortnight after this that, somewhat nettled by the constant chaffing we had to put up with—it was a standing joke to ask us when we were going to the Sunderbunds, and one wag induced a native to advertise and take up to our quarters a Sunderbund topee, needless to say, to the bazaar wallah's great personal discomfort after the interview—Tilson, Johnson, and Gordon suddenly came into the mess, where I was sitting ruminating over a weed and some gin-and-tonic water, and said—

"Look here, old man, we are hanged if we will stand this any longer! Are you game to start?"

"Start! where?" I asked.

"Why, to the Sunderbunds, of course. Every d—d fellow we meet is always asking us when we are going, and I'm blowed if we don't go!" they replied.

I suggested mildly that we could not afford it, or get sufficient leave, but Tilson said—

"Bother the X's and leave! I have had a chat with

a skipper of one of the pilot brigs, and he says there is heaps of good shooting round Diamond Harbour. He will take us down there the day after to-morrow in a tug, and we can hire a boat, or we can sleep on board his brig if he does not get under way."

"That's all very nice," I ventured to remark; "but Diamond Harbour is not the Sunderbunds, and, from what I remember of it, it is rather a dreary spot."

"What does that matter?" they all chorused; "we shall have a cheery outing, lots of shooting, and the chaps up here won't know whether we have gone to the Sunderbunds, Diamond Harbour, or Timbuctoo. Who knows but what we may tumble across a tiger, after all? and then the chaff will be all on our side. You go and get leave, and then we will see about the provisions and boat. We must get old McSweeny to go too, as medical director of the expedition; it will be grand sport."

I was, I confess, rather bitten with the idea, and the end of it was that, after some little difficulty, we all got ten days' leave, supplemented by forty-eight hours' regimental leave, and made our preparations for a start on the following day. We had the greatest trouble to persuade McSweeny to make one of the party, for he said he was by no means anxious to be mixed up with a lot of hair-brained subalterns, who were sure to get into a mess, and he steadfastly refused to believe in tigers, or shooting of any kind at Diamond Harbour. However, when he saw that we were determined to go, with or without him, he consented to come "just in case of an accident, ye ken;" and of us all, the old humbug was in reality the keenest.

We laid in a goodly stock of provisions—tinned meats, soups, beer, whisky, etc.; and McSweeny insisted on us each having a waterproof sheet besides our bedding, and carefully selected himself a stock of medicine sufficient to poison the whole regiment. We then proceeded to inspect our boat, which Tilson had hired already. It looked all right, and seemed quite sweet and clean at first sight, but before we had been on board half an hour we found that it was a regular menagerie of the insect tribe, and we had to close it up and fumigate with a mixture of sulphur and other abominations of Mac's compounding, which had the desired effect, and destroyed the creatures by cart-loads.

We had to be off at six in the morning, so we embarked on our ship after dinner, and having made John, my bearer, who, much to his disgust, was impressed into the service, prepare our couches and get us a sort of supper ready, we started to make a night of it. The skipper of the pilot brig joined us from the tug alongside, and what with whisky-pegs and 'baccy, to say nothing of some of the stories that were told, we managed to asphixiate the few remaining creatures of the insect world that were left over from McSweeny's matutinal incense. It was three a.m. before we broke up, but as we had the whole of the next day before us to sleep in, it did not matter, and before any of us awoke we had been more than an hour under way, although we were rather late in starting. I forgot to say that the pilot skipper was a Scotchman called David Lawrie, who hailed from the same part of the thistle kingdom as our dear old medico; and the way the two of them yarned, lied, toddied, and "Oh! Ai! A'd!" to each other was a caution. However, they ended by falling on each other's necks, breathing whisky-and-water into each other's ears, and vowing eternal friendship; so we were quite assured of having "a friend at court" during our trip.

The first thing that roused us in the morning was John knocking the breakfast-things about, and the sound of a stentorian voice hailing us from the tug. "Hoo are ye the noo?" it said, and, like a war-horse that hears the trumpet, McSweeny responded by shaking himself awake and roaring out, "I'm recht, Davie, and hoo's yoursel'? Air you coming o'er for breakfast?" Davie informed us that he had already finished his "parritch," so we were left to ourselves; and after having various buckets of water poured over our heads, we were all as fit as fiddles, and did ample justice to John's meal. Breakfast over, we amused ourselves by potting at empty bottles thrown out astern, and by looking out for a chance mugger, which never appeared; and then, after a game of whist, we took another nap until tiffin and Davie arrived together.

Nothing further occurred of interest till we arrived at Diamond Harbour, where, having carefully moored our ship, we adjourned on board Davie's brig and spent another festive evening. We sent off to make inquiries ashore as to the shooting, and found that there was a capital jheel close handy, with some excellent paddy fields for snipe surrounding the same.

So we determined on an early start, and six o'clock a.m. saw us partaking of chota-hazari, and then we made a move, taking the paddy fields in line up to the lower end of the jheel, which lay to the right of the harbour. Contrary to the usual custom, the report of the shooting had not been exaggerated, for the snipe simply swarmed, and long before we had arrived at the end of our first beat our guns were quite hot and our bag fairly full. I don't think I ever saw so many painted snipe as I did on that occasion—every other bird was of that genus; and, as either we were holding extra straight or the birds were extra easy, we made some remarkably pretty shooting, and were in great form. We were lucky enough, too, to get here and there, out of some high reeds and small pools of water, an odd duck or two, and by lunch-time we had to send back our spoils to the ship to give the game-bearers a chance of emptying the bag.

In the evening we had a grand bit of flighting as the duck came into the jheel, and got no end of all sorts, though I am bound to confess that they looked better than they ate, for they were apt to taste somewhat piscatorial, or fishy. However, we were in high feather, and even McSweeny was fain to admit that it was worth while coming out for. When at last we got back to our boat, he insisted on dosing us all with quinine to keep off the fever, a performance at which we all gibbed, but on which point he would take no refusal, so we were bound to submit with the best grace we could.

The following day we tried the other side of the harbour with fair success; but we did not score such a good bag as on the first essay. Perhaps one reason was that Captain Lawrie—honest Davie—accompanied us, and he and Mac talked the broadest Scotch all the time at the top of their voices, and made noise enough to frighten away every bird within a radius of two miles. We dined early that night on board our own craft, and had just lit up after dinner and commenced the whisky toddy, when John put his head through the screen which formed part of our cabin, and informed us that the headman of a village had come in to say that a tiger had killed a goat.

After duly interrogating the individual in conjunction with the gentleman who was officiating as head shikari, we found that the village was some three miles off on the borders of the jungle. If it had been fifty miles away we should have gone, so we sent off post haste to make arrangements for machauns to be built, and prepared to sit up. We were afraid—at least our shikari was afraid, for we did not know much about it—that we should be too late by the time that we arrived; but nothing venture nothing have, so away we went, determined if we saw nothing that night, to organize a beat the following day.

McSweeny and myself shared a machaun together, and deuced uncomfortable it was, I remember, as the mosquitoes made it pretty lively, and we could not smoke. Directly opposite us were Gordon and Johnson, while Tilson occupied a tree close handy. I don't suppose that so many guns ever sat up over one kill before; but we were all enthusiasts and green, and spoiling to bring back a tiger from the Sunderbunds to confute our Calcutta friends with. Turn and turn about we took to keep watch till the moon was down, and then, stiff and sore, we were fetched away to stumble home empty-handed and half asleep.

McSweeny and I were leading the party, just behind the headman who had brought khubber, and our shikari, when suddenly they both disappeared, and then right in the path was what we thought was a tiger, who, with a sort of snarling purr, seemed crouched for a spring. "Gude Lord, save us!" exclaimed Mac, who was about a pace ahead of me; and then the report of his rifle rang out, both barrels in quick succession, and such a tearing and snarling in the jungle commenced that showed us plainly the bullets had gone home. It was almost too dark for us to see anything clearly, but I could just distinguish a heaving mass tumbling about by the side of the path, at which I promptly fired; and then from a tree the voice of the shikari was heard saying, "Gholee kia," and signifying the death of the animal. It was necessary to proceed with great caution, so we all five dvanced with our rifles at full cock till we came upon the body of a large panther lying stone dead, and the undoubted prize of McSweeny. Of course he was in raptures, and nearly cried with joy at his luck; and when we got Spot's jacket off, his owner could do nothing but walk round it and say, "Ay, but it's a beauty, ye ken. It's just lucky I managed to catch him in the recht place." And precious lucky it was, for had not Mac's shot been a fatal one, there is little doubt but that Spots would have made it extremely sultry for some of us.

We did not go out till late the next day, and then borrowed a boat from the brig to row across to a sort of island at the entrance of the harbour. We had somewhat indifferent sport, and were thinking of returning home, when we noticed it suddenly get quite dark, while the wind began to rise and a small sea got up.

"By jove!" said Johnson, "this don't look nice; we have a pull across right in the teeth of the wind. It looks all like a gale coming. All aboard at once;" and we embarked. The further we got the worse things got. We could hardly make any way at all against the wind; and, what was worse, we began to ship a lot of water, and had to stop every now and again to bale. After a lull, during which we made up a good piece, the wind suddenly came down with hurricane force, and as nearly capsized our boat as could be. As it was, she filled, and we lost all the oars but one.

"Nothing for it now," I said, "but to run out to sea, or to try and get behind the island." By good luck I got her before the wind, and while Gordon and Tilson baled, McSweeny and Johnson improvised a mast and sail out of the oar and a coat, and away we flew straight to sea, where the white horses were showing their teeth, and things looked as bad as they could.

In fact, I had given up all hopes of ever seeing land again, when suddenly the sound of a gun close astern caused us to look round. And there, to our joy, we saw the brig under storm canvas coming up hand over fist. "Stand by to catch a line as I pass ye," roared Davie through a speaking-trumpet, as soon as he got within hail, and in a few minutes he was almost alongside. "Port," I heard him say, and then "Heave," and a line came whistling down, to seize which and catch it round the thwart with a toggle was the work of a moment. "Lie down at the bottom of the boat every one," I shouted, "and get the mast down," both of which were done; and then I watched for Davie to round-to, so as to give the boat a sheer off.

To make a long story short, we were soon alongside and the boat hoisted up, and, after a tot round, we found ourselves safe. The honest old skipper was almost breaking down when he grasped us each by the hand and nearly smashed every bone in our fingers. "It was a near touch," he said; "just a wee bit further, and ye could no ha' weathered it. I was main afraid, too, that ye'd no understand hoo to make fast the line. Eh, but ye did it bonny, lad," turning to me. Then there were more "Eh, Oo, Ah, the noo," etc., between the two Scotch cronies, and Davie filled on the brig and stood out to sea.

"Eh, mon," said McSweeny, "you're ganging wrong; it's back we want to go," when he saw where we were heading.

"My dear sir," chipped in the mate, "I am afraid you'll have to put up with twenty-four hours of sea. We shall have to make an offing; it's going to blow great guns."

And blow it did while we were hove-to for thirty-six hours, during which time poor old McSweeny and Gordon parted with their souls in paroxysms of sickness. After that the gale blew itself out, and we beat back to harbour, and picking up our boat and Christian John, who had given us up for lost (indeed, it was reported in Calcutta that we were all drowned), we started off back again, having had as eventful a trip as any one could wish for. Of course, we had all overstayed our leave; but that was easily squared, as it was scarcely our fault, and our story was a good one.

McSweeny proudly exhibited his panther, thereby effectually silencing all chaff about the Sunderbunds, and we all subscribed to give honest Davie a token of our esteem and a memento of our adventure. There is no doubt his promptness saved us, for if he had not seen our predicament, and slipped his cable to follow us, we must have been swamped, and after all the Hooghly, or part of it, would have had its way, and proved the end of me.

CHAPTER XIX.

BLACK POOL.

BEASTLY hot it was in Calcutta, and precious glad was I when I was suddenly ordered up to the hills on some duty connected with the new rifle about to be issued to the army. There were three of us ordered off, and the rendezvous was Darjeeling. Unfortunately I was, at the time the order came down, actively engaged in earning my pay by attending and being a member of one of the numerous and interminable boards for which the City of Palaces, as a military station, is, or was, justly famed. I do not remember what it was all about, but presumably Baboo Chunder Ghose had spilt or made away with an ounce and a half of gram, thereby defrauding her Majesty of that amount, and five officers had to assemble daily to investigate, and, if possible, to find out how the circumstance had occurred. Anyway the consequence was that I was unable to start with the other two, and did not get away till nearly a week later, when, of course, I had the pleasure of travelling all alone.

In those days there was no railway up to the hills; one got as far as Sahibgunge, where one had to get out and cross the river, and then make the best of one's way by dâk to Siligori, and to the foot of the hills, where, if one had laid the dâk properly, one found ponies waiting to take one up. I had plenty of friends at Darjeeling;

and, having written to say the day I expected to be there or thereabouts, I proceeded to get my kit together, not forgetting my guns, and, together with Christian John, I started off for the station amid the envious glances of my less fortunate brother officers.

The first mishap occurred at Sahibgunge, for the steamer, which should have met the train, took it into its head to break down on that special occasion, and we had to get across, mails and all, by a native boat—an exceedingly slow and precarious journey, for it was long odds that we went straight down the river instead of across. Naturally this threw the arrangements for the dâk on the other side into a mess, and when at last I did get over, I found that my gharrywan had taken it into his head that the sahib was not coming, and gone off to enjoy his hubble-bubble Heaven knows where. In fact, he had, like we used to do at Eton, made "a run" of it. For the benefit of those who were not educated at that classic school, I may say that "a run" was a sort of unwritten law, whereby at morning school, if a master did not turn up five minutes after the hour, the boys had a right to assume that he was not coming, and consequently to vanish as fast as they could—in fact, "to run." I remember well how we used to watch the hands as they approached the five minutes' past, and with what a shout we used to bolt away. Strategy also was often brought into play, for one of the smaller boys in the class was sometimes told off to wait for the master outside his own house, and so engage him in conversation, or by asking questions, that he should not arrive at school till after the five minutes' limit had passed, when, of course, he found the nest empty, and all the birds, save the decoy, flown. Naturally he, the master, saw through the game perfectly, having most likely done the same himself in his youth. But I only remember one who tried to break through the old traditions, and he failed ignominiously. He was a new broom, and I have no doubt thought he was going to sweep very clean. However, one try was enough for him, and he promptly gave it up as a bad job. This, however, is a digression; so I must hark back.

After a long search and a certain amount of strong language, at last Christian John and myself managed to dig out the deserter, who, after the usual string of excuses, went off to see after the steeds—a process that occupied him nearly three-quarters of an hour. During this interval I had the satisfaction of witnessing the departure of the mail cart, and I almost wished that, notwithstanding the horrible discomfort of that method of travel, I had taken a passage therein. However, on the principle of "everything comes to him who knows how to wait," eventually we got our luggage on board, and myself duly installed inside. Then commenced the devilment that always precedes the departure of a dâk on its first stage, followed by a jolt that nearly dislocated every bone in my body, sending Christian John straight up in the air like a sky-rocket, and we were off. Everything went on first-rate till we came to a stream which the rains had flooded, and here we caught up Her Majesty's mails. It was a case of ferrying over in boats, for it was far too deep to ford; and so with the ponies swimming, and the gharry and mail cart stowed in a boat to the imminent risk of sinking the same, we managed to get across by the skin of our teeth in safety. After that nothing further happened till nearing our journey's end, when the wheel of the dâk first caught fire, and then immediately afterwards elected to come off, with the result of sending the whole bag of tricks on to its side, and showing me more stars than ever were in the firmament. John was pitched head first into a bush, where he lay howling like a maniac, and for a quarter of an hour everything was chaos. When we had picked up the pieces it was a question what was to be done. We were four miles from the end of the stage, pitch dark and threatening with rain. The driver was frightened to death about tigers and other wild beasts, for we had entered the region of jungle, and I was a perfect stranger to the locality.

The first thing I insisted on was the righting and propping up of the gharrie; and then, by dint of threats and promises of liberal bucksheesh, I persuaded the trembling gharrywan to take a lamp and set out to the next posthouse to engage a palki. I wanted Christian John to go with him for company, but that worthy, who was more afraid of tigers than anything in the world, utterly declined to budge, vowing that his fall had lamed him for life (he was active enough directly the driver had disappeared), and so the poor gharrywan had to go off by himself, while I turned into my rezai and slept the sleep of the just till his return. The poor devil must have run all the way in his fright, for in about an hour and a half I was awakened by his return with a palki, and a gentleman of the coach-building trade to re-adjust the erring wheel. Much to John's disgust, I left him behind to superintend the latter operation and to look after the luggage, giving him strict instructions to follow on as soon as everything was ship-shape; and then I got into the palki and was whisked off quite comfortably to the next dâk bungalow, sleeping peacefully all the way.

Next morning early the gharrie and Christian John turned up, and we proceeded to the foot of the hills, where I found a chit from my old friend Walters, saying he had posted a pony dâk for me up the hill and engaged coolies to carry my baggage. Such coolies, too—great, big, strapping women most of them, who would think nothing of taking up a piano single-handed, and the owner strapped on to the top thereof.

We were to make a halt halfway up the hill at Kurseong, and to dine with some planters, who had a big feed that night. I had not gone very far up the hill when, to my surprise, who should I meet coming down but Walters himself.

"What the deuce have you been doing?" he exclaimed, as soon as he saw me. "I expected you last night, and stayed up waiting for you till all hours."

I explained to him the series of mishaps that had fallen to my lot, and then we rode up to Kurseong together, chatting over old times and exchanging our mutual budget of news. There was very nearly a deuce of a shindy at Kurseong, for the proprietor of the establishment got it into his head that Walters was flirting with a very pretty half-caste girl, who he claimed as his wife (I believe he had four or five elsewhere as well), and consequently he (the proprietor) resented Walters' advances. From words they came to blows, and I am pleased to say Walters settled his man in ten minutes, though he acquired, in so doing, a nose about the size of a large vegetable marrow. Personally I have not the smallest doubt in my own mind that the proprietor of the half-caste girl had perfect right on his side, and that Walters was very much "on the job" there, though, of course, he denied the soft impeachment.

We had a tremendous evening with the tea-planters, who had come in for a jollification and meant having it. They had arranged their sleeping accommodation in a big barn, and placed their beds all round it, the centre being occupied by a long table, on which was spread a lordly feast.

It was nearly four a.m. before I got to my humble couch on the other side of the road, and I found some difficulty in getting up the hill to the hotel, more especially as Walters, who came with me, insisted on bursting into song every five yards, and compelling me to stop and join in the chorus. It was lucky that the proprietor of the show had been left speechless in the barn, for nothing would please Walters (the wine being in and the wit being out) but to serenade his "ladye-love," and she being equally willing, I left the two playing Romeo and Juliet, and took a circuitous course to my room, where I was soon sound asleep, and did not wake till the sun was high in the heavens.

I do not know whether the authorities would have considered that I was carrying out their instructions "to proceed with all despatch," but, as they had delayed me at Sahibgunge, I felt quite justified in delaying myself at the other end.

At two o'clock, after tiffin, Walters managed to tear himself away from Juliet, and we made another upward move, John having gone on some time in advance with the baggage.

I never shall forget my first sight of Darjeeling as we came round the corner, and I saw grand old Kinchinjunga keeping solemn watch and ward over the valleys below. It was only a momentary peep, however, for up rolled a fog and down came the rain (a commodity of which there used to be plenty at that station), and away we galloped best pace for Walters' quarters, where we found a cheerful fire burning, everything unpacked, and John wrapped up in his thickest clothes, looking somewhat like a salamander in an iceberg, but still exceedingly pleased to be at his journey's end. "Very tunda, sahib, here," he said; "not good, too much cold, must have more coat."

John always had an eye to the main chance, and saw a good opening here for a suit on the cheap, which of course, he managed to get.

Walters was president of the mess, and the way we fed was something extraordinary. Moreover, as he was by no means a flyer at accounts, he generally at the end of the month found himself some hundreds of rupees out of pocket. However, it did not seem to trouble him much, and being one of the cheeriest and best of fellows we had a high old time.

The day after my arrival I commenced work, and joined the board with the two members who had come up before me. Two hours in the morning was considered by us ample to begin with, until we had been sufficiently "picked up" by the mountain air to endure a longer strain; so I had the afternoon free, and employed it with Walters and another pal (of whom more anon), Bagges by name, commonly called "the Major," in doing a bit of horse-dealing, and with their combined assistance I managed to purchase a very decent pony at a moderate figure. Certainly he was not much to look at when I bought him, being then unkempt and dirty, but in a week he was a different animal and turned out a real beauty.

There was a capital little club below the station, of which we were all members, the principal attraction being the billiard-table, and most afternoons there was a black pool going on, at which game both Walters and the major were experts. One evening in the week the neighbouring tea-planters used to come in and dine, and then the fun was fast and furious; but the great gathering was always the first Saturday in the month, when everybody from far and near were wont to assemble in the billiard-room, and the stakes at black pool were raised to a rupee a life, increasing, as the evening wore on, sometimes to four rupees. One of these functions was close at hand, and Walters confided to me that he and the major used to have an hour or two's practice on the table every day for the three or four days previously, and advised me to do the same.

"You know, old man," he said, "these planters are first-rate chaps, but they can't play pool a bit, though they fancy themselves tremendously at it, and, as they look on our winning as sheer luck, it generally is good business."

I could not understand why both Walters and the major always played pyramids in preference to billiards till I heard Walters' statement, but then it dawned upon me, and I saw through the whole game. Naturally I took his advice, and for nearly a week I did nothing but make, or endeavour to make, winning hazards till I fancied myself pretty nearly as good as Walters himself, though the major I could never touch. In fact, he was something out of the ordinary, and had he not been a martyr to fever and ague, he would have swept the board on every occasion.

Directly after tiffin on the eventful Saturday, Walters and self rode down to the club, where we found a goodly number already assembled, and, to our delight, Bagges was not among the number.

"Now, old chap," said Walters, "are we going to go into partnership to-day?"

"In what way?" I asked.

"Why," he replied, "like this: some of these chaps do nothing but hit hard and fluke, therefore it's as well to have two strings to one's bow. They have a game of their own: they put so much into the pool, with three lives each as at ordinary following pool, only with a black ball, and then, besides the black, you can take the pool or divide. They generally have two or three games like that, so I propose that in all games of that sort you and I go shares both in lives and pool, but in the ordinary black pool we shall go each for ourselves."

Of course I agreed, and we started with excellent results to the firm, until the arrival of the major, who, finding himself late and not included in the firm's transactions, let himself go, and played like a demon, taking pool after pool and whipping the black down every other shot. This sort of game soon put a stop to the planters' eagerness, and they proposed that we change to the ordinary black, which was done. By that time it had come on to rain hard, and Walters, with evident glee, whispered to me that the major was evidently getting a "go" of fever, and also was trying to stave it off by repeated pegs. I could see that he was getting a bit unsteady, though he was still well on the spot. So we, the firm, agreed to stand out, although it was now every one for himself, and start again after dinner.

As time went on the major got more full and somewhat cantankerous, ending by having a shindy with a doctor and a tea planter—a sort of three-cornered duel, where all the combatants attacked promiscuously. What it was all about no one seemed to know, except that Bagges and the doctor were tight, and Bagges swore that the doctor had tripped him up as he was going to make a stroke, while the planter vowed that both the medico and the major had choused him out of a life. It culminated in a sort of free hustle, during which the doctor and Bagges rolled under the table and were then promptly removed and peace was restored. By this time dinner was ready, and we all adjourned to the dining-room, where the sound of the merry champagne cork was soon in full swing. Dinner did not take long, for, of all keen players, commend me to those planters, so, with a bottle of champagne (in some cases more) under every waistcoat, we promptly made a move into the billiard-room, and the play recommenced.

It was late when we mounted our tats to ride up again to Walters' quarters, and I am proud to say that the pockets of the firm were bulging out with the nimble rupee. Trouser pockets, coat pockets, great-coat pockets, and a small bag carried by Walters' syce represented the spoil, which we duly counted out on arrival, over a night-cap. As far as I can remember, the grand total came to nearly nine hundred rupees, a pretty tidy weight to carry up, and not a bad day's work even when divided by two. And this sort of thing went on every month, besides the Saturday weekly gleanings, so you may imagine I was in no hurry to return to the plains, and by great luck I managed to do what is known as a "shunt," and by volunteering for duty after my board was finished I secured three months' extra ozone in the hills.

During the time I was there we had two expeditions after game, principally of the pheasant order, and in one of these I very nearly lost my trusty henchman—Christian John. It happened thus. We had to cross a river by one of those extraordinary cane or bamboo bridges, which generally commence to swing when you are about in the centre. We had all got over safe excepting John, who brought up the rear, and in the middle the structure commenced its vagaries. Paler and paler grew the wretched man, till at last he completely lost his nerve and fainted clean away. Luckily he did not fall off, and so two stalwart hill-men managed to carry him safely across, but nothing would induce him ever again to trust himself alone on one of those treacherous articles. I confess we did not do very much in the way of sport, but I thoroughly enjoyed myself, and, with the aid of the planters' pool, materially increased my income.

Everything, however, must have an end, and the rule applied to my hill trip, which, in my opinion at least, terminated all too soon. The firm was sorry, I believe, to lose one of the partners, but Walters' feelings could not compare with mine, who knew that it was a case of not only returning to the plains, but also of braving the righteous indignation of my brother officers, they having had to do my duty all the time I was spoiling the Egyptians in the cool. They certainly had their revenge, however, when they got me back amongst them, for if there was any extra duty to be done, or any outside board to attend, the order book was sure to contain my name.

CHAPTER XX.

A NARROW SQUEAK AND HOMEWARD BOUND.

THE time has now arrived when I must perforce bring these reminiscences to a conclusion, so far as Indian sport is concerned; and, consequently, this will be my last chapter on the subject, although I hope to be able to take my readers into other lands and endeavour to give them an account of what befell me there. I will conclude therefore with an account of perhaps the narrowest squeak I ever had, just before I took my final departure for "England, home and beauty."

It was just at the end of the cold weather, and I had already sent in my application for leave to go home, with every expectation of it being granted, that Tilson and Gordon suggested that we should have one last shoot before I left. Johnson was to have come with us (he, by the way, was going to accompany me home). But at the last moment he was put on some court-martial duty, which kept him tied up, so that we had to go off without him.

We only had three or four days' leave given us, which, by starting late on Saturday evening, we managed to turn into five, so, naturally, had to take the nearest spot we could, and after due deliberation, the *locale* was fixed at the foot of a low range of hills some sixty miles away from the station at which we were quartered. There was the usual amount of scrub jungle, with some famous nullahs running down from the hills, which were reported by the native shikarie to be more often than not the temporary home of a tiger; also, as we knew for ourselves, there was always a panther or two knocking about, and in the vicinity of where we proposed to pitch our first camp, a large jheel existed which, failing larger game, would give us some sport in the way of duck and snipe. We managed to secure two elephants from the commissariat, which with tents, our horses, and provender, we sent on two days in advance, and then proceeded to lay a dâk for ourselves. I was very sorry that Johnson could not be of the party, because he had been there twice before, and the native shikaries knew him well; moreover, he had a very good idea of the ground, which would have been exceedingly useful.

However, on the occasion of his last visit, I had accompanied him, so that I was not a complete stranger, and with the numerous hints he gave me I hoped to be able to manage. Neither Tilson nor Gordon had ever been over there, and, indeed, were not well up in the science of venery, so that the direction of affairs fell on to my shoulders, and they both promised to obey my instructions implicitly. Johnson very kindly sent his own shikarie, who acted as his bearer, with me, as he knew all the natives of these parts well, and so, armed with the necessary purwannahs and a stock of high spirits and bright hopes, we started off after an early dinner at mess on our sixty miles dâk journey. Of course, I took Christian John with me. Indeed, I do not believe he would have remained behind if I had told him to, much as he hated tigers, panthers, *et hoc genus omne*, for he was very sad at my approaching departure, and would scarcely leave me for a moment. Poor John! I do believe he was fond of his master. We had been in so many scrapes together, out of which we had contrived to come all right, that he had acquired great faith in me, and danger was the touch of nature which made us kin. He was very anxious to come home with me, but could not make up his mind to face so great a distance of "kala pawnee." Besides, as I had visions of his getting sick and ill in England, to say nothing of his anti Sir Wilfrid Lawson proclivities, I was afraid of the responsiblity, so we parted at Bombay, and the last I saw of him was a dishevelled figure dissolved in tears invoking blessings on the head of his sahib, and saying, "You come back, always find John waiting." I am glad to say I got him an excellent place, and I had a letter from him a year after, a document which I still keep, and of which I confess I am proud. Six years ago I heard he was still alive, and in service, but getting old, and my informant also told me that he still looked forward for my return, and was "still waiting for master." Since then the rest has been "silence." However, this is a digression; so I must get back to our shooting.

We arrived on the ground without any mishap, and found everything all ready and prepared for us by Johnson's man, who had gone on with the elephants. The camp was pitched in a tope of trees, and our beds were all ready for us to turn into, which after a B. and S. round we were glad to do. I was the last to tumble in, as I had to make arrangements about the return dâk at the expiration of our leave, and also hear what the shikarie had arranged for the next day. He told me that he had seen the head men, and settled all about the beat, which was to begin at 7.30 a.m., or thereabouts. As it was close on four a.m. then, I did not get much rest, and it seemed to me as if I had only turned round once, when Christian

John woke me, and giving me a cup of tea told me it was time to show a leg. A mussuck of cold water soon put us all to rights, and over an early breakfast we discussed with the shikaries the programme of the day's proceedings.

It was proposed that we should first beat some of the most likely places and nullahs for tiger, and then try a spot some little distance off where the natives said a panther family had their lair. Having impressed on Gordon and Tilson the necessity of silence, and also that they were not to fire at any lesser game than stripes or spots, under pain of death, we started off. I was on the back of the pad elephant, while Tilson and Gordon occupied a howdah together.

On arriving at the ground, we were all three posted by the head shikarie in advantageous positions, and then the two elephants were sent away with the beaters, one on each flank. Johnson's man told me that they had posted men in trees so as to mark our quarry down, should he, she, or it, appear. This, I believe, is a common way of dealing with "spots"; the men ascend trees and other points of vantage during the small hours, and watch for the gentleman's return from his nocturnal visits to his lair by day, and then, having carefully marked him down, they send a runner into camp to fetch the "sahib logue."

We, however, had neither time nor patience for this course of procedure, and so started out on a regular beat. Soon after we were posted, the signal was given, and the band commenced. The first arrival was a magnificent boar, who trotted leisurely along with his bristles up and seemed quite indignant at being disturbed. Presently there was a tremendous shindy among the beaters, and shouts of *bhāg*, and we each clutched our guns, determined to do or die. From my position, I could see Tilson seated not too comfortably in the fork of a tree, on what looked to me a rotten branch. He was evidently very much on the *qui vive* and excited, and to get a better view was trying to get further along the said branch, when all of a sudden crack it went, off went Tilson's rifle, and down he came on the ground. The way he scuttled back and shinned up the tree again, rifle and all, nearly killed me with laughing, notwithstanding my annoyance in knowing that the noise of the shot must certainly have turned the animal, whatever it was, away from our direction. From the increased noise on the right of the line of beaters, it was evident that our quarry was making in that direction, and so it proved, for very shortly after, Johnson's shikarie arrived post haste to tell us that a large panther had broken cover and been tracked down into the bed of a small nullah about a mile and a half away, where he was lying under some thick scrub. There was no time to lose, so we all made the best of our way to where the head man and the assembled beaters were standing. The vedettes in the trees signified that spots was still there, and so, having divided the guns and formed a circle, we cautiously approached his lair.

When we arrived close, a fresh disposition was made, and the beaters were taken to the upper end, while we, the guns, commanded the front and the two sides. All we had to fear was the beast breaking back where we had no gun, but as we could not make four out of three, we could only hope for the best. At a given signal all the beaters kicked up a most diabolical row, and simultaneously discharged a well-directed volley of stones at the spot where the panther was supposed to be. Dead silence for a moment, and then, with a rush close by where Gordon was posted, out sprang a fine large panther. (The brute had evidently crawled along under the bank, which completely overhung and concealed him, and so got some twenty yards lower down.) For a moment Gordon was too much astonished to fire, and then our three shots rang out like one, and "spots" gave a spasmodic bound in the air, which showed that one bullet, if not more had taken effect. As soon as he was on his legs again the beast turned short round and charged straight at Gordon up the nullah. It was an anxious moment, but he stood perfectly still, and just as his second barrel cracked, I fired, and the panther lay in the agonies of death within ten yards of his intended victim. I don't think I ever saw any one so delighted as Gordon was; he regularly jumped for joy, and was quite like a boy who had just shot his first rabbit. Of course we presented him with the skin, as he so nearly lost some of his own in the affray, and that completed his cup of happiness. We had another beat or two, but nothing further rewarded our exertions, and so we gave up and returned to camp.

Later in the afternoon I thought I would go out and get a duck for dinner, so taking one of the beaters with me to carry the spoil, I went off to the jheel, and it was here I nearly met my fate. I had bagged one duck, and was turning to come home, when a couple got up right under my feet and flew across an arm of the jheel. With the first barrel I got one, and the second fell on a sort of island or rather promontory. My native attendant having gone to retrieve my first bird, I thought I would go round and gather the second for myself. While on my way I heard the man shout out something, but did not pay much attention, as I thought it was only to show me whereabouts the duck had fallen, which I considered I knew better than he did. I had not gone far up the said promontory, when I felt the ground begin to quiver in that peculiar way which denotes a bog. Now, if there is one thing that has always frightened me more than another, it is a bog, and directly I felt I was on one I got the funks on board, and did the very worst thing I could do, viz. to try and get back to *terra firma* by a succession of leaps and bounds. Of course, the second jump I took I broke through, and with a yell which might have been heard miles off, I sank into the treacherous mud. Deeper and deeper I gradually got every moment, and the more I struggled the worse it made matters. I got my gun across, which eased me a bit, but I was slowly and surely sinking to destruction, and I knew that if help did not come soon I was lost. I could not see my beater anywhere about, and I felt I was alone. (What I *did* feel is better imagined than described.) I distinctly remember wondering what Gordon and Tilson would say when I never came back, and also, oddly enough, what they would do with my things.

By this time I had sunk nearly up to my shoulders, and had got into a state of hopeless despair, when I heard a welcome shout from the bank of the jheel of "All right, old man; we will have you out in a moment," and I saw the figure of Johnson's shikarie crawling along with a rope tied to him. I remember feeling him put it under my arms, and then everything became a blank, and, my overstrung nerves giving way, I fainted clean off, and did not come to my senses till I found myself supported with my head on Gordon's knee and Tilson trying to pour some brandy and water down my throat.

"Thank heavens, old man, we were in time," said Gordon, as I came to with a gasp. "There, you are all right now; but it was a narrow shave, and I thought, after we got you out, that we were never going to bring you back to life again. Drink a good dram of brandy, and you'll be yourself again."

They told me as soon as I was quite recovered that they were both lying down fast asleep, when my beater came rushing into camp and told Johnson's man what had happened, and that he immediately dashed off, got a rope, and hurried them down. On the way as they ran he told them that it was one of the most dangerous places in the country, and he wondered that I had never heard of it. When they got down and found me, he also declared that in another ten minutes it would have been all over, and that I should have gone for ever. They said that when they hauled me out I lay like a dead man for nearly twenty minutes and frightened them out of their lives. I have no doubt its seems very foolish to have fainted after all was safe, but, as happily it is not a common experience, I do not think many are qualified to give an opinion. Anyway, I can answer for it, that it was the narrowest squeak I ever wish to have, and one I hope never to try again. I had one other adventure, which perhaps was nearly as bad, when I was in a nullah or drain on a pony when a dam burst, and I only saved myself by the skin of my teeth, and swung myself out by a bush just as the flood came down, carrying away and drowning my luckless steed. But it was sooner over, and, being more exciting, did not seem anything like the helpless agony of slowly sinking inch by inch to one's doom.

We did not do very much more on the trip beyond a snap-shot at a panther, which we all missed—tigers there were none—and getting a fair sprinkling of duck and snipe under the guidance *bien entendu* of the local sportsmen, who knew where it was safe to go and where it was not; but we had a very jolly time, and were all sorry when we were forced to sound the retire and go back to cantonments and duty.

A month or six weeks later, Johnson's leave

together with mine, came back granted, and we were very busy disposing of our goods and chattels to the best advantage to every one who was good-natured enough or foolish enough to purchase them. The things that caused me the most anxiety were my cases of skins and trophies. I knew I could never get them down to Bombay in time to start with me, and I was sure that if I trusted them to be forwarded afterwards, I should not see half of them. In this conjecture I was about right, for it was just about half that I did eventually receive, the second half, which started home in the following steamer, being now with Pharaoh's chariots at the bottom of the Red Sea, the vessel having been wrecked.

At last everything was disposed of, our things packed, dâk laid, and our last night at mess arrived, after which, the good-byes and good wishes from all being over, we made a start—Johnson, self, and Christian John—to join the railway somewhere in the region of Delhi.

By this time it was getting pretty hot, and the prospect of a longish journey in a dâk gharrie was not a joy, but we managed to tide it through somehow, and arrived at our destination, a mass of dust, and with a thirst that would have fetched a long price.

Poor dear old McSweeny, who was terribly cut up at losing two of his bairns, had presented me as a parting gift with a small medicine chest, "just to keep ye fit, ye ken, the whiles ye are awa' from me," as he said, and as a precaution after our journey, we each took, Christian John included, a dose of quinine before we turned in for a night's rest previous to embarking on the train. The following morning we were consequently as fit as fleas, and having taken our tickets and laid in a good stock of sodawater and ice, which we put in a chellumchee under the seat, away we went. All went well till an unlucky thirst seized Johnson, and having poured himself out a goodly portion of brandy, he woke me up to get him a bottle of sodawater out of the chellumchee. I had no sooner put my hand down to reach it, when bang went two bottles, cutting my fingers and right hand all to pieces, and deluging the carriage with blood. What a blessing McSweeny's thoughtful present proved may be well imagined. Johnson having, with the aid of cotton wool and bandages, strapped me up as best he could, telegraphed from the next stoppage to some pals of ours and made all arrangements to stop there the night.

By the time we reached the station I had lost a good deal of blood, and was feeling pretty sick, but the regimental surgeon who met us soon put matters straight, and having extracted the best part of a bottle from various parts of my hand and arm, sowed up and strapped the wounds so well that I was able to dine at mess and "knock spots" out of a bottle of "simkin," and the next day, having bid adieu to our kind friends, we continued our journey and arrived at Bombay without further mishaps; though, of course, I had a "wing up" nearly all the way home. Before starting, I got a wire from McSweeny, who had heard of the accident, saying, "Better come back; not fit to be trusted alone without me; hope medicine chest useful." I wired him back, "All richt the noo, hoos yersel?" and then we went on board, the screw began to turn, and we were off.

We came in for more bloodshed before we arrived in England, as we found ourselves in the thick of the Franco-German war, but beyond being arrested once, and being nearly left behind at a small frontier station, we got through all right, and at last had the pleasure of seeing the white cliffs of Dover, and subsequently dear, smoky old London, looking just the same as the day we had left it some years before.

PART II.

CENTRAL AMERICA.

CHAPTER I.

OUTWARD BOUND TO CENTRAL AMERICA.

In the concluding chapter of Part I. I took leave of the gorgeous East and all the merry days I spent there, and I managed to land myself safe and sound—or fairly so—in dear old England. After a year or so, however, in the old country the spirit of travel and adventure attacked me badly, and I felt I must be up and doing. It was no use trying to fight against it; the feeling was far too strong, and the more I put it off the more it grew, till at last, after a projected expedition to the Rockies had fallen through, it became unbearable, and I was forced to cast about for new ground. Eventually, for many reasons—one of which being that I had become possessed of a share in a coffee plantation, the only visible advantage of which was seemingly that it kept the resident manager in dollars—I determined on visiting South and Central America, ostensibly on business, but mainly with a view of seeing what sort of a country for game it might be. No sooner was my mind made up than it became necessary to find a pal or two to accompany me, and after a good deal of trouble, argument, and persuasion I managed to get two to come—Halifax and Royal—and then commenced the work of fitting out. Of course, none of us knew anything about the country we were going to visit, and there was precious little information to be obtained from books on the subject, although we searched the British Museum diligently for close on a week. The natural consequence of this was that we laid in a stock of articles, the greater portion of which were of no earthly use, and indeed were never used at all. Guns, ammunition, and, happily, clothing, was all right so far as the shooting kit went, but of everything else the least said the better. Messrs. Silver, of Cornhill, were entrusted with the job of the outfit, and even that well-known firm of colonial outfitters knew no more than we did ourselves about the country, and beyond high boots, flannel breeches, and coats were hopelessly at sea. However, it was a case of nothing venture nothing have; and, as I knew it to be tropical, I went in for pretty much the same kit as if I was going out into an Indian jungle.

This matter settled, we booked our places in one of the royal mail steamers starting from Southampton, and awaited events. The first difficulty we had was with our powder, of which we took a fair amount—indeed, far too much. The railway company would only carry it by certain trains, and the ship refused to carry it at all. Here was a pretty kettle of fish to start with. Without our ammunition we could not and would not go, and to all our letters of remonstrance we only got a polite reply to the effect that it was "against the regulations." At last we agreed to d—n the regulations, and to beard the board of direction of the company in their den, and, accordingly, one fine morning, we started off for the city, and after half an hour's argument got the board to say that if we would ship the powder in the magazine, and, provided the captain of the vessel did not object, they would this once relax the rules and allow the stuff to go. The skipper proved a right-down good sort, and when we asked him if he minded, he only said, "Mind! No;

certainly not. Why the plague did not you come to me at first, without making all this fuss? I would have done it for you at once." And so the vexed question was happily settled, and our ammunition got safely on board with the rest of our heavy baggage, we ourselves following in *propriâ personâ*.

I remember it was a beast of a day when we left London for Southampton, a regular thick November fog, which, as we got down the line turned into rain, and right glad we were to get on board and shake ourselves down in our cabin before starting. We had just finished that process, having tossed for choice of bunks, and had come up on deck to look round, when the first catastrophe occurred, which might have been a serious one. They were swaying up the foretopsail yard with the aid of the donkey winch, and the winch man did not stop his engine in time, with the result that the yard slings and parrell broke, and down came the yard, endways, close by Royal's head, and, going right through the upper deck, remained there quivering. By the time they had got it out and the damage repaired, the tender steamed away, and we were off down Southampton Water.

Just as we started the weather cleared, and the sun came out, which brought all our fellow-passengers up from below, so we were able to have an inspection. A pretty mixed lot they were too—all shapes and sizes, nationalities and colours, the most English of the lot being a Jamaica lady, who, if she had been a mare, would have been described as a bright bay, but who informed us (she had been taking leave of her friends in champagne, and having done herself remarkably well she consequently was communicative) that she had been *home* for six months, and was now going out to Jamaica to be married. There was a gay widow, to say nothing of three or four grass widows, some Spanish Americanos, a sprinkling of sugar planters, a civil engineer or two, and some naval officers; besides a lot of others of all sorts. It does not take long on board ship to make acquaintances, and before dinner time our party was made up, and we were all on excellent terms with ourselves, the widow, and the grass widows, and things were going as merry as marriage bells till we got well into the Channel, when the sea made, and the female contingent left us for forty-eight hours.

During that said forty-eight hours we had a real dusting across the Bay of Biscay, and, to make matters more pleasant, Royal succumbed to the "motion of the ocean," and became a corpse in our cabin. His cure was brought about in an odd but very effectual manner. He was occupying the thwart-ship bunk, and lay there moaning and groaning, bewailing his hard fate, and anathematizing the sea and all its ways, when suddenly Halifax's dressing-case, which he had jammed in at the foot of his berth (the upper one) fetched away and landed on the top of the invalid, followed immediately by Halifax himself, who, in his endeavour to avert the catastrophe, carried away himself. This sudden and unexpected assault so astonished Royal and roused his ire, that he forgot all about his illness, and, jumping up, vowed he would break Halifax's head. As he proceeded to put his threat into execution, they both rolled over on to the floor of the cabin, and I was forced to get out, and, though nearly prostrate with laughter, endeavour to separate the combatants. When peace was at last restored, and mutual explanations exchanged, lo and behold! Royal was himself again, the sickness had disappeared like magic, and for the rest of the voyage no amount of bad weather made any difference to him. I do not suggest that this remedy would be effective in every case, or that it is one that would ever become popular; but, in this instance, it answered most perfectly, and saved us all a world of trouble.

The bad weather in the bay being passed, the ladies began to make their appearance again, and *tête-à-têtes* might be seen every evening in the gloaming in various secluded portions of the ship. When we arrived one fine morning off Hayti, we found a deuce of a row going on; the place was in the throes of a revolution, and the insurgents were bombarding the town. Of course we were obliged to lie well off, and as there was a heavy swell it was not the pleasantest thing in the world. Besides, we had great difficulty in landing the mails, and precious nearly lost the mail officer and our medico in so doing; for, in coming out of the harbour or roadstead, some of the more valiant of the invading party formed up on a spit of land which the boat had to pass, and fired three or four volleys at her in succession, luckily without doing any harm; though, if they had been anything in the way of shots, they ought to have killed the whole boat's crew. I do not think any one was sorry to hear the order to turn ahead given, and to see our good ship's bows pointed for sea. We put into the pretty French island of Martinique, where we laid in a large stock of that most excellent stuff called *creme de cocoa*, and also had a look at Barbadoes, the peculiarity of which place is that most of the inhabitants insist that theirs is an English climate, and wear tall hats on every possible occasion. Certainly their capacity for putting away sangaree or brandy-and-water is unlimited, and worthy of a better cause. It was at this place that our especial party of three was nearly reduced to two; for Halifax, who had started out for a ramble with one of the grass widows with whom he had struck up a violent flirtation, went too far, and the pair only caught the vessel by the skin of their teeth, and tumbled on board out of a shore-boat, looking very guilty and foolish, just as the screw began to revolve. Naturally, they got properly chaffed, and for the next few days their lives were a burden to them.

At the Dutch Island of St. Thomas' we varied the entertainment by going ashore on a sandbank, and had to stop there a day and a half while they were overhauling the ship. Half the passengers had to sleep that night at the hotel—and such a place! Royal, Halifax and self got one room with two beds in it between us, and consequently had to divide the night into watches. We began by trying a shake-down on the floor; but no white man could stay more than a quarter of an hour in that berth on account of certain animal life that, to say the least of it, was exceedingly "fine and large." Moreover, the spaces between the flooring boards were nearly a quarter of an inch wide, so that one could see into the room below all that was going on. I remember we were much edified!

At last we arrived at Jamaica, where we had to tranship to a smaller steamer going to Belize, in British Honduras; and what a hunt we had to get our various goods and chattels safe, and everything sorted out. We found time to go to a dignity ball, and enjoyed the fun muchly; also were introduced to the mysteries of pepper-pot. One day we had a try for some snipe at the back of the island, but it was not a great success, though a charming trip. One incident happened which, although I have recorded it elsewhere (viz. in my book called "Sporting Sketches," and under different names), will bear repeating. We had gone up to the hill station at Newcastle to dine and sleep with the regiment quartered there; and it was certainly what would be called "a wet night" at mess.

Royal, who, by the way, had an exceedingly curly head, retired rather early, and made the best of his way to what he believed to be his temporary abode. Unfortunately, however, not being quite as clear about locality as he might have been, he mistook the diggings, and bedded himself comfortably down in some one else's room. The owner of the apartment turned up somewhat later, also slightly mixed, and proceeded to go to bed. But as he tried to get between the sheets his hand came in contact with Royal's curly head, which he immediately took for that of a nigger, and he began to pull the offender out and to administer chastisement. This naturally woke up and sobered Royal at once, and "the band began to play." Round the room they both went in the dark, hammering at each other until the battle was brought to an end and their wild career suddenly checked by both falling headlong into a bath of cold water. This necessitated the striking of a light, and then they discovered their mistake, at which they both had a good laugh. After a drink or two, Royal was piloted safely to his own couch, and the rest of the night —or rather the remaining few short hours of the early morning—was passed in peace.

I confess I was quite sorry when the time was up, and what they called the inter-Colonial steamer was ready to start; but there was no help for it, and we were bound to go. When we got on board we found that we had to take stores out to one of the company's steamers that had been wrecked on a coral reef, so that we should have to turn about a hundred miles out of our course. It was a beautiful bright morning when we sighted the wreck, and as we steamed up to her it required all one's powers of imagination to believe that she was a wreck at all. She had gone on to the reef in the night, going about fifteen knots, and had jumped the outer reef into a small natural basin, which just held her, and there she was, as comfortable as if she was in a dock, with the exception that her lower hold was full of water. As we got nearer and brought up, we became aware of the most overpowering smell from the decaying hides which composed the main portion of her cargo. How the men in charge of her managed to live I can't think; but they had got so used to it that they hardly noticed it. So bad was it that before going on board, which I did, I was advised to leave any gold, such as watch, chain, etc., behind; and even my rings, which I kept on my fingers, were turned quite black.

While they were transferring the stores, we got out some hooks and made a line, terminating in a bit of chain, to fish for barracoutas, a sort of cross between a shark and a pike, about three feet long, and as savage as they make them. We could see the bottom quite plainly, with fish of all sorts and colours swimming about in the coral beds, and, having got a piece of fat pork from the butcher, we commenced operations. Our first hook and line we lost through a big shark, of which there were hundreds all round, taking the bait; but on a second attempt, having rigged up another, we got hold of a barracouta, who gave us some fine sport. It took all hands to get the brute on board; and even when he was on the deck it was no joke going near him to administer the *coup de grace,* for he was as lively as a shark, and somewhat more vicious. We secured three of them, however, before it was time to up anchor, and we had some steaks cooked from one for dinner that evening, which, as far as I remember, were not half bad. One item on board that vessel I do thoroughly recollect, which was the cockroaches. They simply swarmed, big and little; under one's mattress was a colony of them, and the beasts got into everything one had. I don't believe any part of the ship was free from them; and I fancy every vessel that has carried sugar in those latitudes is the same. At first I went in positive dread, but very soon got used to it, and before the end of the voyage from Jamaica I looked upon them as quite part of the passenger list. Halifax and Royal, on the contrary, never got accustomed to them, and used to behave in the cabin very much after the fashion of the cook and the black beetles in some of *Punch's* pictures.

I forgot to say that we left the bronze English (?) lady who had come out to be married, at Jamaica, and there was a deuce of a scene on board before she left because her intended had not come to meet her. If he had seen the way she carried on—or tried to—on the voyage out, if he was a wise man he would never meet her again. She was a lady who evidently recognized the wisdom of having two strings to her bow, for on the way she had made a dead set at the third officer; and when her affianced did not turn up, after a copious flood of tears, she went for her second string, and informed him, in the presence of all assembled, that when he came back she would have him, that she was his now, etc., etc. I believe the poor fellow was so taken aback and so frightened at the idea, that on his return trip he never left his cabin except on duty, until Port Royal was well astern. As, however, she did not come on board after him, I presume that tardy lover, No. 1, turned up, or that she had taken on a No. 3.

After three days' somewhat ticklish navigation among the kays and coral reefs, we arrived off the town of

Belize, a curious settlement, with the houses thereof for the most part built on posts over a swamp, and by no means a prepossessing looking spot to be landed in. I naturally expected the manager of the coffee plantation, which was some hundred and fifty miles further down the coast, to meet us here, and when he did not turn up, and a gentleman who came off put a letter into my hands from him to say that he had been unavoidably detained, I felt somewhat in a fix, and my two pals, Royal and Halifax, began to look on me with an eye of suspicion, and to reckon me up as a fraud. However, there was no help for it, and we had to cast about for lodgings. The gentleman who brought off the letter (he was a merchant there) very kindly offered to put up one of the party, and the governor, to whom I had a letter of introduction, took Halifax and myself in for a night or two, until we found some place to stow ourselves. This we did the following day, and got into comfortable quarters with a Scotch Creole lady. The bathing arrangements were somewhat primitive I own, for the bathroom was in the cellar, and the bath itself was a "dug out" or canoe. Moreover, as the same interstices between the flooring boards, which I noticed at St. Thomas's prevailed equally here, any one in the dining-room above had an excellent view of our tubbing arrangements. However, as everything was as clean as a new pin, and our landlady an excellent cook, besides being a young and pretty woman, we had reason to congratulate ourselves on our luck in striking oil.

The first night after we were domiciled in our new abode, we all dined together at Government House, and, walking home after dinner, we were considerably startled by the huge land crabs, which simply swarmed all over the place. I will back a land crab in the haze of a tropical night, when seen for the first time, against anything I know, for its powers of acting on the nerves; I think, without exception, it is the most "jumpy" object I know. Royal, I believe, thought the devil had got loose, for he was the first to stumble up against one, and yelled blue murder like a maniac. We stayed over a week in Belize before the manager turned up, and then we had to look about for a schooner to take ourselves and our traps down to the nearest port to the plantation—all of which I must reserve till a future chapter. I was deuced glad to see the arrival of the said manager, for both Royal and Halifax were getting very impatient at the delay, which they did not hesitate to lay at my door.

CHAPTER II.

A CENTRAL AMERICAN RACE MEETING.

We were persuaded to put off our departure for a few days, in order that we might be present at some races which were being got up among the good citizens, and which promised to be great fun. Henry, the manager, was selected for the post of judge; not that he knew much about it, but being a big man and manager of a large estate, they thought he would carry weight, and that his ruling would not be so liable to be disputed as that of some of the purely local men. When we consented to stay, none of us had the remotest intention of running anything. Indeed we had nothing bigger than a Cuban bloodhound with four legs that we could enter for a race. But, as luck would have it, one evening we were all asked up to the barracks of the West Indian Regiment quartered there, and after dinner the fun became fairly fast and furious, and the chaff flew freely. Two gentlemen at last became a little too free, and getting on to the subject of the forthcoming races, bantered us about coming out for sport, and not being plucky enough to spend a few dollars on a pony and having a start. This got Royal's back up, and he promptly asked one of the pair if he was going to run anything himself, and on receiving an affirmative answer, said, "All right, we *will* run something, and I'll back our beast against your one to win for a hundred dollars."

The bet was snapped up at once, and a good many of the natives were eager to go a bit more, as they knew all the ponies in the place had been bought up, and considered it a real soft thing. When every one had put on all they could, Royal's friend, who by the way kept an aquadiente store, *i.e.* spirit bar, turned to me, and with an ill-concealed sneer on his face, said, "Which of you are going to ride this dark horse of yours, or can any of you ride at all?" I had been too much astonished at Royal even venturing to say he would run an animal to reply to the question, but Halifax chipped in, and, pointing to me, said, "There is our jockey; and I'll bet he beats you." The gentleman then proceeded to look me over with a supercilious air, and offered to bet me personally that he won. His tone and manner so riled me that I snapped him up to the tune of $200, and then the matter dropped.

After supper we had some boxing, and I did not improve matters by knocking my sneering friend out of time in the bout we had together, and he retired muttering vengeance between his teeth. As we walked home to our diggings in the cool of the morning, we came to the conclusion that we had made considerable asses of ourselves. Here we were in a strange country without a nag, or, so far as we could see, the possibility of getting one, and yet we had backed ourselves to win a race to the tune of nearly £100 amongst us. Something must be done, we all agreed, and whatever it was it must be at once, for time was, as the lawyers have it, the essence of the contract. Accordingly, next day, I went to Government House, and put the matter before the governor. He knew nothing to be bought anywhere, he said, but he was expecting the manager of a mahogany and logwood business in every minute, and there was just the off chance of his having a crock to dispose of. There was also the more than off chance though, amounting to the positive certainty, that if he once came into the place, before we got first run of him, some one else would pick up the much-desired animal, if such a thing existed. So I begged the governor to send out at once and endeavour to waylay him *en route*, which he very kindly undertook to do, and insisted on our coming back to lunch to learn the result of the mission.

We filled up the time before lunch in a fruitless search all round the town, in which we discovered nothing fit to buy, except one which might have had an outside chance, had not our friend of the previous evening been beforehand with us, and, to make matters as he thought quite safe for himself, bought it up on his own account. When Halifax, Royal, and self turned up at Government House, punctually at 1.30 (Henry would not come), we were not in a particularly bright frame of mind, as independently of losing our money we thought we should certainly be the laughing-stock of every one in the place, and we heartily wished the races at the devil. However, the governor's face somewhat reassured us when he told us that the manager had come in, and, what was more to the purpose, had given us the refusal of his pony for £20. (Under ordinary circumstances £12 would have bought it.) The said pony, moreover, was, his master said, very fast and also in hard condition, having been ridden every day long distances, and been out in camp and on the march for nearly three months.

"But come into the dining-room and settle it yourselves," continued the governor, leading the way; and then he introduced us to the manager, Mr. Hiram B. Flood, an American of the most pronounced type.

"Proud to make your acquaintance, gents," he said, shaking us by the hand. "Guess the boss here," pointing to the governor, "has told me your quandary, and how you want something that will just knock spots off these benighted critturs here, and I calculate that Hiram B. Flood is the man to fix it up for you right away. Directly I heard the tale I froze on to the situation at once, and I said, 'Hiram'—that's me—'Hiram,' I said, 'your little mustang is framed for this job. He's fast, sound, and good.' Give me one hundred dollars right down here, and he is yours; and, if he wins, I reckon you'll count H. B. Flood amongst your friends. That's so."

"Where is the beast to be seen?" I asked Mr. Hiram B. Flood, who replied by saying—

"Guess that's coming somewhere near a trade. The fact is I brought him along with me, and he's right there by the stable."

Of course we all adjourned, before we had a mouthful of lunch, to look at the animal, and though a trifle small perhaps, we found a wiry little beast in hard condition, showing a bit of breed, and evidently fast. I could feel that a few gallops would lengthen his stride, and that in a week or less he would be better than most of them; and so, without hesitating a moment, I closed with Flood, and became the possessor of the "mustang" in the name of the syndicate.

"Wall," said his late master, as I counted him over the dollars, "I guess I ought to have traded him away for double; it's a dead cert he wins, and I ought to have asked two hundred dollars. However, a trade's a trade, so put it right there," and he grasped my hand and nearly broke every finger I had.

While we were eating lunch, we arranged that the

pony should remain till the day of the races with Hiram, and that I should ride out every morning to give the beast his gallops, Hiram promising to lend me a mule for the purpose. He was camped about four miles off, on a fairly level grass plain, where some good mile of gallop could be got, and by this method we should be able to do all we could in the short time at our disposal without being interfered with, and without letting anybody know, except our immediate friends.

As the time for the races drew nearer and nearer, the local excitement increased in proportion, and the number of tips that were flying about at "cocktail time," was worthy of some great classic event. Every clerk in a dry goods store had an animal entered, and knew (for the first time in his life) the pride of ownership. Most of them were going to ride, and the learned way in which they were wont to discuss the different methods of "getting off," the proper "time to come," "finishing," etc., gave me the impression that if the worst came to the worst, and an epidemic carried off all our well-known jockeys at one fell swoop, the Old Country would have no need to despair, for here were plenty to take their place, and ready to win any races when called upon, either at Newmarket, Doncaster, or Epsom, in the most approved style.

The training ground was perhaps a little peculiar, but, as every one used the same place, it was equal for all parties. It was nothing more nor less than the centre of a sandy road which ran out of the town under my windows. In that country a sandy road or lane does not belie its name; in fact, there is a good deal more sand than road or lane. It is generally nearly knee deep in dust, and the effect of some twenty or thirty animals galloping over or through this is better imagined than described. The nearest approach I can get to it is the appearance of the atmosphere after four or five batteries of artillery have been firing their hardest on a rather damp morning when the smoke hangs and clings to everything. The time at which it was considered the correct thing to train and gallop the racing crocks was in the evening, and the skurry up and down this road was amusing. Naturally, as I had got my work over early in the morning, I could afford to watch the efforts of our adversaries with keen enjoyment.

The secret of our pony was well kept, and we had to submit to any amount of chaff without a murmur. No one imagined that we had one for a moment, and the originator of all the trouble was very jubilant, not to say insulting. We had entered our animal under the name of "Last Chance," and Royal had taken especial pains to see that all the formalities were complied with. The next difficulty that arose was that of kit. I had no colours, no top boots,—breeches, yes, but I could hardly ride a race in those without the other appurtenances. Of course there was no chance of a local Spanish bootist being able to rig up a pair, so I decided to let the tops go, and ride in a pair of brown Peels. The colours we did manage in a way, with the aid of a local tailor, though the cap was a peculiar and awful-looking object that would have been "guyed" even on the stage of a transpontine theatre (and you do see some queer rigs there), or some country travelling circus.

At last the fateful day dawned, and the whole of the population, black, brown, yellow, and white, flocked up to the racecourse. And such a course! The start was made in one of the sandy lanes, which seemed to be the staple commodity of the place. After about half a mile of that, one emerged on to what was called grass, more level certainly, with a few green leaves on the sand, the finish being on the cricket ground in front of the barracks. The grand stand was the quartermaster's house belonging to the West Indian Regiment, built, like they were all, on piles of pitch pine with a verandah. Under the verandah a staging had been erected with chairs placed thereon, and the judge's box was nothing more nor less than an old sentry box which had been dug out from somewhere and placed in the proper position. The course was marked out by poles with coloured pieces of calico nailed on to them, and on the left of the course coming close up were the waters of the Caribbean Sea. Our race was No. 2 on the list—the cup, fifteen dollars entrance, for all ponies, etc., weight for age. The first race was the Merchants' Purse, catch weights, and for that there was a tremendous field. The riders and their varied turn-out were most amusing. Very few of them had boots on at all, and the colours were for the most part left to the imagination. From the stand one could not see the start, so lost half the fun; but when they appeared round the turn, the effect was most sublime and killing. The various competitors were all over the shop, some half off, some in front of the saddle, and some behind, all screaming and yelling like maniacs, and all of course, flogging their best. The man who won the race happened to be a white man attached to one of the dry goods stores, and if he had won the Derby he could not have been more proud of himself as he strutted about after dismounting, to receive the congratulations of his friends. The next race was ours. We had kept our steed well out of sight, and when I went to weigh there were a good many inquiries after my mount, and my friend was most sceptical on the subject of there being an animal at all. He suggested my paying up there and then, and informed me that it was no use my trying to bounce him. However, I said nothing, and the ceremony with the scales being over, I retired behind the barracks, where I found Last Chance waiting, and, to the surprise of every one not in the swim, I mounted, and cantered on to the course.

I think most of them were somewhat taken aback at the appearance of Last Chance, for the pony certainly looked as fit as a fiddle and as hard as nails. Hiram told me he had invested the twenty pounds he had sold the animal for in bets, and was cocksure of winning his money. As we went down to the post which, as I have said, was in the sandy lane, I took stock of the competitors, and very soon saw I had only one to fear, which was a brown, ridden by a coffee planter, who I could see, with half an eye, had been at the same game before in England, and knew thoroughly well what he was about. If I could beat him, I thought I had the race safe, and consequently on the road down I managed to lay my aggressive friend another fifty dollars that I beat him.

The start was given, not by flags, but by firing a pistol; so I determined to keep an eye on the man who had the weapon in charge, and get off if possible, on the flash. We had a long time to wait, owing to two or three of the riders being deposited on the ground suddenly, and without cause; but at last we all got pretty even together, and directly I saw the jet of smoke puff out I gave Last Chance his head, poached a couple of lengths and took the lead. One mile six furlongs was the length of the course, and as soon as I got clear of the ruck I took a pull, and on entering on the so-called grass, I found myself lying third, with the coffee planter on his brown close at my girths, evidently having singled me out to ride against. For the most part the rest began the whooping and halloing tactics, and their faces, as one by one they were forced to fall back, having pumped their nags, were quite a sight. Before we got to the straight there were only four of us in it. The coffee planter, myself, my aggressive friend, and a Creole gentleman. I thought it was about time to begin something, so I played the old, old trick of punishing my boot, which had, I am glad to say, an immediate success on both the Creole and the other man, but not by any means on the rider of the brown. Directly I commenced, the Creole began to shout, and coming up with a rush, knocked the coffee planter clean out of the course. Then for about three hundred yards there was a ding-ding race between himself and the aggressive gent, during which I kept Last Chance going well within himself, and then seeing that they were both "all out," I called on the gallant little pony, and came away from the distance, closely followed by the coffee planter, who had by this time recovered himself. We had a fair race home, but I had the legs of him all the way, and eventually won easy by three lengths, the coffee planter being second.

Lord, how angry our especial friend was; and how he did swear at having to pay up! And how pleased Hiram was! I thought he was going mad the way he whooped and yelled when the words "all right" were given. He had won about thirty pounds; but what seemed to gratify him more than anything was the fact that, partly through his instrumentality, we had managed to beat what he was pleased to term "the critturs."

There was nearly a shindy afterwards about the race; but, having got our money, we were determined not to be bluffed, and the gentleman who had been so particularly sarcastic about our horse and our riding powers, finding abuse of no avail, tried to drown his sorrow and his chagrin in drink, and the last I saw of him that day was being escorted into the town in a speechless condition. The governor was, I think, as pleased as any one, and celebrated our victory in a dinner that night, over which we made very merry. For we all agreed that it was quite worth while waiting a day or two to be able to say that we had got six to four the best of the natives on their own ground. Personally, I was not sorry when it was all over, for in my get-up and scratch kit I did not feel very comfortable; and if some of my friends could have seen me, I fear I should not have heard the last of it for some time, and for many a long day there would have been a standing joke, which the witty portion of my acquaintances in England would have dearly loved to have constantly raked up against me.

CHAPTER III.

ROUGHISH TIMES.

As soon as we got all our traps together and purchased all the necessary supplies, we had everything shipped on board the schooner we had chartered, which was called the *Enterprise*, and after giving over one whole day to the fumigation, and, if possible, extinction of the cockroach element, we ourselves followed. At the last moment, when everything was ready for a start, Henry, the manager, was found to be missing, and though we all went off in different directions all over the town, we never came across him for two hours, when I luckily spied him going into a dry goods store to have a final cocktail with the proprietor thereof. When questioned and roundly abused by us, he admitted that he had been to say good-bye to a certain pretty little Creole lady, and had stopped there philandering longer than he meant to, and having expressed his contrition, he was for that once pardoned, and we commenced to heave up the anchor.

The worthy skipper of our barque was a real good piece of ebony in the shape of a Dominican nigger. Certainly he excelled in the members of his harem; but, having chartered the vessel right out, we sternly refused to allow any lady passengers on board, and, much to his disgust, he had to clear out without. One thing I will say for him: he was a capital sailor, and his language was quite in keeping with his profession. "Hi, you black nigger there forward, why you no overhaul that jib sheet? D—n you, I give you rope's end! Hoist away, you black swabs, d—n lazy pigs, hoist away!" and so on he kept shouting all the time until he got the canvas on her, confiding every now and then to me that "d—n black men no good sailor men," quite forgetting that, of all on board, he was the blackest and most nigger-like.

I thought at one time he was going to throw "Jane," who, it may be remembered, was our cook and body-servant, overboard, when, after receiving a torrent of abuse, that worthy mildly remonstrated, saying that he was not a nigger. "No nigger!" shouted the skipper; "no nigger! d—n you! No, I s'pose not, not so good. You nothing but yellow-bellied girl no 'lowed aboard. I clear you out, d—n you eye!" and then he went for him, and if Jane had not fallen head over heels backwards down the forescuttle, overboard he would have gone. All the skipper said when he came aft again was, "Fancy, I frightened him; guess he found forecastle harder than water;" and then he took hold of the tiller, and, the vessel gathering way, we were off.

After dinner that night we held a council of war, and decided that it would not do to allow the skipper to abuse any of us or our servants, whatever he did with his own crew. So we called him down into the cabin, and having given him a stiff glass of rum-and-water, we told him that he must clap a stopper over his tongue as long as we were on board, which, after another dose of rum, he promised to do, and we parted the best of friends.

About four a.m. I was woke by hearing a boat lowered, and by finding the ship hove to, and on reaching the deck I saw the captain just vanishing round a point, and ourselves brought to opposite a village on one of the kays.

"What the deuce is the meaning of this?" I said to Jane, who was also on deck; and that polite individual informed me that the captain said he was going to pick up another hand ashore, as he was one short, but that in his (Jane's) opinion he had gone to see one of his wives. On hearing this I went below, and awaking Henry, asked him what was to be done. His reply was not satisfactory, for he said that we could do nothing; that it was quite customary on these coasting voyages for the skippers to pull up for an hour or so and to go ashore to see their friends, and that every one of them were alike.

Well, thought I, this is a rum sort of country! And I began to wonder how long the voyage would last if we had to depend entirely on the skipper's will and pleasure, and the number of establishments he maintained along our course. However, there was nothing for it but bed and resignation; so I turned in, and when I woke again at eight we were bowling along merrily about seven knots, as if nothing had happened.

Three times that day we stopped to allow the Dominican to land and "search for another hand," and each time he returned without the required article; but the breeze luckily held, and while we were going we made good way.

About dark we got into a rather ticklish channel with coral reefs on each side, and here our worthy admiral came out in his best colours as a first-rate pilot. Just before going down to dinner I happened to look at my pocket aneroid, which I always carried, and I found that it had gone back a lot since the morning—a fact which evidently did not meet with the skipper's approval when I communicated the intelligence to him.

"By golly, we going to have a norther—soon, too; I

smell him! We crack on and get to Livingston, or we all food for d—n sharks!" he said, and he promptly proceeded to hang up every rag he could, and to sail all he knew.

There was no sign now of searching for another hand, and I could see from his face that he did not half like it. I did not say anything to the others, though Royal and Halifax both remarked that we were spinning along famously; but Jane let the cat out of the bag just as we were finishing the evening meal by exclaiming, "Captain thinks all right; Livingston only ten mile off now; get there before norther bursts."

"Norther!" said Henry, as soon as he heard him; "I hope to Heaven we are not going to have a norther. It's the most dangerous part of the whole coast here, and if it *does* come down we have not the ghost of a chance."

Here was a real pleasant look-out! a dead lea shore with sand banks, coral reefs, and sharks by the score, and every prospect of one of those dreaded South American hurricanes, called "northers," close on the top of us. Of course we all went on deck, and when we got there it was as black as ink. Far away in the distance we could hear a low humming noise, and the sea was beginning to make unpleasantly. How the skipper managed to steer clear of all the obstacles I cannot imagine, for he had nothing to go by except the compass and an occasional glimpse of white water and breakers. As things grew worse he gave up the helm to his mate and went forward into the bows, and then every minute it was, "Port, d—n you, port!" Then, "Starboard, hard a starboard, you d—n nigger!" All the time the moaning, humming noise got louder and louder, and the night, if possible, got darker and darker, till at last a light flashed out some little way off on our starboard bow, high up on a cliff.

"Tank the Lud, there's Livingston!" shouted the skipper, running aft, and then roared, "All hands shorten sail, d—n lazy pigs; shorten sail!" Off came the foresail and outer jib, also the topsails, and we all worked with a will, for it was a case of neck or nothing. We had been running free before, so the spread of canvas did not signify so much; but now the wind had increased tremendously, and we had to round the boat into the harbour on the starboard tack.

"Reef mainsail!" was the next order, and just as we had hardened down the reef the most vivid flash of lightning, accompanied by a deafening peal of thunder, burst out, and for a second the whole coast and sea was lit up. Right astern of us, about three miles away, so far as I could judge, the sea was one vast boiling pot, and the noise of the wind was something terrible. I heard the captain shout, "By golly, we just do it! Look out, massa! In main sheet;" and then, "Port helm, gently, you nigger!" and we were laid right down almost on our beam ends, steering straight for the light. For about ten minutes it was touch and go, and then we rounded in behind the cliff, and shot into the harbour at the mouth of the river just as the storm burst in all its fury. Away went both anchors, and we brought up short, saved by the skin of our teeth.

Of course we were all wet through; and when we went to find Jane, in order to get some dry clothes, we discovered him in the forecastle, almost in a comatose state, livid with fright. However, the judicious applications of shoe-leather administered by Royal brought him to a sense of what was what, and seeing that everything was still, and that we were in port, he bustled about and soon had a change for us and a cup of hot coffee.

We then broached a bottle of rum, which we served

out to all hands, and before it was finished we were boarded by no less a person than Signor el Commandante, who came down from the Cabilldo on the hill to see who and what we were. He was a jolly old scamp, and a friend of Henry's; so we were all the best of pals in five minutes, though, as he talked nothing but Spanish, the conversation was necessarily somewhat limited. One thing he quite understood and appreciated, viz. a glass, or rather glasses, of brandy; and the way he took his liquor was a picture. Before he got too tight to speak, he informed us that we had had a very narrow escape, and that, watching us from the "castle keep," he never thought we should have weathered the storm. It was two a.m. before we got rid of him, and then we sent him off—tight as a drum, but intensely happy, and the proud possessor of a couple of bottles of *eau de vie*, which, drunk as he was, he took care to wrap up and treasure like jewels of untold value.

By seven o'clock the next morning the hurricane had passed, and given place to a beautiful calm day, with little or no wind—just enough to cross the bar with, and to enable us to stem the tide of the river. The skipper had passed his night ashore, so I presume that he had "another hand" concealed somewhere about there, and he came off at five or six a.m. in the best of tempers, and announced his intention of proceeding to Yzabal, the other side of the lake at the head of the river, at eight o'clock.

Before we got under way Signor el Commandante, in return for our overnight present of brandy, sent us down a basket of eggs, an iguana—a species of yellow lizard which, when cooked, is delicious—and a few fowls, together with his earnest wishes for our success and good health. He would have come himself; but he sent word that he was not feeling quite the thing, and begged us to excuse him, the real fact being that he had a most unmistakable attack of hot coppers.

I was much struck when we started up the river by the magnificent scenery. High cliffs on each bow seeming almost to meet at the top, and a perfect garden of flowering shrubs, orchids, and palms, met the eye on every side. As we rounded the first point, we passed a precipitous wall of rock on the right, at the base of which, below high-water mark, were a mass of hieroglyphics carved and stained red and blue. They were reported to be over two thousand years old, and the extraordinary thing about them was that, although washed by every tide, the colours were as fresh and bright as the day on which they were first put on. They were very similar in character to the hieroglyphics found in Egypt, and were said to be of Indian origin, that is, they were supposed to have been done by the aboriginal Indians ages before the Spanish invasion under Cortez. Whether a wandering tribe from the East originally found their way there I leave others to determine. Certainly the similarity is very remarkable in the figures, and it is an interesting question that will not easily be settled. One thing, however, is quite clear, that the method of staining stone by some species of pigment, and thereby rendering it impervious to water and climatic influences, is one that we have entirely lost, but which the ancients had the knowledge of to perfection; and I doubt if anywhere else in the known world such a record of the lost art is to be seen.

As we got further, the stream narrowed, and we were frequently brought up by the overhanging branches of the trees, till at last the wind died clean away, and we were obliged to let go and wait for the sea breeze, which usually came in about midday or a little after.

Henry told us that he had asked the commandante to

send a messenger up overland to Yzabal for our steam launch—a sixty-feet steel boat with which a mail contract with the Government was carried out—and that if the old gentleman only remembered it in the morning, we might expect her down in about twelve hours, and then we should be all right.

It was quite three o'clock in the afternoon before we got the sea breeze, but at last it did come, dead fair, and we were off flying, passing the fort at the junction of the river and lake, where we had to stop and send our papers ashore to be looked at by the Guatemaltecan sergeant in charge. The fort itself from a distance looked very imposing with its guns and white parapets glistening in the sun; but on a nearer approach we found that the parapets, instead of being of stone, were merely "adobe," or mud painted white, and that the guns were somewhat of the description of those carried, or supposed to be carried, by the *Flying Dutchman*. When we were graciously allowed by the authorities to proceed, we got about a quarter of the way across the fresh-water lake, and then it fell a dead flat calm; so we resigned ourselves to fate, and prepared for another night out.

Just about sundown, however, we saw in the horizon the smoke of a steamer, which Henry assured us was the launch, as no other steamboat ever came up that way. Our only fear now was that she would not be up before it was dark, and that she might pass without seeing us, and go flying down the river to Livingston. To avoid this we hoisted a riding light at the schooner's masthead, and I got my big rifle on deck ready to fire signal guns. We watched the smoke gradually getting nearer for about an hour, till at last the darkness came down—there is scarcely any twilight out there—and we lost sight of her. This was the signal to commence firing, and boom went the rifle, followed by shots at intervals of about five minutes. Presently, to our delight, we heard the launch's whistle ring out over the calm water of the lake, and in a short time she was alongside, and her engineer, Johnson, stepped on board.

He, Johnson, was a queer man, and had seen all sorts of life, at one time being engineer on a blockade runner, at another employed on board a revolutionary war vessel, where he got shot through the leg, and on a subsequent occasion it was rumoured that he had seen service on a piratical craft, though, I must confess, he would never own the soft impeachment. Henry had picked him up half-starving at Belize, and had brought him down to the plantations as engineer at thirty dollars a month, and he occupied his spare time in looking after the launch and running the mails. Certainly he was a most excellent engineer and machinist, but had the one failing which is so common in those countries, viz. drink. Poor chap, he lost his life through it afterwards; for, returning one day from a trip with the mails, he anchored off Yzabal, and forgetting to give sufficient scope of chain, a norther came down and sunk the vessel at her moorings; and when we got her up again, there was Johnson, drowned in the cabin, with a bottle of "aquadiente" by his side. He had evidently taken a heavy pull at the bottle as soon as he considered his work over, and had become too drunk and sleepy to help either himself or the boat when the storm came.

But this is anticipating, so I must return to the subject-matter, which was how we were to get to Yzabal. Henry was for embarking then and there in the launch, and leaving the schooner to come on as best she could; but Johnson put a stop to that proceeding by saying, in his Yankee manner—

"Guess that right enough for you, Mr. Henry; you can fix up for the night at the American Counsel. But where, in the name of thunder, air the other gents to bed out?"

So we decided to remain where we were, on board the *Enterprise*, and let the launch tow us after dinner, of which meal Johnson said he was badly in want. Accordingly, when dinner was over, we got out a warp, and, having filled our engineer up with a rummer of grog, away we went, arriving at Yzabal about two in the morning, when we all turned into our berths and slept the sleep of the just.

The following day we were up pretty early, and disembarked all our goods and chattels, which were loaded on mules under the superintendence of the American vice-consul and Henry, and despatched up to the hacienda, eighteen miles off up the hill. Our own personal effects were the last to land, and it was three o'clock in the afternoon before the captain of the schooner had been paid off and we were ready to make a start for our future *dulce domum*. Henry tried very hard to persuade us to postpone our departure till next day, as he said the weather looked threatening, and that we had not allowed sufficient daylight for going up. Although the distance was only eighteen miles, under favourable circumstances the journey took between four and five hours; and in the dark, besides being dangerous, no one could say how long it might not occupy. He might just as well have spared his breath, for we were all bent on making a move, and the more he argued against it the more determined we were to go. Accordingly, Henry had to give way with a very bad grace, and we all mounted and rode off. The first mishap occurred to Halifax, who was riding a particularly vicious mule, which, having gone about four hundred yards, took it into its head to buck in a most determined manner, and promptly shifted Halifax over its head. Luckily no bones were broken, and, beyond being well laughed at, the unfortunate equestrian got no sympathy, but had to remount and follow us as best he could.

For the first hour everything went on swimmingly, and we were all in high spirits, but the road, or rather track, was something awful. Notwithstanding that I had been accustomed to ride in the hills in India over some pretty bad ground, I had never seen anything like this; it was a succession of leaps and bounds from rock to rock with a nasty precipice, in some places, on each side. How the mules kept their footing as they did I can't imagine, and it fairly frightened me out of my life; nor was I singular in this respect, for both Royal and Halifax were hanging on for dear life, expecting every moment to go over the side. Henry, too, endeavoured to make things more pleasant by saying, "Oh, this is nothing; it is far worse up higher!" Just at the very worst part it became suddenly quite dark, and began to pour torrents of rain, as only it can rain in the tropics, and for the next five hours we were continually picking up the pieces. The only thing that cheered us at all was when the manager came a cropper; then, in the midst of our misery, we *did* laugh, and managed thoroughly to enjoy his discomfiture.

Everything, however, must have an end, and, after close on eight hours, we at last arrived at the hacienda, tired, wet, hungry, bruised, weary and disconsolate. Of course our baggage had not turned up, so there was nothing for it but to take off our soaked things, wrap ourselves in blankets, and stand or sit round the fire. Poor Jane was a sight for the gods; his straw hat, limp and wet, came down on both sides of his head like a large bonnet. He was plastered with mud from head to foot, having been down about twenty times, and was altogether about as wretched as a man could well be. However, he chirped up at the sight of a fire, and was soon bustling about in his blanket getting us something to eat. Our dinner consisted of some tinned soup, some tough beef, and a gallina or garden fowl, washed down with some strong Catalan wine, which, with a cup of coffee, such as you can only get on the spot, and a *chasse* of brandy, made us feel as fit as fiddles, and quite put the thoughts of our recent misery out of our head. We were all of us very glad to turn in though, after we had cleaned our guns, and every one was asleep in a twinkling. Had we not all been roused up by shrieks from Halifax that he was being murdered, we might have had a decent night's rest; but about two o'clock he began to yell blue ruin, and, on striking a light, we found the cause of the disturbance to be a young calf which had walked in through the verandah and started to lick Halifax's face, thereby frightening him to death. We were, I confess, not otherwise than "a merry family," for the hacienda was only one story high, with a high pent roof and an open verandah all round, so that the fowls of the air and the beasts of the field considered it quite as much their house as ours, and occupied it quite as freely. The playful scorpion, too, was not unknown, and though during the time I was out there none of us ever got stung, we had some narrow shaves, and I learnt to detest the beasts heartily.

The next morning we were woke up by the sounds of the unloading of baggage, and, getting up, we found that the animals had all arrived safe and sound, having sheltered in a hut half-way during the storm. Oh, how stiff we all were! I thought I should never be able to move again, as I sat on my bed sipping my morning chocolate; but at last I managed to struggle up, and essayed to get into a grass hammock hung in the verandah. Of course the beastly thing rolled up like a rope, and deposited me on the floor. I had not learnt the knack of getting into it, and it consequently resented the intrusion in that forcible manner. However, I am glad to say I was not the only one, for I had the satisfaction of seeing first Royal, and then Halifax, perform the same acrobatic feat (they had not been present when I tried), and their faces of mingled pain and astonishment as they stood, one after the other, rubbing their heads and looking at the refractory hammock, fully compensated me for the big lumps on my own cranium, and filled me with that unholy joy which we are all so apt to feel when others are served the same as ourselves. Grass hammocks, if not properly managed, are snares and delusions—on that we were all unanimous. But once was quite enough for me to be caught, and before I ventured again I took the precaution of taking lessons in the art of getting into the thing, so that it should not be able a second time to make a fool of me.

CHAPTER IV.

OUR FIRST SHOOT.

THE whole of the day following our awful *trajet* up to the hacienda we spent in recruiting ourselves and in making preparations for our first shoot. The major domo of the estate—who, by the way, was a captain in the Guatemala army, and a great pot in his own estimation—came down about noon, and there was a pow-wow or council of war held there and then as to how things were to be carried out. After a long discussion it was decided that the sport should take the form of a beat. We were to be posted in the most likely places, and the major domo was to enlist all the men he could from far and near, and start them off early to form a circle of some miles, and to beat, on a given signal, inwards towards the guns. When everything was definitely settled, and the major domo's heart made glad with a tot of aquadiente, he retired, and we proceeded to overhaul our shooting irons and get ready for the morrow.

Suddenly I asked Henry what there was for dinner, and, to my dismay, he replied that he did not know if there was anything in the place. It appeared that they only killed meat once a week, and that there was some left of the last batch. Moreover, our supplies of pork, etc., had not come up yet. This would not do at all, I thought; so I hailed Jane, who was out in the kitchen, and interrogated him. I found he had ordered some meat for the next day, but, beyond a fowl, had nothing else. As the fowl was at that moment running about, it looked very much as if we were doomed to the old dâk bungalow fare, which I did not quite relish; so I got my gun, slipped on my long boots, and went out to see what I could get. I had to take one of the plantation hands with me in case I lost my way, but for any other purpose save as guide he was not likely to be of much use; for, besides being no sportsman, he was utterly unable to speak a word of English—and I was equally at sea when it came to the language of Old Castile.

The first thing I saw after leaving the hacienda was a flight of green parrots, and I promptly bagged a couple right and left, which the man retrieved. Then I got two turtle doves—I am ashamed to say they were feeding on the ground, where I shot them both in a most unsportsmanlike way, sitting—and they were gathered. After that I tried for a long time to make the man understand that I wished to go to the river; but for the life of me I could not manage it, till at last I hit on the word "Rio," and the trick was done. The river I found was broad and shallow, but on both sides there was a bit of swampy ground, and some pools wherein I saw visions of duck. I wished that either Royal or Halifax had been with me, because I kept on putting up snipe out of shot, and two of us could have got quite enough for dinner. Anyway, I secured three couple, and coming across the river toward home I "downed" a duck. So my return to the hacienda was greeted with enthusiasm, and Jane's heart was once more full of joy at the prospect of being able to turn out something for dinner besides the tough old fowl. In fact, we had quite a feast, and smoked our cigars afterwards with that feeling of rest and contentment which is so plainly indicative of repletion.

As it was to be an early start, we turned in soon in order to get a good night's rest. Halifax and Royal, during my absence on the foraging expedition, had carefully kicked all the fowls, calves, etc., out of the house, and had put up a barricade of netting to prevent them coming in again, so we thought that on this occasion we were bound to be all right. Fond delusion! We had not been asleep more than an hour or so, when we were all roused out by the devil's own row in the farmyard, which seemed to proceed from a large quince tree in front of the hacienda. Such a flapping and screaming I never heard; and as Henry had told us that he had been losing a lot of his chickens lately, of course we all naturally concluded that there was some one up the tree come after the fowls who roosted there, and whose numbers had been augmented by the contingent Halifax and Royal had turned out of our sleeping apartment. Accordingly, out we all bundled, and slipping on the first things that came to hand, seized our six-shooters and sallied forth. As we got outside into the verandah, we saw, by the light of the moon, an animal slip down the tree and make the best of its way across the open. "Eugh at him, Lion!" shouted Halifax to the bloodhound; and then crack! crack! went everybody's pistol, while we all started to run our best pace after the dog, who was well on the track. Whip! came a bullet into the ground close to my legs; ping! sung another not a hundred miles from my ear; and flop! went a third into a tree within an inch of poor Lion.

"For Heaven's sake cease firing!" I shouted; "somebody will get shot directly." But I might have spared my voice, for no one paid the smallest attention, and they all kept whooping and halloing like demons, loosing off their pistols (presumably at the flying animal) every second.

Why no one was shot I can't imagine, for it was as bad as a general action; and as I caught the contagion, and began to shout and yell and shoot the same as everybody else, I could not complain. At one moment I thought I had been hit; for, running along full pelt after Lion, I caught my foot in something and turned a regular somersault, coming down on my head with a bang that nearly stunned me. At last we ran the beast to ground in a hole under a tree, and I remained with Lion to guard the spot, while Henry and the others went back to the house for spades and axes.

Henry, by the way, had come out in slippers, which, of course, he had lost; and, instead of a pistol, he had snatched up a "machete," or long knife, which he brandished about recklessly over his head as he went hopping along on his bare feet. I think, perhaps, he was more dangerous than any one; for, being a very tall man, with long arms, and not looking the least where he was going to, it was even betting that he took somebody's head off in one of his wild flourishes with the machete.

However, as I have said, no accident happened, and on the return of the mining party we commenced to dig the beast out. About ten minutes sufficed to make a fairly large opening, through which we saw a pair of eyes gleaming, and at which we all three fired. There was a bound, a scuffle, and Lion appeared dragging out of the hole a large opossum, who had been the despoiler of the hen-roost. We skinned the animal there and then; and I confess I was very glad to find myself safe once more in my couch, without being full of lead and with my head still on my shoulders. I still possess the 'possum's skin, and whenever I look at it I am inclined to treat it with almost as much veneration as I should the V.C., by reason of the heavy fire I went through in order to obtain it.

It seemed to me as if I had only just turned round in my bed when I was woke up a second time by the sound of a mule galloping up to the verandah, and the clanking of a pair of long Mexican spurs. This proved to be the major domo, who, hearing the fusilade, and thinking that a revolution had broken out (by no means an uncommon occurrence in that country), and that we were all being murdered, had ridden over from the sugar plantation to see what on earth was the matter, and, if necessary, to collect the fragments that might remain. As we found that it only wanted an hour to the time we had arranged to make a start, we kicked up Jane (the artful gentleman had kept himself snug all the time we were at war with the wild beast), and told him to bustle up with our coffee and breakfast, while we proceeded to make our toilet. The first act of the toilet was to saddle up the mules and to ride down to the river for a dip, where the cold water and the stimulating effects of the common or garden sandfly soon made us all wide awake, and ready for our early meal.

The major domo informed us that the men, under two estate corporals, had started overnight to form the cordon of beaters, and that he had arranged the signal to commence, which was the lighting of a fire under a gigantic mahogany-tree, which stood on a hill and could be seen as a landmark for miles round. As soon as breakfast was over we mounted our respective mules, with our rifles slung across our backs, and started off for the rendezvous. A beautiful ride of about an hour under an avenue of kahoon palms, brought us to a lovely valley, where the major domo proposed to place the guns. It was certainly a lovely spot, with a stream running down the centre, and hills rising abruptly on either side. The freshly-turned earth on each bank of the stream showed plainly that if there was nothing else there were plenty of pig about; and deep down in the forest we could hear the occasional bark of a deer, and the infernal chattering of the laughing monkeys.

Royal was posted on the left bank, about fifty yards up the hill, in an open space behind a large cotton tree, from whence he could command a good sweep in front and on each side, Halifax occupying a similar position on the opposite side. My post was on a rock in the middle of the stream, from which point I could take charge of the head of the gorge, and close on a hundred yards on each flank. I was a little in advance of the other two guns; and on my left was Henry, who being, as he said, a poor shot, took the worst place of the lot. As soon as the disposition of the guns had been made to the major domo's satisfaction, he rode off to the mahogany tree to give the required signal, and for a quarter of an hour or twenty minutes we were left to our own devices, and silence reigned supreme. At the end of that time we could see a thin curl of smoke rising straight up into the morning air, and directly after the sound of the beat commenced. If we had not heard the beaters, we should have been able to note the exact instant that they commenced by the hundreds of parrots and macaws that came screeching over our heads, followed by a whole tribe of monkeys, who, from their chattering, evidently were not accustomed to be so rudely disturbed, and could not make out what the deuce it all meant.

The next thing that appeared was a sounder of pig, which passed close to Henry on my left, but which, for some reason best known to himself, he omitted to pull at. However, the old boar went crashing along to Royal, and coming out into the open about thirty yards from him, received his quietus in the shape of an explosive shell from the right barrel of his express rifle, and so gave Royal (save and excepting the 'possum) the honour and glory of first blood in the virgin forest of Central America. Halifax had a snap-shot at some pig also, but failed to make bacon of any of them much to his disgust, though he swore positively afterwards that he had knocked an immense beast over. By this time the circle was drawing closer, and the tribe of monkeys increased in size, as also did the flocks of birds. Suddenly from out of the forest, right in front of me, walked a stag, with its head up, and evidently scenting danger, as it stopped for a second or two to sniff the air. Taking a careful aim, I pulled, and had the satisfaction of hearing my bullet go home, just as Henry's rifle rang out on my left. To make up for not firing at the pig, he had had a smack right across me, and, of course, had missed; but had I been a second later in firing, he would have spoilt my shot completely. The deer, however, was not killed, for on receiving my bullet he gave a tremendous bound into the bush, falling on his knees, and then staggering up was about to make off, when a lucky snap-shot with my second barrel finished him, and in an instant Lion, who had been crouched at my feet perfectly quiet all the time, was at his throat. I was just about to vacate my post and wade across the stream to where the scuffle was going on, when Henry shouted to me that the bearers were yelling on the right that a tiger was afoot. Sure enough there was a tremendous row going on, and everybody was on the tiptoe of expectation, for we could not tell where the jaguar (the Central American tiger) would break. We knew that the brute was coming our way from the ever-increasing din made by the beaters on the right flank, and I hoped he might present himself at the head of the valley, in which case we should most likely all have a chance of a shot. As the circle closed the uproar got louder and louder, and at last the jaguar bounded out just where I had hoped he might. The four of us caught sight of him at the same time, and the four rifles rang out as one, the united reports being followed by a most awe-inspiring snarl and charge on the part of the jaguar, which showed that, at all events, some one had got home. Straight up the right bank of the stream he came towards Halifax, and I was just going to let go my second barrel when Henry, who was quite mad with excitement, gave a loud shout, and plunging into the water made for my rock.

Now it so happened that just underneath the said rock the water deepened into a pool, into which Henry suddenly flopped with a yell, and finding himself going under he threw out one of his long arms and clutched me by the legs. I had just time to say, "What the devil——" (I was going to say, "are you doing," but had not time to complete my sentence), when head over heels he pulled me souse into the brook, my rifle going off at the same moment in the air. There we were both floundering about in the water, and though luckily I did not get out of my depth, I was in a jolly rage at losing my shot, and getting a thorough ducking through Henry's idiotcy. To make matters more comfortable, the bloodhound Lion, who had witnessed the catastrophe from the bank, came blundering in after us, and of course I thought it was the jaguar at least, and got a fright fit to take the hair off my head.

By the time we all three—Henry, self and Lion—had scrambled out, Royal and Halifax had given "the tiger" the finishing stroke, so there was nothing left for me but to open the floodgates of my wrath upon Henry. However, he presented such a lengthy, woe-begone, dripping appearance, and was so profuse and humble in his apologies, that my anger vanished, and I burst into an uncontrollable fit of laughter, in which both Royal and Halifax joined. Just as the beaters emerged from the forest, a mountain cow broke across to the right, and Halifax covered himself with glory by making a snap-shot at about a hundred and fifty yards, which bowled the animal over stone dead. This ended the beat for the day, for it was too late to send the men off for another, and as I was soaking wet I did not see the fun of sitting about in my sopping clothes, and running the chance of a bout of fever. So after making up the bag, which consisted of a boar, a stag, the jaguar, and a mountain cow, I took a good pull at the brandy flask, and, mounting our mules, we made the best of our way back to the hacienda, leaving the corporals to bring the game along after us.

I have no hesitation in saying that we had exceptionally good luck, for it is almost impossible to beat the virgin forest with any hopes of success; and we might have tried day after day without getting, perhaps, a shot. The major domo was intensely pleased, as he naturally took a good deal of credit to himself for the way in which he had organized the beat and disposed of the forces at his command. We were, on the other hand, nothing loath to accord him all praise, for we had had a first-rate day's sport, and were quite as satisfied and pleased as he was himself.

It was early in the afternoon when we got back to the hacienda, and we were all pretty hungry. I know I did full justice to some food which Jane had got ready; and as soon as I had changed my wet things, and well cleaned my rifle locks and all, for it had been under water, the rest of the men under the corporals turned up, bearing with them the spoils of the day. Lunch over, we commenced to skin the animals, while Henry and the major domo settled up with the beaters, who, as soon as the ceremony was completed, dispersed to their respective homes. Later on Johnson, the engineer, arrived from Yzabal with the mails, and a telegram for Henry from the city of Guatemala. Oddly enough, although there were no roads, and, ten miles outside the capital, very little civilization, there was a Government telegraph right through the country from both the Atlantic and Pacific coasts, and the price of messages was quite reasonable. The contents of the telegram Henry found would necessitate his going to the city shortly, a ride of about two hundred miles; and as we all intended to go up there sooner or later, we agreed to accompany him at the end of the following week, and meanwhile to have as much shooting *chez nous* as we could get before making a start.

The major domo was very anxious for us to go out and sleep at a place on the property called "Los Idoles," where there were some old Indian idols, described in Steven's work as the idols of Quirigua, and where it was rumoured buried treasure existed. We were to start one day, shoot in the evening by "blazing" deer, sleep there, and after a beat the next morning, return. We agreed to come down to the sugar plantations the next morning and discuss the question after a look round the place. With no little trouble, at last we got rid of the gallant army captain, and having digested our dinner and smoked the calumet of peace, we prepared to go to roost. Having been hunting the opossum the great part of the previous night, and also having a fair day's work, we were all pretty tired, and it did not take us long to get to sleep, in which we were happily undisturbed; my first return to consciousness being when Jane came in the early morning with the matutinal chocolate, and also to say that the mules were ready saddled outside to take us down for a bathe in the river, and only awaited orders.

CHAPTER V.

"LOS IDOLES."

As soon as the whole party were roused out of bed we all adjourned to take our matutinal dip in the river, and, mounting the mules, we rode off pretty much in nature's garb, that is to say, with only a pair of breeches, slippers, and a towel apiece. As we neared the bathing place, the demon of mischief seized Royal, and I saw him dismount and tear up a long sapling, to the end of which he affixed something, and then, remounting, rode up astern of Henry, who was leading the cavalcade. I knew that there was some devilment up, by the way Royal kept on chuckling to himself, but what it was I could not imagine till, just as we arrived on the bank of the river, he suddenly couched his wand, and, carrying it lance fashion, ran a tilt against the manager's mule. Now Henry, who was very tall and very thin (we christened him Don Quixote), was by no means a brilliant equestrian, and the moment the mule felt the effect of Royal's lance, which he had armed at the end with a long thorn, the brute gave a mad plunge, which threw poor Henry on to its neck. Another application of the lance produced another plunge, and then souse went the mule and his rider into the river, Royal at the same moment ridding himself of his compromising weapon. Of course he was the loudest in his proffers of assistance and his expressions of sympathy to Henry, who, having lost both his slippers, was doing his best to fish them up from the bottom, and who, every time he emerged from an unsuccessful dive, presented a most woe-begone and ludicrous appearance. It had all happened so suddenly, that Henry had not the remotest suspicion as to how it came about, and consequently vented his wrath on the mule, who was doing its level best to scramble out, and who resented being caught by the tail, anathematized, and hammered, by nearly braining Henry with a couple of vicious kicks. Luckily, however, there was no harm done, and, having handed the mules over to the ariero who had accompanied us, we all jumped in and between us managed to find the lost slippers, and to hustle the bewildered manager up the bank. It was all we could do to keep our countenances at breakfast though, for, all through the meal, Henry kept on calling down the vengeance of the gods on the innocent mule, and vowing that he would get rid of it on the first occasion that offered.

Breakfast over, and a cigar smoked, it was time to be off to the plantations to have a look round and to see the worthy major domo about our projected trip to the idols. The sugar plantations were some little way from the hacienda, and by the time we arrived there the sun was beginning to make itself felt, so we were not sorry to get into the shade of the major domo's house and have a drink of fresh cane juice and vinegar. Royal struck work here, and vowed he would not go a step further; so Halifax and myself went round the place with Don Quixote and the major domo, and were further initiated into the mysteries of making sugar—an industry, by the way, that was, as I have said before, at that time by no means a paying one. When we had finished, and Henry had given a certain number of orders, which, being in

Spanish, I did not understand, we came back to the house to find Royal fast asleep—a proceeding that we immediately nipped in the bud, much to his disgust.

Then the major domo went out to find two corporals, and, on his return, we formed ourselves into a committee of ways and means to arrange the details of our expedition. It was generally admitted by the cognoscenti that the two corporals would have to start early in the afternoon with a sufficient retinue to cut a way through the forest to the idols from the river some four miles down. We were to start the next morning at three a.m. or before, and to go down in canoes to where the path commenced, sending the mules on over night. Here two of the guns raised a preliminary objection. Both Royal and Halifax said that they would be d—d if they were going to turn out in the middle of the night to make one of a water party. After a long and heated argument, however, they were talked over, and very reluctantly consented to the proposed arrangement, swearing all the time that it was rot, and that we had much better make a two days' journey of it than get up at such an ungodly hour. I at first was inclined to their opinion; but the major domo said that none of the men would go there at night, and would only work in the daylight, and that we should never get through the forest on mules if we attempted to do so after sundown. He also informed us that the natives had a superstitious dread of the place, and, unless we were present, not a soul would camp there. They had a tradition that there was a buried treasure, and that "the giants" had placed Los Idoles there to guard it, and consequently not a man would try and unearth the loot, nor would they stay there at night if they could help it, for fear of the said "giants." "Of course," said the major domo, with grandiose superiority, "we all know better; but the superstitions of these poor ignorant men must be respected." I am convinced though, for all his fine speeches, that he himself was just as superstitious and frightened as any one of "the poor ignorant men," and, equally with them, believed in "the giants." The moment the palaver was over, and everything definitely settled, we galloped back to the hacienda to get our traps ready, and to break the news gently to Jane that he would have to accompany us in the early morning, and would also have to submit his beauteous person to the malign influence of the genii of "Los Idoles."

I could see that the unfortunate being did not at all like the prospect, and was frightened out of his wits; but as the only alternative given him was to go off that afternoon and await our arrival, he said he would sooner accompany us, and that as long as we were there he was sure that he would be safe from "the giants." Almost before we had selected our things and put them together, the corporal turned up with a couple of mules, on which were packed some cooking utensils, blankets done up in waterproof sheeting, and provisions, to say nothing of rifles and ammunition; and, as soon as they were ready, he joined the rest of the cavalcade and away they went, while we adjourned to make an early dinner.

It was just before this meal that I gained my first experience of shopkeeping. One room on the right of the hacienda had been turned into a regular village shop, where everything under the sun was kept for the use of the hands on the estate, from pickled pork to a ball of string, and this was "run" something on the truck system, *i.e.* whatever they bought was chalked up against them and deducted from their wages. Henry, Halifax and Royal, had gone to have a tub and change their clothes before dinner, and I was finishing the cleaning of my gun in the verandah, when I was surprised by the appearance of six or seven women, who, after some time, made me understand that they had come to buy some coffee, salt, and thread. There was no one else to serve out the goods, unless Henry turned out *in puris naturalibus;* so there I was, obliged to do shopkeeper, and, in the best Spanish I could muster, to officiate at the counter and assure the good ladies that I had an excellent "line" in this, that, or the other. Of course I had to shout to Henry to know what to charge, and also to find out against whom I was to enter the purchases; but I got through somehow, and gained a novel and amusing experience in the intricacies of sale and barter. I had just finished my commercial transactions when Jane announced dinner, and I had to hurry up to be ready. None of us stopped long after the evening meal. Just a cigar, and then bed was the order, and by nine o'clock we were all sound asleep.

It was somewhere about 2.30 a.m. when we were roused out and very unwillingly made to "show a leg." Indeed, I began to despair of ever getting Halifax and Royal up; but at last it was effected, and after a prodigious amount of stamping about, combined with bad language, we were all dressed and ready for a cup of coffee before starting. As soon as the coffee was finished, everybody, Jane included, was made to have a nip of brandy with a couple of grains of quinine in it to keep off malaria, and then, shouldering our guns, we made a move to walk down to where the boats were waiting for us. Our hammocks (by the way, we had mastered the wiles of the grass hammock by this time), and other *impedimenta* had gone on, so we were in light marching order, and had only ourselves and guns to look after. However, I found that quite enough, for it was almost dark, and walking through the forest, if one once got off the path, was not the easiest matter in the world.

On reaching the plantations by the river, we found the major domo all ready waiting with the canoes, and after the usual salutations and greetings, we delivered ourselves into his hands and embarked. Just as we were about to shove off, a tremendous hullaballo occurred among the rushes and maize stalks which fringed the river, and, with a bound and a splash, Lion, the Cuban bloodhound, dashed into the water and tried to get into my canoe, nearly upsetting the "whole kaboodle" in his frantic endeavours. The poor brute had been left behind by mistake, and forgotten in the early departure; but, having managed to break loose, he had tracked us down, and was wild with joy. After a good deal of trouble, and by carefully jamming the canoe against the bank, we eventually got him on board and persuaded him to lie down in the bows, and then we actually did make a start. For the first half mile or more we had to paddle through a sort of backwater choke-full of snags and weed, and consequently our pace was very slow. Not that that in itself mattered so much, for we were fairly up to time and had the whole day before us; but, unfortunately, it gave ample opportunity for all the mosquitoes, and every other winged abomination that could bite or sting, to attack us. All one could do was to sit still and try and bear it, smoke all one knew, slap and swear one's best—I wonder the language used did not sink the canoes. Royal kept on lamenting his own "d—d idiotcy for getting up at cockcrow to be eaten alive," and wishing himself anywhere but where he was; and in these remarks and sentiments he was ably seconded by Halifax.

There was not much sympathy to be got out of either

Don Quixote or the major domo, both of whom seemed to be uninviting subjects from some reason or other, for they suffered almost perfect immunity from attack. The former merely told us that we should soon get used to it, while the latter laughed and said, "Es nada, signor" ("This is nothing"); and then gave us a long account of how, if we wanted to know what mosquitoes were, the place to go to would be the bar at the mouth of the river. Happily, as soon as we were out of the snaggy backwater, we got into midstream, where the brutes retired, and we went down flying and in peace. In about an hour's time, after getting into the river proper, we arrived at our destination, and, on disembarking, found our riding mules all ready for us, and a corporal and some men hard at work with their machetes, cutting out a path for us through the bush. The sun was just beginning to think of getting up, and the mist was rolling away when we landed, so that things looked a little more cheerful, and when Jane proposed that we should let him brew a cup of coffee (he had had the forethought to bring all the necessary materials with him) before starting, the proposition was carried *nem. con.*, and we called a halt until the fire was lighted and the comforting beverage duly prepared.

As soon as this ceremony was over, we packed up the things, mounted our mules, and, preceded by the men cutting the path, rode off in the direction of the idols. Our pace was of necessity very slow, for we could only move as fast as the men could cut. It was absolutely impossible to force one's way through the tangle of undergrowth, long grass, and creepers that every now and again formed a barrier like a thick wall. How the men managed to slice it down with their machetes was marvellous. They seemed to make no more of it than a mower would of an ordinary swath in a hayfield, and, no matter what it was, grass, creeper, or young tree, the knife went through it like a pat of butter, and the way was opened. Hot is no word for what it was as the day wore on. Not so much from the sun, for the big forest trees kept that off; but there was not a breath of air to be got, and after three hours of it we all felt more or less cooked. As we were about *in extremis*, we suddenly emerged on a beautiful green open space surrounded by mahogany and other trees, with a little stream rippling through the centre of the fairy-like dell. Here we could feel the cool breeze at last, and simultaneously the same idea struck everybody, and in a twinkling the whole party were dismounted and seated on the mossy bank of the brook. It was a perfect paradise, and, after our choking experiences of the last few hours, it seemed all the more beautiful. Moreover, a second surprise was in store for us, and one which crowned Jane with everlasting glory, for he came softly up to me and said—

"If gentlemen wait here half hour, I get breakfast?"

"Breakfast?" I asked. "Where the devil are you going to get that from? There was only some whisky and sandwiches ordered. You don't call that breakfast?"

"Master come with me a moment," was all he replied, and, on my following him, he took me behind a large tree, where, to my astonishment, I found a chicken, some eggs, bread, butter, plates, cups, etc., which the worthy fellow had carried packed up in a bundle, with a saucepan and frying-pan, and in two minutes he had improvised an open range, and the water was boiling, the eggs cooking, and the coffee brewing before I had recovered myself.

When I returned to the others and told them about it, they all voted Jane a crown of laurels, though I fancy the little present, in the shape of dollars, which we presented him with there and then, found more favour in his eyes than any amount of floral or leafy tributes would have done. Anyway, he was immensely pleased with both the dollars and himself, and turned us out a first-rate breakfast that was most acceptable. We were allowed to smoke a cigar in peace afterwards; and then the major domo said we must be moving, as we still had some way to go, and so we had to re-mount and leave our haven of rest with regret.

It was about three o'clock in the afternoon when we reached "Los Idoles," and pretty well tired we all were, but we found everything ready for us—a temporary house of boughs and leaves made, fires all lighted, and our hammocks slung, besides a long shed for the men. The Caribs are very clever at this sort of thing, and had run up our camp in about three hours, we were told. Our leafy bower was exactly facing the idols, which were three (or four, I forget which) large, upright blocks of stone, wonderfully covered with hieroglyphics and curious figures on every side, and surmounted with faces of the most villainous expression it has ever been my lot to see. They were arranged evidently on some plan, and in a semicircle, with a sacrificial altar in the centre. What rites were carried on there in the ancient days, or by whom, or by what race they were set up, is, and must remain, a mystery always, unless some one be found to read the hieroglyphics, or something is discovered elsewhere that will throw fresh light on them.

They are supposed to be over two thousand years old, and, beyond the tradition of the buried treasure and the giants, nothing is known about them. Deep down in the middle of an almost impenetrable virgin forest, with no road, ruins, or even water near by—by water, I mean any river of any size; there was only a small stream—there they have stood for ages, calm and undisturbed, with the carving almost as good as the day on which they were first raised. I have a theory—but it is only a theory—that at some time in that region there was a city of some magnitude which has been either destroyed by earthquake or buried by volcanic eruption, and which now lies overgrown by the growth of centuries, and that these idols were connected with its religion, and were erected at some little distance therefrom. The curious and puzzling thing about them, however, is the similarity in the heiroglyphics to those of ancient Chaldeans or Egyptians, and yet not sufficiently alike to be deciphered. That they were made by savages, or men to whom civilization was a sealed book, is out of the question. There is far too much method in arrangement, and far too much artistic power displayed in construction, for that theory to hold good. Whoever or whatever race set those idols up had some knowledge of the sculptor's art, some idea of transmitting their history to posterity, and certainly a form of religion in which sacrificial offerings played a conspicuous part. Beyond this, everything is mere conjecture, and lost in the dim ages of the past. Nevertheless, it gave me many an hour's thought, and interested me very deeply.

After carefully inspecting the idols, and having unpacked our rifles, ammunition, etc., we all retired to our respective hammocks, and dedicated the next two hours to the god of sleep. Soon after six o'clock, though, we had to turn out for dinner and finally arrange the proceedings for the evening's "blazing." Henry informed us at dinner that he felt far too tired to go out, but would stay behind with Lion to guard the camp, and, in the event of our being lost in the forest, he could guide us there by firing a gun at intervals.

Royal, Halifax, and myself, therefore, as the "shades

of evening" closed in, started with the major domo and two corporals, besides three Caribs carrying torches, and struck right into the virgin forest. Before we lost sight of the camp, I took the precaution to set the bearings by my pocket compass, and from time to time, as we stumbled along over roots and through all sorts of undergrowth, I gave a glance at it to note our course. Halifax, being of a scientific turn of mind, was anxious to take an observation by star, with all the paraphernalia of sextant, false horizon, etc., but this was promptly vetoed as being unnecessary, and as likely to occupy half the night. As we got deeper and deeper into the silent forest, I noticed every now and again one of the Caribs would "blaze" a tree, *i.e.* take a long slice of bark off with his machete in order to direct our return. Occasionally a rustle in the bush on our flanks showed us that some animal had been disturbed, and the monotony of the proceedings was frequently varied by one of the party tripping up over a creeper and falling head over heels.

At last we arrived at the bed of an old water-course, where in places the water had collected in pools, and here it was proposed that we should commence operations. Accordingly, Royal was put on the right flank, Halifax on the left, and the major domo and myself in the middle. Alongside of each gun was placed a Carib bearing a lighted torch, and the order was to advance slowly in line with as little noise as possible. Strict injunctions were given to all and singular, that on no account was a shot to be fired down the line or in rear, but only directly in front. As our line extended nearly half a mile, and no one gun could see the other, this was a very necessary precaution, more especially as it would be absolutely impossible to keep abreast where one of us might find himself advancing in an open space, whilst another would be forced to cut his way through with a machete. On the outskirts of each flank, starting from the water-course, went a corporal whose duty it was to blaze the trees, and when the sport was over every one was to return, as near as possible, on his tracks and *rendezvous* at the starting-point. In addition to the corporals and Caribs who were with the guns, there were six or seven men in rear in order to carry any game that might be shot, and as all of us, *i.e.* Royal, Halifax, and self, carried a loud-sounding whistle apiece, there was little chance of our being lost. Directly all the preliminaries were satisfactorily arranged, at a given signal from the major domo we all moved silently forward.

For about a quarter of an hour nothing occurred, and then suddenly Royal's rifle rang out on the right, and almost at the same moment my Carib with the torch came to a dead stop, and I saw in front of me a pair of glittering eyes, at which I promptly fired, and was rewarded by hearing the thud of the bullet and a heavy fall, showing me that I had got home. A double shot from Halifax on the left, followed by a fiendish snarling yell, gave evidence that he also had seen something, and so we went on. It was awfully tiring work; for what with the darkness and the glare of the torch in our eyes, one could not see a yard before one, and one found one's self just as often prone on mother earth as in an upright position. The next shot I got at eyes I missed, and then we stumbled on a lot of pig, amongst whom was an immense boar. He stopped a second in the full glare of the torch, where I could see him quite plainly as he stood wondering what the sudden light meant, and hesitating whether to charge or no; and, drawing a careful bead on him, I gave him two barrels which promptly converted him into bacon.

By this time the night was well advanced, and, as we had a fairly long tramp back, I gave the signal on my whistle for a retreat, which was answered from each flank. It took us quite an hour to regain the water-course, and then we had to wait for Halifax, who had somehow missed his path, and was only guided by our whistles. When we had all assembled, we found the bag consisted of three deer, a boar, and a tiger cat, which was the author of the fiendish row I had heard. Royal had wounded another animal, what he did not know; but, as he could find no trace except the blood, it could not be reckoned. When we had skinned the animals and taken what we wanted, we made tracks home, and, thanks to the Carib's careful marking of the trees, and my compass, we only got out of the course once. As we neared the camp, a large animal came bounding through the bush, and Halifax was just going to fire, when I saw it was Lion, the Cuban bloodhound, come to meet us, and so shouted to him just in time to save the old doggie's life. He must have winded us from some distance, for we were quite a mile off when he appeared, and he had come a direct line through the bush.

At this juncture every one began to sing out for a drink. We had brought whisky in our flasks, but had forgotten to dilute it, and the question was where were we to find water. However, one of the Caribs, on our wants being made known, soon solved the difficulty by selecting a stout bush rope (a species of creeper) which he cut in two with his machete, and from which issued a stream of pure water, quite cold and good, which, mixed with a drop of the "craythur," pulled us together in no time. These bush ropes, if you happen to know the right ones, always contain water, which they soak up and filter, so that one need never die from thirst if one be "in the know."

About another hour brought us home, where Henry was awaiting our arrival, and very glad he said he was to see us, for we were so late that he was afraid we had missed our way. He told us that Lion, who was lying under his hammock, had suddenly bounded off with a loud bark, and that though he called him back and whistled till he was out of breath, the dog would pay no attention to him, but dashed away into the bush.

Jane had not been idle either in our absence, but had prepared quite a nice supper of cold chicken, which, having devoured and washed down with some whisky and water, we felt all the better for.

It was nearly two in the morning, and we were all ready for bed, as may be imagined; indeed, we were so tired that we decided not to have the drive next day, and right glad I was to tumble into my hammock, from whence I could see the biggest of the idols, as it were, keeping guard over me, and whose hideous face, in the flickering light of the camp fire, seemed, as I dropped asleep, to be bestowing an occasional and patronizing wink.

CHAPTER VI.

BY FLOOD AND FIELD.

I LEFT us comfortably wrapped in our blankets, and safely deposited in our hammocks, wooing the god of sleep, under the shadow of "Los Idoles de Quiriqua." We had agreed *nem. con.* to abandon our drive, so that we might be able to pull ourselves together a bit after the somewhat heavy work of the previous day and night, and had looked forward to an extra hour or so of rest. Vain hope that it was, for, very soon after daylight, the camp began to rouse itself, and the usual "jawbation" amongst the retainers commenced. Added to this, what painters are so fond of calling, "still life" ceased to be still, and the forest resounded with the shrill cry of the macaws, and the chattering of the troops of monkeys. Then the fires were lighted and mules taken away to water, in itself a noisy operation, so that all chances of sleep were at an end, and we had of necessity to do as the Romans did when at Rome, and rouse ourselves. After a wash in a bucket (we could not manage a bath), one felt a little better; but, with the exception of Henry, who had not been blundering through the forest half the night, we were all so stiff that we could hardly move, and sitting down or getting up was a performance of great difficulty and pain. The major domo, like a sensible man, had started off a couple of runners, when we decided to abandon the drive, to the base of operations, viz. the canoes, to say that we should return that afternoon, and to order everything to be in readiness for our arrival, and, early as it was, he seemed particularly anxious to get us *en route* and to have the paraphernalia and *impedimenta* that had to go overland packed and started. Nor where the retainers behindhand in this respect; for although they had passed the night in safety within the sphere of the idols, it was evident that they only attributed their good luck to the presence of the signors, and the fear of "the giants" was still strong upon them.

Accordingly, after an excellent breakfast, in which Jane out-Janed himself, everything was seized upon and loaded up, and by nine a.m. the overland caravan had started for home, and we were left to ourselves. The major domo allowed us one hour's siesta before we had to mount; for, as the road was clear, he calculated we could do the journey to the river under five hours. Personally, I was very grateful for the respite, and, declining with some asperity Halifax's invitation to come out and shoot some oorial (brown birds with beautiful golden tails), which had taken his fancy, I wrapped myself up in my blanket and was sound asleep in forty seconds. By 10.30 a.m. we had all mounted, and, after taking a last look at Los Idoles, we started, Don Quixote and the major domo leading the procession. We halted for half an hour at the stream of the previous day, and had a snack, also filled up the water-bottles, and then, plunging into the thick scrub, we made the best of our way to the river. It took us somewhat longer to reach it, however, than we had calculated, as on one occasion we lost our way trying to make a short cut, and spent nearly an hour wandering about before we struck the path again.

Eventually we arrived at the bank where the canoes were, just as the sun was getting low, and lost no time in embarking. The mules we had ridden had to stay there in charge of the arrieros, as it was ten to one against them finding their way in the dark to the plantation; so, stripping our saddles off and putting them on board, we shoved out into the river, leaving the arrieros busy picketing their charges and making a hut for themselves. Of course, our progress against the stream was a very different matter to coming down, and for some time it was all we could do to hold our own; but we managed, by hugging the bank, to get along somehow. As we rounded the first bend, I saw in the distance a black line along the water, and in a second I made out that they were duck. "Avast paddling!" was the order at once, while we all dived for our guns, and, just as we had got them, whirr came a whole flock right in our faces. They did not see us till they were quite close, and then, directly they caught sight of the canoes, up they went in the air, showing their white breasts and giving us a capital mark. Eight barrels rang out almost simultaneously, and six ducks paid the penalty for their rashness. Of course everybody claimed to have killed their respective couple; but, from former experiences, the conclusion was arrived at that if any one had missed, and somebody must have, the culprit was to be found in the person of Henry. It took us a little time to collect the spoil, and when we had gathered them all the sun had completely disappeared, and, what was worse, a dense miasma-like fog began to roll down the river, which gradually increased in volume, till we could not see ten yards in front of us.

The navigation against the stream was difficult enough in broad daylight, when one was able to take advantage of the slack water, and to avoid the numerous snags with which the river was crowded; but in a fog it became next door to impossible, besides being pretty dangerous. We had not gone far after the fog came down, before the first casualty occurred, and the canoe in which Don Quixote and the major domo were seated, and which was the leading one of the flotilla, ran end on to a snag and commenced to sink. We in the rear could not see what had happened, but could only judge that it was something grave, from the shouts for help which Don Quixote gave out with no uncertain sound. In endeavouring to go to his assistance, my canoe, in which also was Halifax, went upon a sandbank, hard and fast, and Royal's bark was as nearly in the same predicament as makes no matter. My crew, to their credit be it said, promptly jumped overboard and floated us again; but Lion, who occupied his usual position in the bows, seeing every one else get out, thought he ought to follow suit, and bounded into the water as well, giving us thereby a deal of trouble in getting him on board again. By the time we had ranged up alongside of Henry's craft, we found her with her bows stove in and full of water, while the unfortunate manager and his second in command had quite made up their minds that their last hour had come. We had to tranship everything into our canoe, which brought her nearly level with the water, and then to wait till Royal found us, in order to make a fair distribution. After a prodigious amount of shouting and whistling, we at last got him alongside, when I transferred half my shipload to his care, and we proceeded with two canoes, leaving the third to sink at its own sweet will. Three or four hundred yards further on we were both on another sandbank; and so it went on till at last we arrived opposite the plantation, which we could just make out by the lights, dead tired and dripping wet, about eleven o'clock at night. Even then our troubles were not over, for it took us a long time to hit off the back-water and get alongside the landing-place, and both of us were as near as a toucher capsized forcing our way through the weeds in order to arrive at the haven where we would be.

I never shall forget poor Jane's face, when he once more found himself safe on dry land. He had been in a blue funk all the way up, was perished with cold, and the most complete martyr you can possibly imagine, but directly he touched *terra firma*, his whole appearance changed, and he was all for cooking one of the duck for our supper, before we rode up to the hacienda. This, however, did not accord with our views of comfort, as we did not quite see the force of having to wait in our drenched condition, while our *cordon bleu* performed his culinary operations. So we hustled him off on the first mule that was brought, with orders to open a couple of tins of soup and to make a good brew the moment he reached the house. We were not long in following him, and I can answer for it that I have seldom enjoyed a basin of soup so much as I did on that occasion; while some mulled Catalan wine that we compounded afterwards, made us forget all our troubles and look on the rosy side of nature.

When I say that we forgot all our troubles, I am not quite exact, for there was one thing we found on our return which annoyed us exceedingly. It was a telegram which had been forwarded through the city of Guatemala, recalling Royal back to England on urgent business as soon as ever he could start. It was a great disappointment to him, for he had made up his mind to see the capital of the country, and had been looking forward to the expedition for some time. "Anyhow," he used to say: "I suppose, when I get up to Guatemala, I shall be able to get something decent to eat, served on plates, like civilized beings; and I may possibly have some chance of getting a night's rest;" and, when things were extra rough, he would always cheer himself up by saying: "Never mind, I'll make up for it when I get to the city." Now, however, that was at an end, and there was nothing for it but to pack up and go. He was quite furious with Halifax, who chaffingly said: "Well, old man, you'll get some decent food now, and can sleep all the way home," and poured forth such a torrent of dreadful language, that poor old Lion thought some of it at least must apply to him, and slunk away out of sight with his tail between his legs.

We found on calculating, that there was a good week or eight days before the mail left Belize, so that if we could arrange the *trajet* from Yzabal or Livingston to that port, Royal would have plenty of time. The next morning I volunteered to ride down to Yzabal and see what chance there was of a boat, and, much to my delight, Royal insisted on coming with me. We had to make an early start in order to do the job in one day; for although it was only eighteen miles, it took nearly three hours and a half going down, and about four hours and a half to come up again, and we were bound to give the mules a rest before returning. So, shortly after six a.m., we were off, and beyond a cropper apiece through bustling our mules over some bad ground, arrived safely at the American Consulate at Yzabal shortly after 10.30, just in time to help him out with breakfast. We found that there was a schooner going to start for Belize on the following afternoon, and, having interviewed the skipper, we engaged a passage there and then. We tried all we could to persuade him to postpone his departure for a day, as it would be impossible to get Royal and his traps down in time, if he sailed the next afternoon; but he said he could not do it, for love or money, as he had to wait two days at Livingston to load some government stuff, and was bound to be up at Belize in time to catch the mail.

"What the deuce is to be done?" said Royal. "I must go, if I start as I am, without my kit."

I was as much puzzled as he was, till a happy thought struck me, and I exclaimed: "It's all right, we will start in the steam launch the day after to-morrow, run down to Livingston and pick the boat up there. Johnson is bound to go down for the mail."

No sooner thought of than done. We dug out Johnson, the engineer, and told him to have the boat ready with fuel on board (we had to burn wood for the most part), and steam up at the time appointed.

Then having arranged with the American vice-consul to put some food and drink on board, we had a bit of lunch, saddled our mules, and after a "last stirrup cup," set out for our return journey up the hill. Before we arrived at the level plateau, whereon stood the hacienda, it had got pitch dark, and we had to trust to the instinct and sense of our animals to keep us in the right path. I was a little bit in advance of Royal, and was riding along, thinking of nothing in particular, when suddenly my bridle was seized and a loud voice rang out, "Halta!" Oddly enough the vice-consul at luncheon had been telling us that the country was in rather a disturbed state, and laughingly warned us on starting to be careful we were not taken by brigands. In a moment it flashed across me that there was some meaning in his words, and the next instant I had my six-shooter out and levelled at the dark object that was holding back my mule. I was in the very act of pulling, when to my horror I heard Halifax's voice say, "For God's sake, don't shoot!" and instinctively I threw my hand up as the pistol went off. For a few moments I sat there in my saddle trembling like an aspen leaf, while all my blood seemed to turn to ice, and then suddenly to rush back through my veins like molten lead. Another second it would have been too late, and I should have dropped my pal in his tracks, and the bare thought of it quite stunned me. At last, however, to use a Biblical expression, "my tongue was loosed, and I spake," and I called Halifax every name I could think of for being such an arrant fool. After I had finished pouring out my torrents of abuse, he replied—

"My dear old chap, I am awfully sorry; I only did it for a lark, to scare you. Henry and I thought it would be an excellent joke, and I never imagined that you would have drawn so promptly on me."

"Oh!" I said, "Henry thought it would be a good joke, did he! At all events he took jolly good care to keep his own d—d carcase out of harm's way. It would have been an excellent joke if I had put a bullet through you, would not it? and I should most undoubtedly have done so in another second if you had not shouted out. Take my advice once and for all, never try to play a practical joke on an armed man after dark in a lawless country like this, and thank your lucky stars that you are alive at this moment."

Just then Henry, who had heard the shot, came running up to know what was the matter, and both Royal and myself gave him such a dressing that he did not know whether he was standing on his head or his heels. He did not improve matters either by turning sulky, and muttering something about "people not being able to stand chaff," which only got my back up rather more, and brought down a fresh outburst of wrath on his head. Throughout the whole of dinner he would not speak a word; and when I told him that we should want mules to take Royal's things down, he said that they could not be spared. This was coming it a bit too strong, so I had to assert myself and to remind him what his position was in relation to myself, and to inform him that if he did not choose to carry out my orders, I should take steps to find some one who would—a proceeding which seemed to bring him to his senses; for, after a devil of a row, he apologized, and harmony was once more restored.

The next day we were all very busy packing Royal's kit, and the poor old chap went about quite subdued and crestfallen at the idea of leaving us. He was very keen about taking home a skin or two as a trophy to show, so we packed him up the jaguar skin, a deer skin, and a macaw or so, with which he was quite content. He insisted on leaving us all his ammunition and anything that might be of use, and wanted to make me a present of his rifle; but this I firmly refused, so it went in with the rest of his things. That night we had a great farewell dinner, with which Jane took the greatest pains; and we broached a couple of bottles of champagne out of our little store of half a dozen which we had brought up with us from Belize. During dinner it suddenly occurred to Royal to ask how in the name of fortune he was to get on in the way of feeding between Livingston and Belize without a body-servant; for on the coasting schooners all passengers were supposed to provide their own food, and also the individual to cook the same. Indeed, in most cases, it would be impossible to eat anything cooked by the ship's cook, so it was a case of starvation if one had not taken the proper precautions. It had never occurred to any of us before to think of this very necessary adjunct to travel, and here, at the eleventh hour, was our guest about to depart *solus* and comfortless. What was to be done? Why, clearly Jane was the only person who could help us in our dilemma; he might possibly know some one who for a consideration would undertake the post of head-cook and bottle-washer as far as Belize, so we promptly called him in and interrogated him on the subject. Jane thought diligently for some minutes, and then said—

"No, I not know no one, all stranger here; but if massa like, I go with massa Royal so far as Belize, then come back. Manuel, massa Henry's boy, he good cook for hacienda, can do all. No good for sea, but good here."

"That's all very well, Jane," I said, "but when you once get to Belize, how do I know you will ever return? You might go and get married. When you get among the girls there, no knowing what may happen."

"'Pon my word, as a gentleman, I come back," replied Jane; and added, "No me gusta the girls."

So it was eventually decided that Jane was to go, though Royal pointed out that it was still an open question whether Jane was not a girl himself (or herself), and that he or she had not given an undertaking not to marry a man.

By eight the next morning the pack mules were loaded with Royal's things and sent off down the hill, with a note to our friend the American vice-consul to get them on board the launch directly they arrived; and at eleven, Royal and myself mounted, and having drunk a last glass for old lang syne, we rode away together for the last time. Halifax was to have come down with us as far as Yzabal, but unfortunately he had developed (tell it not in Gath) a boil, which utterly precluded his riding. So he was forced to abandon the idea, and to take his farewell at the door of the hacienda.

"Good-bye, old chap—good luck to you—God bless you, old man!" and we cantered off, Royal with a lump in his throat that prevented him from speaking.

When we reached Yzabal we found everything in readiness—all the traps on board, steam up, and, for a wonder, Johnson fairly sober; while, thanks to the consul's kindness, an excellent repast laid out in the cabin. He, the consul, confided to me that there were two bottles of whisky in the locker, and half a dozen bottles of beer, all of which he had carefully put under lock and key, *a cause de* Johnson, so that there was no fear of our starving *en route.*

I elected to dispense with the services of the second hand, as I was capable of taking charge of the engines myself, and thought that five of us would somewhat overcrowd the ship; so, as soon as the anchor was up, we landed him and prepared to steam off. Luckily, as it turned out, just before we started for good, a mail came down from the city, and having taken it on board, we ran up the mail flags. I say luckily, for at that time they had peculiar ideas of customs duty, and wanted to levy a tax on both exports and imports; consequently, if we had not had the Government mails on board, the customs officers would have mulcted us properly over Royal's kit. As it was, they came off in a boat and wanted to search the ship; but in our contract for carrying the mails it was distinctly laid down that with mails on board we were free of the custom-house, so I pointed to the mail flag and refused to allow them on board. This did not suit the gentlemen at all, seemingly, for they did their level best to obtain a footing, and I had to go ahead full speed to get clear of them, leaving them in a few seconds astern gesticulating and vituperating to their hearts' content.

After a good square meal and a tot of grog all round, Johnson included, I made Royal lie down and try to get some sleep, while I steered the vessel across the lake. We had been going about half an hour when Royal emerged from the cabin with the perspiration streaming down his face, and vowed he would never go in there again, the heat being something awful. I just put my nose in, and found it as he had stated; so he coiled up in the cock-pit aft, and was asleep in no time.

We could not get more than about five knots out of the boat with the wood fuel at the best, and it was no easy matter keeping steam at all, so our progress was not very rapid; and after steaming a couple of hours longer, I knocked Royal up to steer, as I could not trust Jane, while I relieved Johnson at the engines, he turning in in the cabin, utterly regardless of the heat.

I had been firing and driving about three-quarters of an hour, and was as hot and tired as I could well be, when suddenly there was a rush of steam and a cessation of movement, and I found that the packing of the slide-valve had given out. "All hands repair damage," was the order, and it took us nearly an hour before we put matters straight and were off again.

More by good luck than good management, we were able to hit off the opening into the river, and steamed past the fort I have described before, bringing up for the night in the bay on the far side. I don't fancy any of us were sorry when the time came for letting go the anchor, for we were all fairly tired out; and after spreading the awning, notwithstanding the mosquitoes, the whole ship's company were soon sound asleep.

As soon as it was light, Johnson started lighting the fires, and Jane compounded some coffee; and about half an hour later we got steam, and, heaving up the anchor, made our way down the river towards Livingston, where we arrived early that afternoon and found the schooner half loaded.

I had not forgotten to bring down with me a couple of bottles of brandy for our friend the commandante, who received us with open arms, and had a couple of bedrooms rigged up for us in no time; celebrating the arrival, by the way of ourselves and the brandy, by getting right royally drunk that evening. I am sorry to say that his example was promptly followed by Johnson, who, till the small hours in the morning, kicked up such a shindy that we thought more than once of putting him into the guard-house. However, before that catastrophe occurred, we had transferred all Royal's baggage to the schooner and our light baggage up to the cabildo, leaving Jane on board to keep guard and watch.

I paid the erring engineer out the next day, though, by starting him off with a couple of men to cut wood for the launch for the return journey; and as he came in smiling about noon with a full load, he must have worked his headache off successfully.

At four o'clock in the afternoon the schooner was ready and hove-short, and the time came to bid Royal a last farewell. I took him on board in a most melancholy frame of mind, and having given Jane his final orders, I left him, and shortly after the schooner got under way and sailed out with a fair wind for Belize.

That evening we got the mails, and I gave orders for

an early start back to Yzabal the following morning, also imposing upon Johnson the necessity of steering clear of fire-water. His heart was gladdened by the arrival of a few bags of coal by the same vessel that brought up the mail, which would enable us to do the return journey in half the time, so he promised faithfully to be on his best behaviour and to have everything ready.

The commandante and myself had another symposium that night, at which he again succumbed to the potency of my brandy, and when I turned in I left him under the table snoring like a pig. Nor did he turn up next morning at five, when I got the launch under way, to bid adieu and a safe journey to his friend and benefactor.

CHAPTER VII.

A TRIAL AND A START.

We had, thanks to the coal, a quick run back to Yzabal, and, on my arrival with the mail, I found both Halifax and Henry waiting for me at the American Consulate. Directly Henry saw me, he told me that there had been the deuce and all to pay about my steaming off and leaving the custom-house people lamenting. It appeared that they were exceedingly irate, and immediately on their return had telegraphed up to the city of Guatemala a garbled version of the story, with the result that the Commandante of Yzabal had received peremptory instructions from Signor el Ministro to investigate the matter, while the American vice-consul had also been instructed by our minister to watch the case on my behalf.

Oddly enough our major domo on the estate, from his position as a captain in the Guatemaltecan army, happened to be the commandante, and consequently I was to be judged by one of my own servants. Not that I minded that in the least, for I was quite certain that I was in the right, and knew very well that, even if I had not been, the major domo would have made out that I was; but it struck me that the whole proceeding was an anomaly, and bordered very closely on the ludicrous.

As soon as it was intimated to the commandante that I was on shore (he was at his own office sitting in state, and would not have come near us for untold gold), I was politely requested to walk over, and the investigation began. The proceedings opened by a long speech in Spanish by the boss custom-house official, in which he told more lies than I should think it was possible for the recording angel to jot down. Of course I did not understand half what he said, but the American vice-consul interpreted it, and told me that I "had the floor." I began mildly by stating that the gentleman who had just finished was a parlous liar. I fancy, as everybody seemed satisfied with my opening sentence, that the consul must have toned it down a bit; and I then gave my version of the affair, produced the mail contract, and called Johnson as a witness. As three or four more orators were itching, I could see, to speak, I sat down shortly after examining the engineer, not forgetting to make a low bow to the president of the honourable court, who returned it with what I could swear was a very palpable wink. When the budding statesmen had delivered themselves of their pent-up eloquence, the major domo, or rather, I should say, the commandante, asked if any one else wanted to have a go at the subject; and finding no one ready, he proceeded to sum up in what I have not the slightest doubt was a most eloquent speech, but which unfortunately I did not grasp.

However, the upshot of the whole thing was that the customs were defeated and severely reprimanded, and I left the court without a stain on my character. I never quite made out, though, what position I occupied throughout the affair. I was not a prisoner, and I was not charged, neither was I a prosecutor—the only conclusion at which I arrived after mature thought being that I must have been in much the same category as that of the corpse at an inquest.

Directly the function at the court was over, we adjourned to the American vice-consul's house to drink "success to crime"; and shortly afterwards the major domo appeared, accompanied by the head of the customs, who had come, he informed me, to tender a humble apology, and to make it up with me. Of course I pretended to highly appreciate the honour, and having exchanged cigarettes and numerous bows, to say nothing of pretty speeches, over various glasses of "aquadiente" (by the way, I was uncommonly glad when the said speeches came to an end, for my vocabulary was exceedingly limited), we parted the best of friends—outwardly—though I was quite certain that the gentleman retired fully determined to have his revenge in some way on a future occasion.

As soon as he had turned the corner and was out of sight, we all gave vent to our feelings in a peal of laughter, in which no one joined more heartily than Signor el Commandante. He said, though, as soon as he had recovered himself, that he was very glad to see the mail contract, where it expressly stated that the custom-house people were on no account to interfere with the launch when running the mails, for he had been puzzling his head all the morning how he was to get out of the cleft stick he had got into between his duties as major domo and his duties as commandante. Poor old chap, he was not what one might call a "fellow of infinite jest of most excellent fancy," and in matters social and political was a babe. For on a subsequent occasion, when he heard that the British minister was coming down to Yzabal, he, in his capacity of commandante, assembled the populace and addressed them somewhat as follows: "Know, oh people, of the great honour that is about to be conferred on you. Signor, the Minister of the Queen of England is coming amongst you. Think of that, ye dogs! Signor el Ministro!! Ay mas. It is more, Signor the Consul is coming. Think of that!! Signor el Consul!!! Ay mas, it is more than that even. The *Vice*-Consul is arriving!!! Think of that and tremble!!!! Signor el *Vice*-Consul!!!!" Thus, without meaning or knowing it, running down the scale, and making out the vice-consul to be a far greater man than the minister of Her Most Gracious Majesty Queen Victoria.

It was about noon when the proceedings terminated at the inquest, or whatever it was called, and by the time we had finished breakfast and exhausted the usages of polite society towards the humbled custom-house official, it was close on two p.m.; so that it became necessary for us to make a move up the hill to the hacienda, unless we wanted another experience similar to our first journey. Accordingly the mules were saddled up and brought round—my baggage, by the way, having been despatched some hours previously—and we bade adieu to the hospitable vice-consul and his wife, and started on our return journey, my late judge leading the way. We left one mule behind with the consul for Jane to ride up when he came back, asking that he might be forwarded on the instant he put his foot on shore.

It was dark when we got to the plateau where I nearly shot Halifax, but we had no catastrophe, as on the former occasion, and were all as cheery as possible though, I confess, we missed Royal's sallies of wit and jovial laugh considerably. Halifax had galloped on ahead about a couple of hundred yards, and we were all preparing to follow, when suddenly I saw him pull up short and fire two barrels of his six-shooter into the bush. This was followed by a fiendish row, and, as I dashed forward, I heard him shout, "Look out, old man!" just as a huge tiger-cat bounded out under my mule's nose, frightening that worthy animal out of his wits, and very nearly causing my downfall. However, I managed to let drive one barrel of my revolver at him, which took effect, and stretched him out a corpse then and there. When we picked the beast up we found two bullets in him, and consequently Halifax claimed the skin, to which he had a perfect right. He was (the tiger-cat) a magnificent specimen, full grown and beautifully marked, so we were in luck, and we bore the body home to the hacienda in great state, where we skinned him and pegged him out.

Henry's boy, we found, had prepared us an excellent dinner, as he knew, by the arrival of my baggage about an hour before, that we were *en route;* and right glad I was to find myself once more under the familiar old thatched roof. The major domo stayed to dinner, and we fought the battle of the customs over again, packing him off, fairly full of Catalan wine and rum, about eleven o'clock to his own house by the plantation. He must have done himself pretty well, for he confessed afterwards that he fell off three times on his way home, and narrowly escaped breaking his neck in his acrobatic feats. As he was an excellent rider—after the Mexican fashion—there must have been something wrong with the works, and I have little doubt that the last go-down of rum-and-water had much to say to it.

For the next few days we were as busy as possible, making our arrangements for our projected visit to the city, which, as I have said, was a six days' journey. If the country had been in a settled state there would have been no bother at all, for we could have despatched our baggage in advance some three or four days, and followed on ourselves in light marching order; but, as things were, this was out of the question. War between Guatemala and San Salvador was imminent, and the whole country was in a state of ferment; moreover, as is always the case in a revolution or war in those parts, the hills were infested with bands of robbers, who would have been only too ready to pounce on our bullock trunks and to carry them off, together with the baggage mules. Consequently it necessitated the baggage coming with us under our protection, which, as might be expected, would materially lengthen the time we might reckon on taking to cover the distance to the city.

Our first stage was an easy one—Henry said about fourteen miles—to the hacienda of a Frenchman, who had established himself there with a view of prospecting for gold. He had found a fair amount by washing a small stream, and, having traced it to its source, he was bound to the city to obtain a claim and authority to crush the rock, or to form a company; and as he heard we were going up, he had written down to ask if he might join our party, there being, in his opinion, in which we agreed, a certain amount of safety in numbers. Poor chap! his mining scheme did not turn out very successful for him; for, after he had obtained the necessary licence to work the mine, and had staked out his claim, the Government suddenly sent him word to say that, by the laws of the country, no alien, they found, could hold any mining rights, and that if he wanted to do so he must become a naturalized Guatamaltecan subject. He, with the thirst for gold on him, did not care twopence what nation claimed him for its own, and consequently agreed then and there, looking on it merely as a matter of form. However, the Government did not take quite the same lax view of it, and, directly they got him properly fixed and in their power, they took him off to serve five years in the army as a conscript. So that all he got for his claim and expenditure was the honour (?) of carrying a rifle in the ranks of a semi-civilized force, with little or no pay, and little or no food, and by the time his service expired his licence to work the mine would have run out, unless he had started something going thereon.

I never heard what the end of it all was, but I know that, although the Republic gained an unwilling recruit, they, for the time, absolutely knocked on the head all chances of the country being opened up for mining purposes by foreigners. Of course, having once become a naturalized subject of the Republic, the French authorities could do nothing, although they tried their best, as did we all. The Government was obdurate, and would listen to no argument, and consequently, as I have shown, the last state of that man was worse than the first.

After mature consideration we decided that, instead of taking Jane up, we would take Henry's boy as our body-servant, as he was handier with mules and baggage, and was quite equal to anything in the cooking line that we should be likely to require on the road; indeed, it was more than likely that in many instances our dinners would consist solely of tortillas (cakes somewhat similar to a chow-pattie, and serving the purposes of knife, fork, and spoon combined) and frajoles (white beans). In fact, we found that this prognostication was pretty correct, excepting on occasions when we were able to buy a kind of gallina, or barn-door fowl, or to shoot something.

Two days later we decided to make a start with the baggage, as escort thereto as far as the Frenchman's house, and, leaving it there, to return to the hacienda, and wait the arrival of Jane and the mails. Then, having put him in charge of the house during our absence, to make a final departure from the base where our luggage was, and so travel up all together.

We carried this part of the programme out satisfactorily, and having slept one night at the Frenchman's house, who, by the way, was delighted to see us, and entertained us right royally, Henry, Halifax, and myself, with the boy, returned to Quirigua.

We waited three or four days without hearing anything of Jane, who ought to have been back easily by this time, till we began to think something must have happened, and so sent Johnson off with the launch to Livingston to see if he could hear anything of him.

Meanwhile, Halifax and myself had a very successful day at duck on the river, getting between us fifteen couple. As we were walking back in the evening to the house, we had to pass a potato-patch, which Henry had planted as an experiment to see if he could get them to grow in that country, and, on getting near it, I noticed three or four black forms dodging about inside, which, on careful inspection, turned out to be pig, which had broken through the palings, and were too busy rooting among the tubers to notice us. It was unusual for them to begin their foraging at that time, so it was an exceptional piece of good luck. As soon as I discovered what they were, I whispered to Halifax to slip in a wire cartridge in his right and a bullet in his left barrel (we always carried these with us, in case of big game turning up), and then to creep round the far side, where they had obtained an entrance, so as to be ready for them when they made a bolt. Directly he got there he was to blow his whistle, and when I heard it I would climb the fence and come down on them that way. By this means we were sure, if we held straight, of getting one, if not two, or, at all events, some bacon. While Halifax was going round I took further stock of our quarry, and made out two boar and three or four sows; and a nice mess they were making of the manager's garden. One was a magnificent specimen, which I singled out for myself, and as he was at the upper end furthest away from the exit, I determined to scale the fence in the centre. Ten minutes later I heard Halifax's whistle, and over I went, as bad luck would have it, catching my coat in the top and coming down on all fours.

Such a scuttle as there was inside! The old gentleman at the top end, as I expected, made straight for the broken-down part where he had got in, and, in doing so, had to pass within about fifteen yards of me. Luckily I had picked myself up and was ready for him, giving him my right barrel behind the shoulder as he came by, and tumbling him head over heels. I thought I had killed him on the spot, but I soon found out my mistake, for he recovered himself in a second, and with a snort and a grunt charged straight at me. If I did not stop him with my second barrel, I knew I should have a rough time of it, and although, I confess, I was somewhat excited, I managed to draw a pretty straight bead and let him have it at about ten yards' distance, jumping on one side directly I fired. It was just as well that I did so, for though he dropped stone dead close against the fence, he charged right home to where I had been standing, and if I had not cleared out of his way, would have inevitably ripped me.

Halifax meantime was having a high old time of it at the bottom end. He had killed the first pig as it came out, a sow, and with his second barrel had wounded the boar, which had laid up in some thick stuff just outside, the others going round the garden like mad things. Before I could re-load they had passed me, and, flying down the other side, charged the fence all together and broke through, thereby getting clear away. Hearing

Halifax shouting, I came down to him, and found him standing by the thick shrub where the boar had gone in. As I came up he said, "The brute is badly hit, but I don't see how we can get him out without Lion or something." I did not quite see my way either, as it was too green and wet to burn, and we had no fireworks, nor was it oversafe to go polling about too near, as one did not know quite from which point he would charge.

Luckily one of the plantation hands came by, and I sent him up to the hacienda to fetch the bloodhound, and to tell the manager, if he had come back, to hurry down to us. I had by this time mastered sufficient Spanish to make myself understood. I then went the far side of the patch of thick stuff, while Halifax remained where he was. After waiting nearly twenty minutes, from my position I could see Henry running down the hill with Lion in a leash, so I shouted to him to loose the animal, which he did, and the brave old doggie came bounding down to us. As he neared the place, his bristles went up, and he began to growl, and required little encouragement from me to make him dash into the thicket. Once in, there was the devil to pay—growls, grunts, roars, and a conglomeration of sounds, ending in the sudden exit of the pig, followed closely by Lion, who, happily, had escaped unhurt. The beast came out close by Halifax, and charged him so instantaneously that had it not been for the bloodhound hanging on to his ear, and thereby turning him, the consequences might have been serious. However, as he turned and presented a fair broadside, Halifax let drive, and bowled him over, much to Lion's surprise, and before he could struggle up, I ran down, and, putting my gun close to his head, gave him a finishing stroke.

So our day's duck-shooting ended in the slaughter of

three members of the porcine tribe, and we had for dinner that night some very excellent pork chops, which I can answer for it, were fully appreciated. Henry was much distressed at the damage the brutes had done to his experiment in potato-raising; but the idea of ham somewhat mollified him, and he gave orders that no time should be lost in pickling some portion of the robbers' bodies to take with us on our way to the city.

Two days later Jane and the mails turned up. He was in rather a dilapidated condition, for the schooner on which he had come from Belize had been nearly wrecked on one of the coral reefs, going through the passage outside Livingston that I mentioned in a previous chapter. It was bumping for twelve hours, and they only escaped sharks and shipwreck by the skin of their teeth. However, he had kept all the letters dry, and told us that Royal had caught the steamer all right and gave off. The old chap (Royal) did me, after all, for amongst the baggage that came up the following day was the case containing his rifle, which I had already refused to accept, and a note from Royal saying that, as I could not possibly return it to him, I was in duty bound to take it as a memento of the cheery time he had spent with his pal.

CHAPTER VIII.

ON THE ROAD TO THE CITY.

We now had to see about making our final start for the city of Guatemala. Jane was visibly depressed at our leaving him behind, and at the eleventh hour begged hard to be allowed to accompany us; but, as all our arrangements were made, and he would have been little or no use, we were obdurate, and started off back to the Frenchman's hacienda without him. By leaving fairly early we arrived at our Gallic host's house in time for dinner, and also in time to view some mules that had been scraped together, from heaven knows where, for our inspection and possible purchase.

It is a very extraordinary thing; but no matter what part of the globe one may find one's self in, or what the general manners of the country may be, there is always one bond of sympathy which is apparently alike to all viz. a deal in horse-flesh, or, if you like to be more particular and accurate, a deal in any article destined to carry about mankind. No sooner does it become known that you are a possible purchaser of a stud, than the whole district for miles round is let into the secret, and every one who can beg, borrow, or steal the required article comes in from far and near and offers his wares. Certainly I admit that horse-dealing in Spanish is an operation of more diplomacy, and takes a longer time than in other languages; but the broad outline is much the same: the seller endeavours to praise his animal up to the skies, and to hide any defects there may be; whilst the buyer goes on the other tack and does his best to run it down and depreciate the value in every possible way.

In Spanish, before you come to the actual deal, there are a lot of civil amenities to go through which take up the time. For instance, a man brings you an animal, you go and look at it and form your opinion without a word. Then you adjourn with the owner, and having offered him a cigarette, proceed to ask him about his steed. If you imagine for a moment that you are going to hear anything about that you are vastly mistaken. "Hurry no man's cattle" is his motto, and he will promptly ask you how you are, what news you have, how your father and mother, sisters, brothers, cousins, and aunts are comporting themselves, and then proceed to enter into a confidential chat on his own family history. You subsequently try and lead him gently back to the subject of the animal, and he replies in an off-hand way, "Oh, the animal. Ah, that is an animal! He can go such and such a pace for such and such a time;" and before you can pick him up he is off at score again on something absolutely foreign to the matter in hand. In perhaps half an hour you may manage to arrive at a price—his price—which it is generally safe to reckon on as about three times as much as he will take. Eventually, after another half-hour, more or less, you will come to terms, and having paid the money and offered the gentleman (they are all gentlemen) another cigarette, the deal is over, and he departs, quite happy in the conviction that he has done you.

As I wanted two animals, I had a double dose of that sort of thing, and it was late before I concluded my bargains and became the proud possessor of a very large mule which they called "El Macho Grande," and which, of course, I immediately nicknamed Major Grundy, and a very pretty little strawberry roan. I paid too much money for the latter I know, even taking into consideration the vast amount of family history I acquired gratis; but I was so dead tired of haggling that I named a price on the take-it-or-leave-it principle, and promptly got landed for the article. This part of the business being finished, and the mules turned over to the keeping of the arriero, we adjourned to dinner, which our host cooked himself, and then, after a cigar, we went to bed early for the last time for some days, as we started next morning at cockcrow, and would not get between the sheets again until our arrival at the hotel in the city.

It seemed to me as if I had only just closed my eyes, when our boy roused me up, and presented me with some coffee and toast. All the baggage mules were packed and sent on about half an hour in advance, with connecting files between them and ourselves—the bodyguard—as a precaution in case of attack, and then, having seen everything all right, our pistols and guns loaded, flasks full, and hammocks hung at our saddle-bow, we mounted, and set off on our journey. Halifax again was the first to come to grief, for he was much taken with my little strawberry roan mule, and insisted on riding it. He carried, slung over his saddle, two bags of dollars, one on each side, for our use on the road, and as the mule was a bit skittish, these began to jingle, when it jumped about and frightened the animal all the more, till at last it took to bucking most viciously, and sent Halifax, together with his bags, flying over its head about ten yards, while one of the bags burst, and the dollars were all over the shop.

However, no bones were broken, and after a little

delay in picking up the pieces (literally), we got matters ship-shape and went on. Major Grundy, who carried me, evidently looked on the whole proceeding with supreme contempt, for he never did anything until we had gathered up the fragments and were just on the move again, and then he gently sidled up to the strawberry roan and planted such a couple of well-delivered rib binders in the shape of kicks on the unfortunate brute's carcase as nearly to send both mule and Halifax endways. It was precious lucky for the latter that it missed his leg, for, if it had not, the kick was bound to have smashed it, which would have ended our journey somewhat abruptly.

It was close on 1.30 p.m. when we came to our first halting-place, and unloaded for a couple of hours to give ourselves and our animals rest and something to eat. It was a lovely spot in a valley, with a stream running down it, and a waterfall crashing down about a hundred yards off. There were three or four houses of sorts, "adobe" or mud-built, and an enormous cotton tree, under which we laid ourselves out until fairly routed by fleas, which swarmed. However, we beat them by slinging our hammocks, and having bought some eggs and goat's milk from an old lady, who also undertook to make some frajoles and tortillas for our midday meal, we waited peacefully and perspiringly—for it was awfully hot—till it was ready. When the beans and cakes came I cannot say that they were particularly appetizing; but we were all pretty sharp set, and the Frenchman managed to compound a capital omelette, which was a good wind-up, and another half-hour's snooze saw us quite ready for the second half of our day's march.

Weary work it was for the first hour or so up a steep hill, chiefly composed of quartz, which, baked by the sun, was like tramping over the hot plate of an oven, and radiated a heat all round that would have almost cooked the proverbial beefsteak. Precious glad I was, I remember, when we came to the top and struck through a pine wood into some open cultivation with a white hacienda in the middle of the maize fields.

The spot selected for our first night *al fresco* dormitory was about three miles the other side of the corn fields where the hacienda stood; but by the path we had to take it made close on six, as we had to make a long detour to avoid a cañon. Consequently we were rather late getting in, and the shades of evening had closed round us long before we arrived. It was not long, though, before we had a good fire blazing, the mules hobbled, and the boy very busy cooking our dinner.

I am grieved to say that at that dinner we, all and singular, as they say in legal documents, compounded a felony, for coming through the maize fields our baggage mules suddenly came on a lot of hens, and before anybody could stop him, our young body servant seized one, wrung its neck, and transferred it to the bottom of the cooking utensil basket. Of course the fowls belonged to the owner of the hacienda, and the act was one of robbery, accompanied with violence, if not murder; but we had it for dinner, and, what is more, thoroughly enjoyed it, and consequently all became *particeps criminis.*

Dinner over, we wrapped ourselves in our blankets, and with our revolvers under our pillows, tumbled into our respective hammocks, which were hung under the trees. We had to sleep in our boots, on account of the mosquitoes, and it took me some time to get used to it; but at last I dozed off, and never woke till it was time for boot and saddle the next morning.

As one day was pretty much the same as another, I

will not attempt to describe the journey in detail; nor had we any very startling adventures beyond Major Grundy bolting one day with me and nearly going headlong over a precipice, which was an experience I never wish to repeat. Henry told me afterwards that he was quite certain we had both gone over, and thought nothing could possibly save us; also that it turned him so sick that he could not look for the finale. When the Major pulled up, and I went back to inspect the spot, I found that there was barely three inches between the marks of his hoofs and the edge of the precipice, so that it was quite near enough for me.

Anyhow, we arrived all safe and sound at Antigua, the ancient capital of the country, which had been destroyed by a volcanic eruption, and there we stopped at a house which had been a palace, and enjoyed the luxury of a lovely cold bath in a marble tank.

We agreed to devote a day to sight-seeing, and also to have a crack at the duck on a lake about two miles out. Accordingly, early next morning, we started off—Henry, Halifax, and myself—to ride through some fields of cochineal to the lake, and reached it just as the sun was rising. All round the shores grew beautiful high rushes, and we could see from the high ground above before we got there that the place was swarming with duck, so we looked forward to some real good sport. However, we were rather out in our calculations, for, after we had fired about four shots apiece and bagged two and a half couple, the whole *pouse comistatus* of the duck tribe suddenly took flight, going off to some other lake in a big cloud, and we never found another bird during the next hour. This being the case, we thought it better policy to give it up as a bad job, and return to the city and sight-seeing with our spoil. Our friend the Frenchman was delighted when he saw the duck, and promised us a real good feed for the evening, which promise he duly kept.

Antigua must have been a fine city in old days, for the remains of the monastery and cathedral are very fine still, and the architecture magnificent. Some of the old houses and palaces are also very grand, though their walls are cracked in many instances right through their whole length, and show evident signs of earthquake. The few people who still live there are in daily fear of another visitation, and consequently take no trouble to repair the place, which makes the town look somewhat dilapidated.

We were warned to be very careful on our next stage, as we had to pass through some low hills, which they said were the stronghold of a band of robbers. Acting on this information, we kept the mules and baggage with us, and rode with our pistols ready for emergencies. Whether they thought we were too strong for them or not I can't say; anyhow, we were not attacked, though I did notice two or three wild-looking figures, evidently armed and watching our cavalcade from a distance.

That night we had a scene, for we took it in turn to keep watch, and Henry, who relieved me, suddenly roused the camp and swore that the robbers were on us. Of course we all jumped up and got our six-shooters ready for action, when suddenly there was a rush, and four of the mules, led by Major Grundy, stampeded through the camp, followed by the arriero in *deshabille.* We all had to put our best leg foremost to circumvent the brutes, as we knew that if we once let them get away we should never see them again. After nearly an hour's hard running and stumbling over trees and rocks in the dim religious light, we managed to turn them back and to secure the ringleader, on whom the arriero vented his wrath, accompanied by a choice selection of Spanish epithets, and we then retired to get what rest we could.

Three days later we came in to the next stage to the city about four in the afternoon, and encamped on the banks of a river, which we thought was a capital opportunity for a bath, and accordingly we stopped and plunged in. No sooner, however, had we done this, than, to my astonishment, the bank was suddenly lined with an admiring crowd of women, who had come down to wash clothes and draw water. They evidently considered it a sort of gratis show, and stood there indulging in somewhat pointed chaff. The position was, to say the least of it, embarrassing for a modest young man; but, as the water was icy cold, it amounted to a question of staying in and being frozen, or coming out and feeling shy, and the latter carried the day. Our appearance *in puris naturalibus* did not in the least diminish our audience, but they waxed exceeding merry at Henry's expense, calling each other's attention to his long and lanky proportions, a proceeding that roused his ire to boiling pitch. He endeavoured to retaliate by shouting back some rather broad Spanish, but it had as much effect as water on a duck's back, and only drew down more chaff from the ladies on his devoted head. As soon as we had donned a certain amount of wearing apparel and were presentable, we returned to our camp utterly routed, and firmly convinced that modesty was not one of the petty vices of these children of the forest.

That evening we were visited by the *padre* of the place, who came, he said, to apologize to us for the conduct of his flock, and to assure us that they meant no harm—dear little innocents!—but from the merry twinkle in his eye when he looked at Don Quixote, I could see that he had a full and true description of the scene, and that he thoroughly appreciated the ludicrous side of the question. He was very good company, although I had some difficulty in understanding his Spanish (the only language he could talk), and he took his grog like a man, leaving us at a late hour perfectly happy. Before going, he took me on one side and begged me to let him know when we were coming back, and that we were to be sure to "posada" at his house on that occasion, when he would show us round, and then he went off singing to himself a singularly secular, not to say highly spiced, Spanish carol.

The next day we struck the broad high-road just then commencing, and arrived at last at the city of Guatemala. From a distance it looked most imposing, and even when we got there it was by no means a bad place, though the streets are paved with great whole stones, something after the fashion of Mexico, which makes travelling not altogether a bed of roses. We passed the opera-house, the piazza, and cathedral, and then turned into our hotel, where the landlord, having been duly advised by telegraph, was awaiting our arrival, and promptly escorted us to our rooms.

The whole city was very full of soldiers, as they had drafted two regiments in that day, and were mobilizing the second army corps for the war.

We found in our room heaps of cards and invitations to dinners, suppers, balls, etc., so that we were in for a cheery time. In fact, if we had been emperors, kings, or princes, they could not have made more of us, and almost before we had a wash and a brush-up and got into our "Europe clothes," a fresh influx of visitors commenced to arrive. How many cigarettes I smoked before dinner, or how much marsala, which seemed to be the fashionable tipple, I imbibed with our new friends I can't say. All

I remember is that I was precious glad when the visits came to an end, and we were left in peace for that evening to settle down.

In the hotel we found the opera company were staying, and, oddly enough, two of the "boss" ladies had come out with us as far as Jamaica in the same ship. So we claimed acquaintance, and as it was an off night, we had some music in the drawing-room. Some of the very fierce-looking Guatemaltecan officers who came in, evidently did not half like Halifax and self being on such good terms with the ladies, and looked pistols and daggers at us. But it had no effect, and the more they scowled the more attentive we became, till at last they left in dudgeon, and the party broke up.

Oh, the luxury of a bed and clean sheets that night! It was quite a novel experience, after all the time in the open air under trees, and I revelled in it, dropping off into the land of dreams in no time. Roughing it in the bush is all very well for a change, and possibly a very healthy occupation, but I came to the conclusion that civilization was decidedly preferable now and then.

CHAPTER IX.

CIVILIZATION AGAIN.

The day after our arrival at the city of Guatemala we devoted to business pure and simple, and after calling at the legation, also on the president and state officials, we had a long interview—that is to say, Henry and myself had—with a leading Guatemaltecan lawyer on some matters connected with the title-deeds of the estate, etc. Legal consultations are not particularly lively entertainments at any time or in any place, but I will back a consultation in a Central American republic, carried out with all the punctilio of Old Castille, to beat anything.

We were at least an hour and a half before we arrived at anything approaching the matter in hand. I whispered to Henry that I thought horse-dealing in Spanish was about as long a transaction as was made, but that this legal business seemed to be able to give it two stone and a beating. However, he replied it was the custom of the country, and from my old Indian experience on the subject of dustoor I recognized at once the necessity of grinning and bearing it. When, eventually, we did get to business, the Spanish law of property was so utterly beyond my comprehension that the legal luminary might have told me anything, and I left the seance just as wise as when I first entered the lawyer's room.

Certainly the Spanish method of tendering advice to a client has an advantage over the procedure of most other nationalities—from the adviser's point of view—for the lawyer charges by time! Like a four-wheeler, or hansom, you engage him by the hour—only it is considerably more than half a crown—that is, you so engage and pay him, unless you are well up in the ways, customs, and manners of the country.

If you are "in the know" you will make a bundobust, or arrangement, with him beforehand by letter. You state your case, what you expect him to do, and you ask him what his fee will be for carrying out your instructions and advising you on all legal points. He will reply naming a sum, which you immediately divide by two or three, and after a couple or so more letters the bargain is struck and you go for your interview. By adopting this method you save both time and money, for the preliminary civilities are considerably shortened, and the actual matter in hand, in consequence, is arrived at much sooner. Unfortunately for me, neither myself nor Henry knew the ropes, although the latter ought to have done so, and so I was condemned to undergo the extra hour and a half's preliminary conversation, which, of course, was included in the bill of costs as so much time.

When we got back to the hotel, we found that we had been invited to the presidential box at the opera that evening, and to supper afterwards at the house of one of the chief commanders of the army so shortly to take the field. I had just time to have a tub and to tumble into a clean boiled rag and evening kit, which I must confess seemed quite strange to me, before it was time to have dinner.

Halifax, who turned up late, told me he had been

all round the city with Signor el Minestro and had seen a review of the troops, with which he was highly delighted. He, moreover, informed me that he had been offered a command in the army, and that the president intended offering me the command of the artillery, consisting of two mule batteries. I somewhat damped his military ardour by telling him that, if they did make me such an offer I should most undoubtedly decline it, and that, although he could please himself what he did, I should advise him very strongly not to mix himself up in any way with the affairs of a foreign republic. I then inquired for our little French companion, and was told that the return to civilization had been too much for him, and that, meeting two or three *confrères* in the city, he had succumbed to the potency of absinthe and aquadiente, and was now upstairs in bed as tight as the proverbial drum, which, under the circumstances, was, we all agreed, the best place for him.

As soon as dinner was over we slipped on our coats, putting our six-shooters into our pockets, which we were warned was a very necessary precaution, and adjourned to the opera house and the presidential box. I forget what the opera was, but I know it was very well rendered. Indeed, if it had not been, there would have been a shindy at once, for of all the critical audiences I have ever seen none have ever come near the good people of Guatemala. A false note or a carelessly rendered number drove them nearly wild, and woe betide the unfortunate artist who incurred their displeasure. They, the audience, did not hesitate for a moment to express their disapproval, and the odds were that the artist—he or she—was hissed off the stage, and might consider themselves lucky if they were not pelted with various missiles from the cheaper parts of the house. On the other hand, I will say they were equally unstinting in their applause, and any song rendered extra well, or that took their fancy particularly, had just as maddening an effect on them the other way, and they would shower plaudits and often money on the lucky singer for the moment.

One of the tenors told me one day that he never saw such people, and that he was never so frightened at singing in his life, for he never knew when he got on the stage what was going to happen. If he had a bit of a cold, or was out of voice, he was just as likely as not to get his head broke, whereas, on the previous occasion on which he appeared, he very possibly had been the temporary idol of the public, and had had dollars, half dollars, and ten-dollar pieces showered on to the stage for him. *Sic transit gloria mundi.*

That night, I am pleased to say, everything went off most satisfactorily. The audience was in a good temper, the president was most affable, and the company on the stage were in excellent voice, and, as I have previously stated, gave a very good representation, so, as may be imagined, we all thoroughly enjoyed ourselves. At the fall of the curtain the president announced his intention of walking to supper with me. Sending his aide-de-camp with Halifax and Henry, and dismissing his carriage, I could not make out what the game was at first, but I soon found out, for we had not gone a hundred yards before he broached the subject of the artillery command, and at the same time confided to me that he wanted some one he could trust, which, to say the least of it, did not place his officers in the very highest light. I told him at once that I was very sorry, but that it was quite out of the question. In the first place, I was precluded from doing so even if I wanted to, and, secondly, under any circumstances, I could not mix myself up in the affairs of a country which had no claim on my services. He pressed me very hard, but seeing I was firm, he took a sensible view of things, and dropped the subject, merely asking me to go with him to inspect the batteries, and to give him any hints, which I promised to do. Nor did my refusal, I am glad to say, make any difference in our relations, for the whole time I was in the city he was most cordial, and could never do enough for either myself or the rest of the party.

As we turned down the street leading to the house of the commander, where we were bound for supper, I had an opportunity afforded me of witnessing the progress that civilization had made in the city. At the corner on the darker side of the street I noticed a man walking slowly along humming one of the airs we had just heard in the opera, and a short way behind another following him stealthily. They were both about fifty yards in front of us, and the president, who saw them at the same moment, evidently knew what was up, for he immediately whipped out a formidable six-shooter, motioning me to do the same. Almost before I could get mine out of my pocket I saw to my horror the man who was dogging the footsteps of the other suddenly rush forward, and jump on to the back of the first man. There was a flash of steel, a blow, a heavy groan, and No. 1 was lying on the pavement stabbed through the shoulder with a fatal down stroke. At the same instant the report of the president's pistol rang out, and No. 2 turned turtle, and then, recovering himself, did his best to get away, evidently badly wounded. However, before he had gone many yards, the police, who had heard the sound of the pistol shot, were after him, and soon had him in custody. They then turned their attention to us, and were mightily astonished to find the president and an Englishman engaged in the sport of men-shooting at twelve a.m. for no ostensible reason. A few words from the president put matters straight, and the assassin was promptly taken off, together with his victim, who was stone dead. The next day the murderer was tried by a summary court at 10.30 a.m., and shot by the president's order at three p.m., about as quick a job as could well be imagined.

As soon as this latter episode was ended, we continued our route, and arrived at the house about half an hour late, where we found everybody waiting for us. Such a supper too! Every conceivable dish in place and out of place! Everything to my insular mind seemed to be topsy-turvy—sweets came when one expected fish, and soups when one looked for sweets, and between every course the whole table, ladies and all, smoked a little cigarette. This, by the way, the ladies do at a ball directly a dance is over, and at first it strikes one as peculiar to see one's fair (or dark) partner suddenly dive into a little bag hanging at her side, and quick as thought make two little cigarettes, one of which she presents to you, and the other takes herself, but one soon gets used to it, and learns to consider it rather pretty than otherwise. However, notwithstanding the odd sequences of dishes, I thoroughly enjoyed my supper, and took a leading part in the *impromptu* dance which followed, arriving back at the hotel dead tired somewhere about five a.m., and I remember to this day how I blessed the aide-de-camp who knocked me up at 9.30 a.m. to tell me that my presence was required at the trial of the murderer of the previous night, and I have vivid recollections of the splitting headache that inaugurated my return to civilization and a "claw hammer" coat. But I had to go, putting the best face on it I could, and although I refused to witness the execution, I confess I was not at all sorry to hear the man sentenced, for was not his action in stabbing the man behind his back a cowardly one? and was not it owing to that action that I had been hauled out of bed and compelled to attend a stuffy court with a head that felt the size of the cathedral dome and a mouth like a lime kiln?

The trial over, I lunched with the president at his house, and there I met an American, whom I will call Brown, who had volunteered to take charge of the artillery post that had been offered to me. He was a most amusing man, quite a youngster, but full of fun and dash, with a fund of anecdote that never ceased. He told me that if he got the appointment he meant business, though he did not reckon to know much about either mules or guns. "However," he said, "if the darned thing is pointed the right road and is touched off, I guess it will knock h—ll out of something." During lunch the president asked me *sotto voce* if I thought he—Brown—would do (why he should have made a confidant of me I can't think), and as I said I thought he was a good sort, he gave him the billet for what it was worth, and very good service he did afterwards. One thing he struck at, and that was wearing a Gautemaltecan uniform. "No," he said, "if I've got to hand in my checks, I reckon I'll do it better in my own clothes; and suppose I got hit, you may bet they would mislay me in that beautiful kit, so" (to the president), "boss, I guess we'll clinch on plain clothes." As he had afterwards to render this into Spanish for the president's edification, it made it all the funnier; but he got his own way, and fought his batteries in a shooting-coat.

That night I made him dine with us, and introduced him to Henry, Halifax, and our Gallic friend, who had by this time recovered. All through dinner and up to a late hour he kept the whole place in a roar of laughter, and went off about midnight as happy as a bird, having made Halifax and myself promise to come down with him the next day to take over his new command and see the mules and screw guns before the president came to inspect them.

The following morning saw us on the parade with Brown and his charge; and such a game I never saw. The mules were half broke, and as soon as they got their respective loads on board, up went their heels and down went their heads, kicking and squeaking, bucking and plunging, until the ground was literally strewn with portions of gun-carriages and field equipment. There was one brute in particular which was worse than all the rest put together; he had to carry the breech portion of the screw guns, and no power on earth could do anything with him. In the first place, he had to be cast to load up, and immediately the hobble was loosed he was all over the place. After bearing very patiently with the brute's tantrums for some time, Brown at last lost his temper, and having amongst his other paraphernalia a stock whip, in the use of which he was an adept, he sent for it, and let the obstinate brute have a taste of the article that fairly astonished him. However, he was just as bad the next day, and so it went on for nearly a week, till the commandant of the artillery was nearly at his wit's end, more especially as the president had announced his intention of inspecting the battery in two days, previous to sending it to the front.

The day that the announcement appeared, Brown was in deep thought up to dinner-time, when suddenly his whole manner changed, and with a yell that would not have disgraced a Commanchee Indian, he informed us that he had solved the problem. "Yes, sir," he said, "I guess I've fixed that mule right away, you bet." He would not divulge his scheme, but told us that if we came down the next morning he would put us up to a wrinkle in mule-breaking that would astonish us. Of course we all went, anxious to see what our volatile friend was about to do ; and on our arrival at the parade ground, we found the battery drawn up, with the obstinate cuss in front. I noticed at once that the brute had been loaded with a double load, in that he carried the whole gun put together, and lashed firmly on to his pack-saddle. Leading from the breech was a long string, one end of which was held by Brown himself, and the other I found to be attached to a fuse. As we came near, Brown shouted out, "See here, mind your heads." And the brute feeling the increased weight, began to caper round more than ever, followed in his gyrations by Brown. It seemed as if the animal had made up his mind to select us for attack, for no matter how we dodged we always found the muzzle of that infernal gun pointed right at our heads or else a pair of heels whistling close by our ears. At last Brown got a clear space in front, and just as the mule gave a more vigorous kick than usual, he pulled the lanyard, and, to my astonishment, bang went the gun, and over on his back went the mule. "Guess that fixed him," said Brown. "Reckon he thought the world had cracked right down there." And he was right; for the poor animal was so frightened that all the devil was knocked out of him, and ever after he was the most docile of creatures.

It certainly was a novel idea, and did the inventor great credit; and I can answer for its being one of the most ludicrous sights I have ever seen. I can sit and laugh now when I picture to myself the somersault that mule turned, and the evident expression of bewilderment that came over it, as it lay on its back on the top of the discharged screw gun.

The president was much amused at the description of the scene, and Brown rose points in his estimation at once. At all events he was very complimentary at the inspection, and quite effusive. The only man who was dissatisfied was the unfortunate officer of artillery, who had been superseded and forced to take a back seat. He was naturally very indignant, and turned sulky. In fact, he went so far as to try and pick a quarrel with Brown, and finding that would not wash, he turned his attention to me. However, I was not going to be drawn, and had not the smallest intention of going out with the gentleman. So I had it politely conveyed to him that if he gave me any cheek, I should treat him to a dose of the English method of avenging an insult, and give him a good hiding. I confess I was not altogether certain that he would not hire some individual to play the knife trick on me behind my back some dark night; and I fancy the authorities had the same idea, for two or three days later the sportsman got his marching orders, and was sent off then and there to the front. I saw him depart, and from the malignant scowl he gave me, I expect, if he be still alive and I happened to come across him, that it would afford him intense gratification to make an end of me, and so rid the world of a man who, in his opinion, unwarrantably interfered with him. I am convinced that he would not believe me if I told him that I had nothing to do with it, but would say that next to Ananias I was the biggest liar that earth ever contained.

CHAPTER X.

A FORCED MARCH.

A COUPLE of days later we got news from the front that the Guatemaltecan forces had been successful in their first engagement, chiefly owing to the gallantry of our Yankee friend and his mule battery. At one time it seemed as if the day was going to end in a general rout of our army, and some of the officers had already begun to make tracks; notably the brigadier commanding the 1st Brigade, who, previous to the troops marching out, had been the chief figure of attraction in the city, dashing and clattering about all over the place in a most magnificent uniform. Directly, however, the first shot was fired, he was completely transmogrified, and bolted like a gun-shy dog, being found, after all was over, some three miles in rear of the scene of action, curled up in a mortal fright behind a large stone. When the San Salvador troops thought the day was theirs, and were pressing on to complete the Guatemaltecan defeat, they were suddenly met in a narrow pass by the mule battery, and so well did the American dispose and serve his guns, that he completely changed the aspect of affairs, and the San Salvadoraneans turned tail and gave it up.

The poor devil of a brigadier was brought in a prisoner under arrest, and was tried by court-martial for cowardice, and sentenced to be publicly stripped of his uniform, degraded, and then shot. The first two sentences were duly carried out; but, at the last moment, in deference to the respect in which the erring young gentleman's father was held (he was quite young, not more than thirty), the president remitted the death sentence, and substituted expulsion. I could not help feeling sorry for the man; he looked such a whipped cur after all his swashbuckling swagger of a short time before. But there is no doubt that he richly deserved all he got, and that he was one of the most chicken-hearted cowards ever born. I found out afterwards that he had been one of the principal agitators against me with reference to the command of the mule battery, so that my sorrow for him was tempered with a certain amount of satisfaction at his discomfiture.

Of course, as is the usual custom, there was, on receipt of the war intelligence and the chronicle of the victory, tremendous rejoicings, illuminations of the city at night, bells ringing all day, and a grand gala entertainment at the opera. To this latter function we were duly invited, and went with the president, and such a row as the people made on the entrance of the latter functionary I never heard. The whole audience rose *en masse*, and yelled and cheered themselves hoarse. It was a good twenty minutes before the artists could resume the opera. The president seemed highly pleased at his reception, and bowed and scraped till I thought he would have pitched over the front of the box. Then they began to cheer the English and strangers, "Viva les estraneros!" which was meant as a compliment to ourselves and the American who had won the fight for them; and up we had to get, and bow and scrape. I will say this, that, demonstrative as they were in our favour on that occasion, I am quite certain that, if the battle had gone the other way, they would have been just as bitter against the president and ourselves, and would have hissed and hooted us out of the place. However, everything was *couleur de rose*, and it was quite a pleasure to be on the winning side. I am sure the artists on the stage found it so, for they were playing the *Puritana*, and the deafening way in which "Suona la tromba" was cheered must have been highly flattering to them.

After the opera we were taken off to the cathedral to hear a thanksgiving mass. I thought it an odd time to choose for the function—twelve at midnight—but I said nothing, and having stood the overpowering smell of the incense for about three-quarters of an hour, at the end of which I was nearly asphyxiated, I was much relieved to find myself once more in the president's carriage *en route* for his house, where there was a great supper banquet ready prepared, at which so many loyal toasts and "Success to our arms" were drunk, that more than three parts of the assembled guests were very soon in that state which is known as "unfit for duty."

Just before the news came in we had made arrangements to leave the city and return homeward bound to the plantation, but, of course, we had to postpone our departure, as, with the San Salvador troops routed and all over the country, it was by no means likely to be a safe proceeding. We decided, therefore, to put off going for a week till matters had quieted down, and had given, or were just about to give, orders to that effect, when I received a telegram which made it an absolute necessity for me to go at once. Halifax had, unfortunately, contracted a go of fever, with a slight touch of the sun, and the doctors said he would not be able to travel for a week, or perhaps more; so, as our minister volunteered to look after him, I had no compunction in leaving him behind to follow on later, and in starting off myself with Henry. We discussed the *pros* and *cons* very carefully, and after due deliberation decided to travel in light marching order, sending our heavy baggage on to the hacienda in company with an escorted treasure convoy that the president was, luckily, just about to despatch to Yzabal. Comfort we could not expect, but in the troubled state of the country expedition was the main question to be thought of. I cannot say I particularly looked forward to the journey, for my return to civilization and clean shirts in the city had somewhat damped my ardour for roughing it in hammock and saddle; but "needs must," etc., and as we had to go, I determined to make the best of a bad job.

For the first two stages, about thirty miles, all was plain sailing and safe, so we sent on our mules, etc., two days in advance, and laid a dâk, *i.e.* we had a relay of fresh mules half way, so that we could do the whole thirty miles at one fell swoop. By this means we should save two days, and also we might hope to get ahead of the news of our journey.

Accordingly the next morning off went Major Grundy and the rest under the charge of the arrieros and Henry's boy, and for the last time we donned our evening kits and attended the opera. The arrieros, I may mention, were in the most ghastly funk at the whole business, and I fancy spent most of the night previous to their departure in alternate nips of "aquadiente" and votive offerings to their respective patron saints. I am sure none of the party ever expected to see Quirigua again, for, as usual, the terrors and possible dangers of the road had been painted by kind friends in the blackest of colours.

We had quite a crowd to see us off, when Henry and

myself started at daybreak on the morning of the second day; and with many a good-bye, and wishes for good luck, we clattered out of the yard of the hotel over the cobble stones punctual to time, but feeling anything but "chirpy." For the first ten miles or so it was an excellent broad road, and we scarcely drew rein, but did the journey almost at a hard canter. We must have presented a somewhat banditti-looking appearance, for we both had rifles slung on our shoulders, and a brace of six-shooters, one in each holster, besides the one we carried in our breast-pockets. Our hammocks were slung at our saddlebow and a net also containing some bread, etc., while on to the back of the saddle was strapped a large water-bottle. I had personally the honour of carrying two of these latter articles, one on each side, but the second one contained, not Adam's ale, but some very fine old white rum which one of our friends had sent up at the last moment *en route*.

Our old acquaintance, the padre, whom I mentioned before, had heard of our probable coming from our advance guard, and as we cantered up was there to receive us with some light refreshment. He did his best to persuade us to turn back, as he said that the road was not safe, and that it was fifty to one that we should never get through alive; not only was the whole country, he informed us, overrun with the demoralized San Salvadoraneans, but there were also a whole heap of robbers and bushrangers out, hanging on the flanks of the two armies, and seeking whom they might devour. I told him that I would willingly forego the journey, but that business and a telegraph made it imperative that I should try and push on; so, when he saw that it was no good, and that I was determined, he shut up and dismissed us with his blessing. By the way, I found out that among his other accomplishments the worthy man was an excellent judge of rum, for he had a taste of the gift bottle, and pronounced it most grateful and comforting. Indeed, I think, if he had had the time, or if I had been willing to give him the opportunity, that he would have finished the lot. He was very anxious to know where I got such splendid stuff, and when I mentioned the donor's name he seemed perfectly happy, for he sighed a sigh of deep relief, and said he knew him well, and that he was a good man and devoted to the Church, which I took to mean that the right reverend father saw his way to a bottle or two of the same at some future date.

We met with no further adventure after parting from the good man, and arrived in good time at the end of our thirty miles, hot, tired and dusty. We found our mules and people all assembled and in working order, but still with a terrible fit of the funks aboard. Directly we got in we had some dinner, and, slinging our hammocks, turned in for six hours the moment we had finished, giving the order to start for the next stage at two a.m. This system we meant to adopt, as far as we could, all through, as we thought we were less likely to tumble into a hornet's nest at night than in the daytime, and where the road was fairly good going by this means we could often do a double journey.

Punctually at two a.m. we were roused up, and in a quarter of an hour were off, arriving at our next halting-place by eleven o'clock a.m. without mishap. Here we heard the unwelcome news that the two armies had changed their front, and were now lying right across our route. To go round was out of the question, so the only thing for it was either to turn back and give the journey up as an impossibility, or to go bang through the two lines, which would not only be difficult, but very risky, as one would be just as liable to be shot by friends as enemies, and probably robbed by both.

Henry and I debated the question for a good two hours, and had rather a heated discussion on the subject. He was for turning back, whilst I was equally strongly in favour of pushing on, and, the arguments on both sides being about even, there did not seem at first much chance of arriving at any definite conclusion. Eventually, however, I carried the day; and then came the question as to how we were to arrange the plan of campaign. Whatever had to be done in the way of a dash through, it was clear would have to take place at night. Our one difficulty was to find out the position of the troops. No one could or would give us any information on this point, and the reports were so conflicting and contradictory that it seemed hopeless. Moreover, when we pointed out to any more virulent liar than the rest that his information could not by any possibility be correct, he would merely shrug his shoulders, and, saying "Quien sabe," walk off and leave us.

It was at this crisis that Henry's boy came to the rescue, and turned out a trump. After asking leave to speak, he suggested that we should at once go on to the next stage, which happened to be a garrison town, where we could await further developments. "It is quite certain," he said, "that there are no troops between here and there, for I have noticed supplies going in by the road, which would not be the case if there were troops, because the people would be too frightened to travel. When we have arrived there, if the signor cannot get any proper information, I will, if allowed to do so, go on myself and reconnoitre, bringing back word. No one will notice a boy like myself, and I can find out a lot." Of course, this speech was all in Spanish, and said with a grave conviction of his own importance. I confess I was mightily surprised, as I never for a moment imagined that the boy had it in him, but the advice was so sensible that we immediately closed with it, and gave orders for boot and saddle instanter.

Our first difficulty was met at the gates of the town, for the guard refused point-blank to let us in, and, there being seemingly no officer present, were inclined to be insolent.

Before leaving the city I had received from my friend the president a document in the shape of a pass, giving orders to every one to forward our journey in every way. But, on producing this, which I naturally thought would prove conclusive, to my surprise it was treated with contempt, the sergeant of the guard saying he could not read. I then demanded to see or be taken to the officer commanding the garrison. This was also refused, and we were told to clear out, unless we wanted to get shot.

Here was a pretty fix, I thought, and I did not know what to do for the best. I felt exceedingly inclined to form line and charge the guard there and then, but even if we knocked half of them over and got through, I knew that we should of a certainty be shot in the back as we were galloping off, so that the game would not be worth the candle. Henry and I, therefore, withdrew our forces, and retired a little distance to hold a council of war. We had been talking the matter over for about five minutes, when I suddenly saw a small troop of men coming up the road dressed in a uniform that I knew.

Leaving Henry staring open-mouthed at my precipitate movements, I promptly galloped off to them, and, to my delight, found that my surmises were right, and that they formed part of the well-known mule battery, the main body of which, with Signor el Commandante in charge, being, they informed me, about a mile in the rear, and marching into the town to get supplies before rejoining the army of attack. This was real good news, and Henry was quite as pleased as I was, so we left our retainers where they were, and rode away ourselves in the direction of the advancing battery, which we fell in with in about ten minutes or so. It was a great meeting with Signor el Commandante.

"Well, damn my boots," he said; "this is prime! Guess I'm that pleased to see you that you won't go again till we've had a fight together; no, sir."

I told him about the little difficulty with the guard at the gate, and on our arrival there together there was a scene enacted with that sergeant that fairly took the hair off him, and we all rode through in triumph. Not content with that, our Yankee pal insisted on our coming with him straight to the officer commanding the garrison, in order to obtain an apology to ourselves for the rudeness we had experienced, and also to report the non-compliance with the orders in writing of the president. I begged him not to make a fuss about it; but he would not listen to me, and said, "It does the damned cusses good; kinder takes the starch out of 'em, see?"

So we went and got all we wanted, while the sergeant and his guard got a rough time of it for their pains. When I propounded my views about getting through the lines, and the necessity for pushing on, the gallant artilleryman, after thinking a few minutes, looked up, and suddenly said, "Guess you ain't afraid of bullets, eh?"

"No," I replied, "so long as there are not too many of them about."

"Well, then," he continued, "I have fixed it up. You

all come along with me this afternoon. Guess I've got to get my barkers in position by to-morrow morn first thing, and then we open the ball. With any luck, we shall give the other lot beans, and when they scatter, guess you'll all ride right away through till you strike the road, and then gallop as if the devil had kicked you till you have put some miles of this benighted country between yourselves and ructions. What say?"

This struck me as being by no means a bad idea, although Henry and the arrieros did not quite appreciate going into action, and Henry's boy was evidently disappointed at the chance of his playing the part of scout being over. However, the latter's heart was made glad by being sent on in advance with some of the battery to find out what they could. After a good square meal and more than one cocktail, which was brewed by our American cousin, we had a siesta, and at about eight p.m. boot and saddle sounded, and the artillery moved off, accompanied by our worthy selves. Strict silence was ordered, so that we were not allowed to speak above a whisper for fear of attracting attention. We had gone about four miles along the road like this, when we were met by a couple of men from the advance guard, who had been sent back to guide us. They said the enemy were holding the road in force about six miles further on, but that they had neglected to block a path which the guide knew, whereby we could, if not detected, manage to get the battery on to a hill slightly in the right rear of their position, and completely commanding the same. The commander then gave the order to halt, and the men loaded their rifles, an armed party being sent on in advance with connecting files. Where we had pulled up was a stream, so we watered the mules and rum and watered ourselves, and then moved on as silently and cautiously as we could.

For about three miles we had to make our way almost at right angles to the proper course, through the bush, and then we suddenly came on a narrow path leading off to the left, where we found a man posted. As we got nearer and nearer the enemy, we had to use more and more caution, and I confess it was very exciting work, as, pistol in hand, we three, Signor el Commandante, Henry, and self, rode in front of the columns. Presently the ground began to rise, and we commenced to climb the hill. About halfway up we came upon Henry's boy, who motioned to us to halt the battery, and after dismounting to come with him. This we did, and after crawling along on our hands and knees for a couple of hundred yards, we came to the edge of a cliff, and peeping through the scrub, saw the whole of the Salvadoraneans about five hundred yards off and a couple of hundred feet below us. The path unfortunately for about twenty yards skirted the edge of the cliff, and we should have to run the gauntlet in full view of the opposing forces, which would never do. So some other means had to be found to get by. We dare not use a machete to cut our way through for fear of making too much noise, and the only alternative left was to send out men in all directions to try and find some way round. This occupied a good hour, during which time we sat tight on tenterhooks for fear the mules should scream and betray our position. However, they behaved like angels, and at the end of the time the men all returned, two of them having found a difficult but possible road round out of sight. I don't think I shall ever forget the struggle and hard work we had to get the screw guns through the underwood, but we did manage it at last, and eventually arrived at the plateau on the top of the hill, where, having put the guns together and masked them with grass and boughs, we laid down thoroughly worn out. From where we were we had a magnificent view of the enemy, and found that it was perfectly true what the scouts had said, viz. that we commanded the whole of their position. At the first streak of dawn we were all up and on the alert, and I took particular care to note the lay of the country and take the compass bearings, so that I might be able to hit off the road again after our dash. The mules had had an extra feed, and very plain instructions given to the arrieros as to what they had to do likewise. I pointed out to them the road in the distance where they were to make for when I gave the signal, and they were clearly made to understand that it was to be a case of every one for himself and the devil take the hindermost. This ceremony being over, we lay down and awaited events, filling up the time by eating a cold breakfast; we could not light a fire for fear of the smoke.

It must have been close on two hours and the sun was getting up in the sky before we, with the aid of our glasses, observed any movement of the troops below. The American commander was just beginning to get impatient and to swear at the commander of the Guatemaltecan army for being behind time, when suddenly there rang out in the clear air the sound of a rifle shot away on our left, and the Salvadoraneans stood to their arms and fell in in a mass of columns.

Immediately after this the musketry fire began, and everything was bustle. Our guns were promptly loaded with shell and trained on the column below, and as the Guatemala troops emerged from the bush into sight, Signor el Commandante fired the first gun himself, saying, as he did so, "Reckon that will make 'em fool around for a bit." Bang went the gun, and smash went the shell slap into the thick of the unsuspecting Salvador people, where it exploded and did fearful execution. They evidently could not make out where it had come from, and three more equally well planted did not make things more comfortable for them. I must say the guns were splendidly served, and in about half an hour's time the battle for the second time became a regular rout, the Salvadoraneans scuttling in every direction.

"Now's your time," shouted our American. "Good luck to you! So long!" and, with a last grasp of the hand, we mounted, and I gave the signal for a start.

Down the hill we went helter-skelter into the plain below, and then everybody made a bee line for the road, passing through the scattered troops like a whirlwind. Luckily they were too much occupied in seeking safety for themselves to pay any attention to us, and our retreat was covered by the battery on the hill. I knew that our pal up there was watching us, for as we all got through safe I heard a distant hurrah, and turning round for a second, caught sight of a small flag being waved from the top of a tree. We all struck the road pretty well together, and away we went full split. It was something like a quick thing in the old country and quite as exciting, with the exception that on this occasion, we might be in the position of the hunted instead of the hunter. For a couple of hours we tore along best pace, till both ourselves and the mules cried enough, and we had to pull up and rest for a bit, continuing our journey as soon as they were ready. Nearly all that afternoon we pushed on, till about six o'clock we thought we had gone far enough, and so camped near a village for the night.

The next morning we were off again early, and had to go down a steep hill through a very thick bit of forest. Here, as bad luck would have it, Major Grundy picked up a stone, and I had to get off and extract it, the others riding on. Just as I had completed the operation, and had remounted, three or four beauties jumped out of the bush, and, covering me with their guns, demanded my money or my life. To parley with them would be fatal, and it flashed across me that the rest of the party could not be very far off, so I laid right along Major Grundy's neck, and, giving him both spurs, away I went with a dash. Whiz went a bullet past my head, and then I pulled out my six-shooter, and, without taking any aim, I fired into the brown of the scoundrels. The man who had fired at me was just taking aim for another pot shot, when my bullet caught him in the centre of the forehead, and he fell in his tracks. This so astonished and flabbergasted the rest that for a minute they stood stock still, which gave me an advantage, and before they started off to follow me I was three-parts of the way down the hill, and going strong. All I was afraid of was that the mule would come down with me before I came up with the rest. Luckily he kept on his legs, and Henry, having heard my shot, turned back with his boy, so that when my gentlemen came round the corner they found themselves face to face with three double-barrelled rifles, all ready for them, and they promptly fled in all directions before we could even pull our triggers. This was an eminently satisfactory conclusion to the episode, for I certainly did not want any more big-game shooting of that sort, and was personally very glad to have got off so cheap.

We made a short march of it that day, and encamped for the evening under the same old tree that had sheltered us on the way up. After all we had gone through during the last few days we were pretty well tired out, mules and all, and so were glad of the rest. Most of the animals appeared pretty well tucked-up I know, while as for Henry, he looked more like Don Quixote then ever; and as I turned over the second time in my hammock that night I quite made up my mind that the dash through the fighting-lines and subsequent adventure with the bushranging crowd had been quite enough excitement in one week.

CHAPTER XI.

HOME BY LAND AND WATER.

AFTER my previous experiences of the state of the country, I confess I was not particularly wrapt up in the idea of trusting myself longer than I could help in the wilds thereof. Nor was I very happy regarding the friends and relations of the gentleman who had fallen a victim to my pistol. Certainly he richly deserved all that he got, and it was solely and entirely in self-defence that the deed was perpetrated, but his "compradors" would not, I thought, take these matters into serious consideration, and if they got half a chance at me would be for repaying the debt with interest, more especially if they scented the smallest possibility of picking up a dollar by so doing. Accordingly I was urgent in my request that we should push on at all hazards. The ariero was for making a day's halt to get his animals fit again after their bucketing, but I would not listen to such a proposal, and insisted on making an early start next morning. Henry joined in the forces against me, and cried out loudly for a day of rest, but it was no good. I had made up my mind; and so next day at cockcrow we were again *en route*. How right I was was very shortly afterwards shown, for one of our retainers had an uncle, a cousin, or an aunt—it might possibly have been a wife or a sweetheart—in the village where we had stayed for the night, and after we had gone about six or seven miles a messenger arrived post-haste to let us know that a band had been organized by the friends of the defunct robber, all of whom had sworn to have their revenge on the cause of his sudden demise.

"Another double stage," groaned Henry, when he heard the news, and another double stage it was, dead tired though we all were. I remember well that for at least six miles I rode fast asleep, and when we halted at the banks of a stream in the night to water the animals, the moment I was off Major Grundy and on the ground I was asleep again as fast as a church. However, the ariero, who was now more frightened than anybody, soon roused me up, and was the most anxious of the whole party to get on.

At about five a.m., just as the dawn was breaking, my mule began to exhibit symptoms of collapse, which rapidly increased as we proceeded, and at last down he went all of a sudden, pitching me over his head. As soon as I had picked myself up and collected the pieces and my wits, I saw that the poor brute was in the acute stage of colic, and rolling about on the ground in agony, screaming like a stuck pig. It was doubtless the effect of a heavy drink of cold water on an empty stomach, and on the top of the severe work of the last few days.

"What is to be done now?" said I to the ariero, who stood there calmly contemplating the scene. "Quien sabe," was, as usual, the reply, till I suggested that if we did not bestir ourselves the avenging party would be on us in a few hours—a remark that seemed to galvanize him into new life. As soon as I had said this, he dashed off to a village, which, luckily, was at hand, and in a few moments returned with about six or eight eggs. Then he proceeded to administer shells and all as a species of enema, much to my astonishment, for I have never seen such a remedy for colic before.

After having passed about five in this way he asked for some whisky, and made a compound of whisky, chilies, pepper and hot water, with which he drenched the unfortunate Major Grundy, and then covered the beast over with a blanket and some maize straw.

This being done, he said, "We will stop here for an hour, in which time the mule will be either dead or quite well." Strange to say, between that time either the eggs or the strong drench had the desired effect, and the mule, having got on its legs and shaken itself well, began to "cavort around," and was as if nothing had happened, beyond being, perhaps, a little bit weak. The ariero insisted on our starting onward there and then, for he said that the next day the animal, though cured, would be *hors de combat* for nearly a week.

It was certainly to me a novelty in the veterinary art, but as it answered, I had nothing to say, but could only admire the effect of egg shells and aquadiente. Happily, we had only about five miles and a half to go before we struck the river and a fairly large town, where we should be quite safe. So we bucketed on best pace, and arrived without further mishap shortly after noon. The first thing was to find stabling for the animals, and a "posada" for ourselves; and having luckily secured this in the residence of the head boss, Henry suggested that we might possibly charter a couple of canoes and go down the river in them to Quirigua, leaving the mules to follow in a few days. This I considered a particularly happy thought. So we immediately, with the aid of the commandante, went round, and after no little trouble, managed to find what we wanted, and made a bargain with the owners of the two canoes to find boats and crew to take us down the river for so much money.

After consultation, we arrived at the conclusion that we could with safety spend a night in the town without fear of molestation, so we decided to start the following day on our aquatic excursion. No one was more pleased at this solution than myself, for I was completely played out, and wanted a night's rest very badly indeed. I don't believe either of us turned in our hammocks from the time we got in till morning dawned, that is to say, after we had fairly started the night, for we made a mistake to begin with by slinging our hammocks inside the cabildo, and found that after sleeping in the open air we could not stand the close atmosphere of a room, consequently we had to shift out under a big tree in the courtyard.

Early next morning Henry's boy brought us our chocolate, and after a sluice down, we sallied forth to provision and pack our boats, also to make arrangements for the mules coming on later, and to leave money with the ariero. One thing we were very glad to hear, which was that the head boss of the town was going to send down an escort, so that our animals would be able to join them and travel down without fear. He himself was most obliging, and promised to do everything that he could for us. Of course this necessitated a little present; but by this time I was quite *au fait* at the manners and customs of the country, so I did not in the least mind bribing where it was of any use. We managed to get the greater part of our kits on board, and plenty of provisions of sorts, though we had been very short of liquor fit to drink, and consequently had to eke matters out with aquadiente. Having got everything in order we bid an affectionate farewell to Major Grundy and company, and then, after a good square breakfast of fish and eggs, we embarked about eleven a.m., and shoved off into the stream. I had the leading canoe, while Henry brought up the rear in the second boat. This arrangement was somewhat solitary perhaps, but as we had to shoot some rather nasty rapids on our first stage, we thought it just as well for each boat to have a responsible member on board. As soon as we were out in mid-stream we waved adieu to the servants we had left behind and to the commandante and suite, and departed amid wishes for success and shouts of "Con Dios Signor."

For the first few miles all was pleasant enough, as we shot down the stream, a boat's length separating the two canoes, and then, as we rounded a corner, the rapids hove in sight, and our boatmen prepared for the fray. I must confess I did not half like the look of them as we got nearer, for the whole stream seemed to be a regular boil, and I was by no means sure of the prowess of our crew; but as they did not seem to be the least anxious about it, I concluded it was all right, and beyond spreading a mackintosh sheet over the guns and as much of the kit as I could cover, I did nothing but sit still and await developments. Just as we got into the head of the rapid, the chief boatman and pilot shifted me out of the bows, where I had taken up my position, and taking my place, assumed command. A minute later we were in the thick of it, and went down at railway speed, avoiding a rock by the skin of our teeth. So near was it that it fairly took my breath away, for I thought we had gone for good. The head man spoke never a word, but simply gave directions by signs with his paddle, standing erect in the bows to give a timely shove-off if necessary. Almost before I knew where we were, we had shot through, and were now gliding into smooth water at the foot of the rapid, having shipped scarcely a drop of water.

I confess I breathed more freely when I found myself safe, and from the expression on Henry's face when I looked back and saw the boat emerge from the foam and tumble, I fancy he was equally glad to have got that part of the business over.

Nothing more exciting occurred till just before we were about to bring up for the night abreast of an island in mid stream, when I had a long shot at a "gator," a fairly large specimen of alligator, who was warming himself on a mud bank in the rays of the declining sun. He was considerably astonished at the shot, and went off in a hurry, but my bullet evidently glanced off his armour without doing him much harm, save the shock. The boatmen were not best pleased at my having fired at all, for they said the bend of the river was not far off the rear of the Salvadoranean army, and the shot might bring down upon us some loafers, who would ask impertinent questions, and very probably try a little looting. I never thought of this at the time, but saw the force of it directly they called my attention to the fact. After a consultation between the two headmen of the boats, it was decided that, under the circumstances, it would not be safe to remain where we were, but that we must go on for another three miles or so, where we should be more out of the way. It was lucky that we decided on this, for, on looking back just as we turned the corner of a broad sweep, I could see through my glasses a party of men running down to the bank of the river, evidently to find out who had fired, and what it was about. They were too much occupied in hunting about the spot we had left to notice us, happily, and in another three minutes we were round the bend and out of view.

A paddle of two miles brought us to the haven of rest—a beautiful grassy glade sloping down to the river

—and here we landed and hauled the canoes up, covering them with branches and grass reeds so as to be out of sight. We then lit a bright fire in a hollow where the smoke would not be seen, and had our evening meal under way in a jiffy for all hands, and our hammocks slung under the trees. There was no doubt about the spot being beautiful enough, but the insects were something awful. Tobacco smoke they seemed to revel in, and as we dared not make any wood smoke from the fire, we had about as lively a night of it as I ever remember to have passed. I was very glad when the morning dawned and we prepared to make a fresh start.

Having been bitten in every conceivable part of the body during the night, Henry and I agreed that we could not be much worse for a little more, and so boldly had a plunge into the river, which was very refreshing. Meanwhile the boy had arranged a sort of cooking-range in the bows of one of the canoes out of large stones, and having lit a fire, was busy cooking our morning chocolate. This time Henry and I boarded the same craft, transferring his weight in luggage to the other boat, and away we went gaily down the stream till we arrived at the house of our Gallic friend, from whence we had made our departure for the city. Here we found everything in disorder, for they had not heard anything about him, and were beginning to get anxious and to wonder what had happened. They little expected that their master and patron was about to be bottled for service in the army, or they would have been in a dreadful stew.

However, they were very glad to see us, and his "best girl" killed the fatted calf for us in the shape of a fowl, and we had our midday meal and siesta at his house. The boatmen said it would take us about three hours to get down to the plantations from where we were, if there was water enough in the river to get over a nasty shoal that lay between ourselves and Quirigua. But they thought it was all right, so I decided to stay where we were till 3.30, and then move on, and I occupied the time flirting with our French friend's young woman, who, by the way, seemed nothing loth. Punctually to time we embarked, and there being luckily plenty of water in the stream, we arrived all safe and sound shortly after 6.30 at the plantation, much to the major domo's delight and surprise.

He immediately sent off to the hacienda to inform Jane of our arrival, and also to get some mules down to transport ourselves and baggage up to the house, and then made arrangements for the accommodation of our worthy boatmen. Jane was almost beside himself with pleasure when we arrived at the hacienda, and informed me that he thought we had been killed in the war; but that he had determined, if the robbers came to the house, to sell his life dearly, for which purpose he had double loaded an old percussion gun belonging to Johnson the engineer. There is no doubt that he would have "sold his life" if he had fired it, for the weapon was as rusty as it could be, and if it had gone off, would inevitably have burst, and blown him to pieces. However, the worthy fellow was intensely pleased to see us back, and did his best to surpass any of his previous performances in the culinary art.

That night I heard Henry's boy giving him thrilling details of the glories of the city of Guatemala, and harrowing his feelings with a description of our ride through the contending armies and my adventure with the bush rangers.

Of course we found an immense accumulation of business and estate work to clear up, and some of it had to be transacted at Belize, so that, although my departure for England was imperative at an early date, I had to send Henry off post-haste to catch the schooner for Belize, which he could just do by starting next day. He did not much like the idea, for he said that he had had quite enough of travelling by land and water to last him for some time. Nor did I particularly look forward to being left alone by myself for a fortnight, with no one to speak to except the major domo and the estate hands. However, "needs must where the devil drives," so at dinner that night we settled the question, and Henry arranged to go next morning down to Yzabal, while I tackled as much of the business at the estate as I could.

One individual who welcomed our return with boisterous glee I must not forget, and that was the old doggie Lion. He would not leave me for a moment, not even after lights were out and we had turned in; for although Jane tried all he knew to get him out of the room, he would have none of it, treating force and coaxing in the same way, till at last I told Jane to let him be, at which he gave a bark of triumphant delight, and passed the night under my bed.

CHAPTER XII.

A BAD START.

WHEN Henry got back to Yzabal from Belize—I had met him at Livingston in the launch—the American vice-consul told us he had been anxiously expecting us every day, and that we must go up to the plantation at once.

"What for, and why so violent a hurry?" I ventured to ask.

"Haven't you heard?" he replied. "The Salvador army has been badly beaten, and are coming down to the coast, devastating everything and everywhere on their road. I have been dreading their arrival before you turned up, for if they do come, guess there won't be much of your hacienda left."

This was somewhat serious, I thought, and, notwithstanding Henry's argument that we two could not do much against a host of dissolute blackguards, I decided to push up the hill at once. The major domo, in his capacity of captain-general of the district, had already called out the local forces, and marched them up to Quirigua to garrison the hacienda. So that anyway we had the foundation of a defence, if the worst came to the worst, and two white men would be a great addition, I knew.

Consequently, tired as we were, we started off there and then, leaving Johnson with orders to keep the launch ready in case of emergencies, and making the consul promise to provision her, so that we might be able to scoot if the beggars proved too much for us. It was dark when we arrived at the house, and I confess I was in deadly fear of being potted by mistake every moment. However, the local army, for a wonder, kept their heads, and were evidently exceedingly glad to see us. Our friend the major-domo was quite in his element, and a big pot in his own estimation. He had posted a chain of sentries all round, and a picquet along the road, which he visited seemingly every half-hour during the night. He was very anxious that I should accompany him on his "grand rounds" to view the disposition of his forces; but, having had no sleep the previous night, I declined, and rolled into my hammock straight off.

The next morning we went into the question of attack and defence, and having turned out all the estate hands, carpenter included, we managed to throw up a very creditable earth-work commanding the road, and also to put the house itself in a position to withstand a siege.

The major-domo had already inaugurated an intelligence department in the shape of a relay of runners, who had been sent out twenty-five or thirty miles to give us timely notice of the approach of an enemy. The only thing now was to secure our retreat. Doubtless it would have been more heroic to have burnt our ships and fought it out; but as I had not come out to Central America for war purposes, I preferred, if possible, getting away with a whole skin. Accordingly we packed up such things as were necessary, and having loaded three mules, sent our traps off to Yzabal to be stowed on board the launch, giving the men instructions to return at once with the mules—an order which they did not half like, as they felt safer away from the seat of war. However, as we sent with them an armed escort under the command of a corporal, they had to obey, and started off full of grief and grumblings.

For three days we waited in anticipation of attack, but as nothing came in in the way of news from the front I determined to ride out and inspect our intelligence department; so, taking with me a corporal and Henry's boy, I started off very early in the morning. On arriving at the first stage, just as I had pitched my camp, which consisted of swinging my hammock and lighting a fire, two of our scouts came in with the gratifying news that the war was over, and that the Salvador people had retired into their own country, also that everything was quiet.

This being so, I only stayed the night, and on the following day returned to the Hacienda to inform Henry and the major-domo of the welcome change in the state of affairs. When I arrived within sight of the dwelling-house I could see that something was up, for there was (for that part of the world) a large crowd assembled round the potato patch, who were evidently much interested in something that was going on inside. Galloping up, I found that during the night a full-grown tiger cat had been caught in one of the traps the manager had set, and was consequently trying its best to make things pleasant and get off. Being a box-trap, it was not in the least injured, and was, moreover, a splendid specimen. Henry had already set the carpenter to work to make a suitable cage for the beast, and was there supervising the construction of the same.

When he saw me back so soon he quite thought that the enemy were in sight, and did not half like it; but when he heard my news he was evidently much relieved, and informed me that the English mail had arrived, and that there were letters for me at the house.

Amongst them I found an urgent summons to England which could not be neglected, so that I made up my mind on the spot to catch the next mail home, and started off a messenger to Yzabal to know when the next schooner for Belize was going to start. I had had enough of the steam launch, and preferred the trajet by schooner, even if it was slower. This being done, I commenced to pack what things I had not already sent down, and also wrote a note to Halifax in the city, explaining why I had been called away. I had already sent him a telegram to be forwarded from Yzabal, saying I was off as soon as possible.

At dinner that evening I conceived the notion of taking the tiger cat home to England with me, and presenting it to the Zoo, and although Henry warned me it would be a terrible bore and trouble I would not give in, but made up my mind to try. The great difficulty was how to transport the brute to Yzabal, for the cage was rather an unwieldy thing in itself, and the moment we tried to fix it on a mule, the animal went nearly mad with fright at its contents. Eventually, however, we found one mule who did not mind it, and, oddly enough, it was my old friend Major Grundy; so it was decided that he should have the honour of taking the beast down.

The next day I got the consul's answer to my note, saying a schooner would leave in five days for Belize, and by which, although it would not catch the mail, he strongly advised me to go, as she was a capital boat, with far greater comfort on board than usual.

Accordingly I made my arrangements to do so, and having said good-bye to the major domo, and presented him with a little present, also something for the estate hands, Henry, Jane, and self started off, for the last time as far as I was concerned, for Yzabal, where we arrived without mishap, and found all my goods, including the tiger cat, on board the schooner, which was, as the consul had said, a new and capital boat, commanded by an American from New Orleans.

We were to start at daybreak the next morning, so I slept on board that night, as did Henry, for he said he intended coming a certain distance with me, and would return in the launch from the fort the other side of the lake. It was just as well he did go, for next morning we had not a breath of wind, and consequently found the launch very useful in towing us across.

The sea breeze came in strong rather earlier than usual that day, which Johnson said was a sign of bad weather, so that we got across to the fort before we expected, and Henry decided to come on to Livingston, as we had plenty of coal in the launch. Of course, at Livingston I had to take an affectionate farewell of the commandante, who equally, of course, celebrated the event by getting blind drunk again, and then the anchor was hove up, and with a fair wind we stood out over the bar, and laid our course for Belize.

The last I saw of Henry and Johnson, they were both standing on the top of the cabin of the launch waving their hats, and a shout came over the water of "Good-bye, good-luck, sir!" from poor Johnson, who was really sorry to see me go. I say poor Johnson, for before I left Belize I got a letter from Henry to say that the launch had sunk at anchor with Johnson on board, and that he had been drowned. I have mentioned this circumstance in one of my former chapters, I think, but it was at this time that the accident occurred, and all through the unfortunate fellow having taken a drop too much, and not giving the boat any chain when the norther came down.

We had a quick run to Belize, for the schooner sailed like a witch; and I confess I had a real comfortable time of it, and was quite sorry to find ourselves inside the kay and standing up for the harbour. There was a deuce of a fuss over the cage and the tiger cat, and for a long time I thought I should not have been allowed to land it, but should have had to accept the Yankee shipper's offer to buy it from me. Eventually, however, I squared matters, and it was duly transferred from the deck of the schooner to the back yard of the house where I was going to lodge until the Royal Mail Steamer for Jamaica came in. I soon repented of my decision with regard to the brute, and wished that I had listened to Henry's advice, for of all the mischievous beasts in creation I never met its equal. It would lie perfectly still, and by carefully putting a bit of food just outside the bars of its cage, would manage to entice one of my landlady's fowls within reach. Directly the fowl tried to peck the food, like a flash of lightning a long little paw would shoot out and the wretched fowl was inside the cage, and its days ended before it knew what had happened. Doubtless very clever and interesting to look on at, but when one had to pay for the fowl, besides rousing the landlady's wrath, it became a bore. I managed to defeat the little game after a time by getting some wire netting and putting it round the cage so that the fowls could not get near, but this seemed to annoy the animal exceedingly, and it daily grew more and more savage till at last the *dénouement* came.

It was the day before the steamer was expected, and I had already entered the cat as part of my goods and chattels with some difficulty, and had also been round and left my P. P. C. cards on the governor and other friends in the town, and was dining that evening at Government House. While we were at dinner we heard a devil of a bobbery, as if the whole town was in revolt, and saw a crowd of natives and people of all shapes, sizes, and colours, flying up the road, and even putting off from the shore in boats, while occasionally the sound of a shot would be heard.

"What on earth is the matter?" said the governor to his secretary. "Go and see." But before the worthy secretary could leave the room the head butler, accompanied by Jane in a very dishevelled state, burst in, and Jane immediately began—

"Master, it's gone; we all die!"

"What's gone? and who dies, you idiot?" I asked.

"The cat, sir, gone away; eat every one," replied Jane, who was evidently frightened out of his wits; and so it was.

The tiger cat had managed to gnaw through the bars of its cage, and when Jane went to give it its evening meal it suddenly, to his horror and amazement, dashed out over his head, and over the wall into the town, dispersing the populace like chaff before the wind, and causing a general panic. I could not help laughing, the whole affair was so utterly ludicrous; but it was really no laughing matter, for there were some serious complications among the fair sex, and through my beastly tiger cat, the registrar of births, deaths, and marriages had more than his daily allowance of the first-named to register, and the indignant husbands wanted me to pay the doctors' bills. After a time, quiet having been to a certain extent restored, a party was organized to try and hunt the brute down, but it was no good. The feline having once more tasted the sweets of liberty, was not going to run any risks, and having performed the functions of accoucheur-general to the town, made off into the jungle, and was never, to my knowledge, seen again. As may be imagined, there was not much sleep for me that night, for the whole town congregated outside my lodging and discussed the situation. Jane told me that they had serious thoughts of making it unpleasant for me; but before they had decided whether they would indite me as a public nuisance, bring a civil action against me for damages, or lynch me, I was safe on board the Royal Mail steamer, and in a position to defy them. Anyway, I left South America somewhat under a cloud, having lost not only my tiger cat, but the good opinion of the populace. Just before we started, Jane came off to say good-bye, and brought me his parting present in the shape of a wonderful green parrot, which was the best talker I ever saw. Poor Jane begged hard to be taken on to Jamaica as he did not at all relish the idea of going back to Quirigua, but I did not see my way to complying with his request, so took a final adieu of him as the anchor was hove short, and from that day to this have heard nothing of him.

There were not many passengers on board, so that there was plenty of room, and I had a large cabin all to myself, and therefore was in clover. Besides, as I knew all the officers of the ship well, we settled down to a rubber of whist the first night, a custom which we kept up till the time came to transfer myself and baggage into the large boat for England, the account of which I will defer to my next. I cannot say that I was particularly sorry to see the kays of Belize disappear, for although we had had a fairly good time of it on the whole, and it had been an entirely new experience to me, the original party was all broken up, and the weather was getting a deal too hot to be pleasant. Moreover, I don't care where one is, or what one is doing in a foreign land, there is always a certain amount of home-sickness concealed about one's person, and a latent longing to see once more the shores of the Old Country. At least, I can vouch for it as a fact in my own case, and I am prepared to lay long odds that the majority of my fellow-men share the same feelings.

CHAPTER XIII.

HOME.

In my last chapter I had safely cleared from Belize, and gradually settled down for the homeward journey. As I said before, we had very few passengers, and only two of the fair sex, one being a grass widow, who, as she was accompanied as far as Jamaica by her *cavaliere servente*, was not of much account to anybody else, though afterwards she appeared again in another light.

When we arrived at Port Royal, Jamaica, the superintendent came off with the pleasing intelligence that everybody would have to land immediately and wait for the English boat at the hotel, as our present vessel was to sail at once to St. Thomas's to go into the floating dock there for scrubbing purposes. It was suggested to the gentleman that, as the homeward mail called at the Island of St. Thomas, and was not due at Jamaica for another four days, it would be far simpler if all the passengers went on to that port and made their transfer there; but he was inexorable, and insisted on every one turning out bag and baggage, which, with the exception of myself, they all did. I had visions of what five days in a Jamaica hotel would be like, and so determined, by hook or by crook, to remain where I was.

Luckily for me, I had staunch allies in the skipper and the purser, and between us we managed to work the oracle. My heavy baggage, of course, was landed for transhipment and placed under the care of the company officials, and at the same time I saw that my berth was properly booked, but my portmanteau, etc., remained on board carefully stowed away in the purser's cabin, and about half an hour before the vessel sailed, I sneaked off in a shore boat, and, having arrived on board myself, was hidden away in the bath-room till after the departure of the superintendent. As soon as the anchor was up and the screw began to turn, I was released from durance vile, and in a very short time made myself extremely comfortable in the ladies' cabin, which I had all to myself.

As may be imagined, we had a very cheery dinner that night, with our rubber of whist undisturbed, and a cigar afterwards on the bridge, where I kept the chief officer company during his watch, was smoked with great satisfaction. Altogether it was like being on board one's own yacht. No rules or restrictions for passengers, breakfast when one liked, and meals or drinks at all hours. In fact, I do not think I have ever enjoyed a trip so much in my life.

It was beautifully calm weather, and the only fear one had was that we should not get into St. Thomas's in time, which, I confess, was rather a serious consideration, not only for myself, but for all concerned in the stowaway, as, if I missed the mail, the whole story would come out, and there would have been ructions. The reason we were doubtful about it was that, although we had four days clear start, the vessel's bottom was so dirty that, do what we would, we could not manage to get more than five or six knots, at the outside, out of her, and that was scarcely enough to do the trick. Moreover, we had been sent off in such a hurry that no time had been allowed to fill up the coal bunkers, and it was even betting that we ran short.

About noon, however, the following day, a nice breeze sprang up well abaft the beam, which looked like freshening, and so the chief officer and myself laid our heads together with a view to getting some sail on the craft. I may mention here that she was brig-rigged; but, with the exception of the fore and aft sails, I don't think the other canvas had ever been cast loose. And it was a question whether the crew knew anything about topsails, etc. Nevertheless, we determined to have a try, and the first step was to obtain the permission of the skipper, or, as he was familiarly termed, "the old man." I was deputed to arrange this, and so I descended to his cabin and made known my request.

At first he hummed and hawed a good deal, and said it was so long since he had done any sailing that he did not like .to risk it, and that, with the exception of the chief officer, no one knew anything about it, which meant that he and the chief would have to keep watch and watch. I was not going to give in, however, without a fight, so I told him that I knew something about the job, and was quite willing to take a watch with one of the officers, and give him the benefit of my experience, and also pointed out that, at all events, we could try it during the daylight; and at last, after a long argument, I managed to talk him over and to obtain his sanction, provided that the quartermaster and boatswain could muster a crew to work the sails.

When I went on deck again we soon had these two worthies aft, and though they both said they had never seen the gaskets cast off, they thought that they could muster a sufficient number of the black Dominican negroes (excellent sailors, by the way) to work the ship, and, happily, were both as keen as mustard. In about half an hour the crew was mustered, and I ran down and fetched the old man up to commence operations. It was great fun to see him when he did come on to the bridge, for he evidently had forgotten everything he ever knew about square-rigged business, but did not quite like to own it. At last, however, he got out of it by saying to the chief officer, "Look here, H——, I should like to see you make sail, just to be sure that you know what you are about."

And then the fun began. The chief promptly took command, while I went forward to superintend. Never did I see such a mess as the sails were in when we began to hoist away! They were black with months and months of smoke and coal-dust, and, as we sweated on the topsail halyards, clouds of it came pouring down and nearly smothered us. However, after about an hour's hard work, we got everything set and the yards properly braced, and were bowling along a good ten knots or more. The old man was quite pleased; so much so that he took all the credit to himself, and kept on impressing on me what a good idea it was of his to put sail on the vessel, and how well he had carried it all out. Naturally I did not contradict him, for I was too glad to see us making tracks as we were. The one thing that I was afraid of was that the breeze would pipe up too strong, and necessitate sending the hands aloft to reef—an operation which I was by no means sure of them being able to accomplish. It is one thing making sail, and another taking it in, and the chief and I had a long discussion on the subject, being at the end much relieved by the black boatswain saying that he had quite enough hands who were "all there" at the work, and that we need have no fear whatever.

Just as I expected, about dinner-time the wind freshened considerably, and we logged twelve and a half knots, which, considering the state of her bottom, was good going. In obedience to a wink from the chief, I went up with him on deck, and together we managed to put a reef in the topsails and took in the top-gallant sails before the evening meal. I must confess it was not done very artistically, but luckily without an accident, which was something, and the men worked with a will. Just as we had finished, up comes the skipper in a tear to see what had happened, as from the noise he evidently thought that the masts had gone over the side. When he saw that everything was snug, however, he quieted down, and although he expressed his intention of taking everything off her before night, we managed to calm him down, and after dinner, over his rubber of whist, he forgot all about it.

I had the middle watch with the second officer, and about three bells, or 1.30 a.m., it came on to blow hard, but luckily right aft, so we managed to hold on, for which I was mighty glad, for I doubt if we should have got the sail off without losing some one overboard. By the time the watch was over and the skipper came up, the wind had moderated, and we were slipping along quite comfortably. I knew that the old man would not play any pranks if he could help it, so I turned in quite happy, and certain that I should find ourselves under the same condition next morning, in which conjecture I was correct, though they told me that the skipper was in a deuce of a fidget all the time he was on the bridge.

The breeze held all the way to St. Thomas, and a rare game we had coming in round the point. We had drilled the men thoroughly as what to do when we rounded in and had to brace up, so that when the time came they were all smart, and we came up to the anchorage, shortened sail, and let go quite man-o'-war fashion, and fired a gun to let the good people ashore know we were there. I believe they would have saluted us in another minute if it had not been early in the morning when we arrived, for I heard that they could not make out what we were at all, never having seen one of the mail boats under sail before.

When the superintendent at St. Thomas came off I was again relegated to the bath-room, and I heard the skipper again taking all the credit to himself. But the superintendent turned out a regular brick, so he was let into the secret of my presence, and I had the pleasure of taking eight dollars off him that evening at whist, without having any more to do penance in the bath-room. We had made such a good passage that I had three days to wait for the mail, and the last night I was obliged to sleep at the hotel, which I alluded to in my first article. At least they called it an hotel; but of all the wretched holes I ever saw, commend me to the Auberge at St. Thomas.

As I have said before, there was scarcely any floor to speak of, and no windows to my room, the furniture consisting of a camp bed, a washing-stand, and one chair with three legs. The next day I was mighty glad to see the homeward-bound steamer coming in, and, much to every one's surprise, I made my number on board, and took possession of my berth. The purser quite thought I had missed the boat, and had promised my berth to another passenger on board, who on my appearance had to take a back seat, which he did not evidently relish. I found that our grass widow had lost no time after dropping her faithful tame cat at Jamaica, but had duly ingratiated herself with the captain, and they were as thick as thieves, being quite the joke of the ship. With reference to this a rather amusing incident occurred on our way to Barbadoes. Of course, everybody who could, picked out a best girl to "beau about," as the Americans call it, and to relieve the monotony of ship life, and I struck up a desperate flirtation with a young Jewess from Jamaica, who, besides being perfectly able to take care of herself, had a remarkable gift of language more forcible than polite. I had one evening escorted the young lady forward under the lee of a convenient boat, where together we "held sweet converse" and "watched the silvery stars," and my movements had been watched by the gallant skipper, who that same night took me on one side and said, in broad Scotch (he was a pronounced Scotchman): "Young mon, I canna have ye interfering with the leddy passengers aboard my ship." I said nothing, but, like the parrot, thought a good deal, and later, having laid my plans and posted my deck-chair in a convenient spot, I had the satisfaction of seeing my worthy Scotch friend bestow a most undeniable kiss on the features of our grass widow. A loud cough from me showed the delinquents that they had been observed, and after the grass widow had fled, I walked up to the skipper, and, imitating him as best I could, said, "Look here, I canna have ye interfering with the leddy passengers aboard this ship." The effect was good, for after a moment's hesitation, and looking somewhat flabbergasted, he said: "Young mon, we had best keep our own counsel, I'm thinking;" and from that day I was free of the ship.

During our stay of fourteen hours or so at Barbadoes, we managed to capture a shark, which gave all hands full employment for half an hour, and even after he was hauled on deck kept things pretty lively for some time. One thing I again particularly noticed about the place, which was that everybody still praised the climate—the European population, I mean—and insisted on it that it was just the same as England. Moreover, to back up their opinions, they still walked about in tall silk hats, utterly regardless of the burning sun and the imminent risk of sunstroke which they one and all ran.

I don't think I have before alluded to one passenger who was on board. He had come out to the West Indies in the same vessel with Royal, Halifax, and myself for a year's cruise, to set himself up against his approaching marriage, and oddly enough was now returning to England with me. He was the worst sailor I think I ever came across, and no sooner was the anchor catted and the ship under way, than he retired to his bunk and refused all food till we got into the next port, when he made up for lost time, and devoured everything that came within his reach, only to repeat the operation *de novo*. As may be surmised, he had not benefited much by his cruise, and as we got in a gale of wind dead ahead directly after leaving Barbadoes, it was for two days a toss up whether he battled through it or not. Indeed, one day the doctor gave him up, and said that unless he took some nourishment, he was bound to go out. However, he just managed to save his bacon, and arrived at Southampton a perfect wreck, so much so that when the pilot boat came off and he thought of sending a telegram to his lady love to come down and meet him, I advised him strongly to do no such thing, for I was convinced that, if she came and saw him in the state he was then in, the marriage would have at once been declared off. I am glad to say, for his sake, that he took my advice, and had a week on *terra firma* before he let any one know that he was back, by which time he had recovered himself sufficiently to be presentable. I never have seen him again, but I know this to be the case, as he wrote me a most grateful letter, thanking me for my suggestions, and telling me he was going to be married that week.

This, however, is anticipating somewhat, as I broke off just as we got into the thick of a gale outside Barbadoes. It was a real snorter, and we could only make two knots against it.

Everything was miserable, water everywhere on deck, meals anyhow, and grass widows and best girls all invisible. This lasted for four or five days, when it blew itself out, and we ran into lovely weather, which lasted us all the way home. The evening before we got in, coming up the Channel, I was on the bridge with my friend the skipper, and was much amused at the earnest conversation we could see going on between the various couples, leaning over the rail in the most secluded spots they could find. I am not ashamed to confess that my Jewess had basely deserted me for the ship's doctor, and even the grass widow had found a second string to her bow, which gave me an ample fund of chaff against the Scotch captain. There was the usual hurry and scurry at the docks, and examination of baggage, but at last it was all over, and I found myself at the station, having said good-bye to all the friends I had made on board, and once more in an English railway carriage on English soil, bound for an English home. I cannot say I was particularly sorry, for, although I had broken new ground and seen sights that I should never be likely to see again, also visited places where few, if any, white men had been, the trip on the whole had not been a very successful one. From a sporting point of view it had been decidedly the reverse, as the sudden break up of our party had entirely spoiled any chance there might have been of doing any good. Personally I cannot truly say that I consider Central America a good field for sport. There are wild animals there in plenty, no doubt, but the virgin forest is too big a business to beat successfully, and it is a pure matter of chance. Then the living is something awful—I mean in the way of food; nor is the climate on the low ground all that could be desired, for the malaria is in places a deadly enemy, not only to the white man, but also to the native element. Properly developed there is no doubt that the country is rolling in wealth, and doubtless at some future date will prove a gold mine; but before that can take place proper roads and means of communication must be made, and capital expended. Also the various states or republics must learn to keep within their own borders, and not interfere with their neighbours, or else, which would be far better, they ought all to amalgamate under one central government. At present life is too short to go shooting in those parts, and until matters are a little more settled, and civilization a little more advanced, I do not fancy that Guatemala will have the extreme honour of again welcoming me to its shores.

THE END.